WRITTEN UNDER THE SKIN

Blood and Intergenerational Memory in South Africa

AFRICAN ARTICULATIONS

ISSN 2054-5673

SERIES EDITORS
Stephanie Newell & Ranka Primorac

EDITORIAL ADVISORY BOARD
Akin Adesokan (Indiana University)
Jane Bryce (University of the West Indies)
James Ferguson (Stanford University)
Simon Gikandi (Princeton University)
Stefan Helgesson (Stockholm University)
Isabel Hofmeyr (University of the Witwatersrand)
Madhu Krishnan (University of Bristol)
Lydie Moudileno (University of Southern California)
Grace A. Musila (University of the Witwatersrand)
Caroline Rooney (University of Kent)
Meg Samuelson (University of Adelaide)
Jennifer Wenzel (Columbia University)

The series is open to submissions from the disciplines related to literature, cultural history, cultural studies, music and the arts.

African Articulations showcases cutting-edge research into Africa's cultural texts and practices, broadly understood to include written and oral literatures, visual arts, music, and public discourse and media of all kinds. Building on the idea of 'articulation' as a series of cultural connections, as a clearly voiced argument and as a dynamic social encounter, the series features monographs that open up innovative perspectives on the richness of African locations and networks. Refusing to concentrate solely on the internationally visible above the supposedly ephemeral local cultural spaces and networks, African Articulations provides indispensable resources for students and teachers of contemporary culture.

Please contact the series editors with an outline, or download the proposal form www.jamescurrey.com. Only send a full manuscript if requested to do so.

Stephanie Newell, Professor of English, Yale University   stephanie.newell@yale.edu
Ranka Primorac, Lecturer in English, University of Southampton   r.primorac@soton.ac.uk

Previously published volumes are listed at the back of this book

WRITTEN UNDER THE SKIN

Blood and Intergenerational Memory in South Africa

Carli Coetzee

James Currey
is an imprint of
Boydell & Brewer Ltd
PO Box 9, Woodbridge
Suffolk IP12 3DF (GB)
www.jamescurrey.com
and of
Boydell & Brewer Inc.
668 Mt Hope Avenue
Rochester, NY 14620-2731 (US)
www.boydellandbrewer.com

Published in paperback in Southern Africa in 2019
(South Africa, Namibia, Lesotho, Zimbabwe & Swaziland)
by Wits University Press
1 Jan Smuts Avenue
Braamfontein
Johannesburg 2017
South Africa

© Carli Coetzee 2019
First published 2019
First published in paperback in World excluding Southern Africa by James Currey 2022

All rights reserved. No part of this book may be reproduced in any form, or by electronic or mechanical means, including information storage and retrieval systems, without permission in writing from the publishers, except by a reviewer who may quote brief passages in a review

The right of Carli Coetzee to be identified as the author of this work has been asserted in accordance with sections 77 and 78 of the Copyright, Designs and Patents Act 1988

British Library Cataloguing in Publication Data
A catalogue record for this book is available on request from the British Library

ISBN 978-1-84701-221-0 (James Currey cloth)
ISBN 978-1-77614-326-9 (Wits University Press)
ISBN 978-1-84701-324-8 (James Currey paperback)

The publisher has no responsibility for the continued existence or accuracy of URLs for external or third-party internet websites referred to in this book, and does not guarantee that any content on such websites is, or will remain, accurate or appropriate

In memory of my Pa, 1939–2018

Contents

Preface ix

Introduction: Piercing the Skin of the Present 1

Part I

1 Reading Mandela's Blood: The Transition, and the Cell as Portal into Bloodless Time 19

2 He Must Not Circulate: Eugene de Kock's Blood Relations and his Prison Visitors 39

3 Ruth First's Red Suitcase: In and Out of the Strongroom of Memory 61

4 A Life Transplanted and Deleted: Hamilton Naki and his Archivists 81

Part II

5 Show Them What Cleaning Is: This Time It's for Mama 103

6 Who Can See this Bleeding? Women's Blood and Men's Blood in these #Fallist Times 121

7 The Bloody Fingerprint: We Must Document 147

Bibliography 155

Index 173

Preface

The term 'intergenerational' in the title of this book refers in the first place to the conventional way in which the transmission of knowledge and memory is understood, from an older to a younger generation. The argument of this book is that intergenerational conversations and collaborations do not only result in such vertical transmission from elders to younger ones, but that the gains and transfers are instead distributed up and down the bloodlines in a mutually interactive generation and regeneration of knowledge. The book is inspired by the incisive and critical ways in which a younger generation of scholars (some of whom identify as #Fallists) have redefined literary and cultural studies, and by their radical demands about how the very terms of knowledge production must be debated and thereby regenerated.

The method outlined here is intended as a resource for the work to come, which will be to redesign the curriculum and reassess what will be handed on to the next generation of students and readers. My generation of teachers and readers cannot claim to have the answers, but we shall be there to watch as the questions are reformulated by younger generations, who will shape the future and debate the terms of our disciplines anew. The tropes through which South Africa has often been read (transformation, emergence, entanglement, reconciliation, diagnostically in search of a cure) are replaced in the argument of this book by vigilant, careful and ethical reading practices that break the skin to extract history-rich bloods through which to interpret the present. This book wishes to challenge the discourses of newness, unburdened 'born-free' birth and emergence, now generally held to be inadequate descriptors of those born after South Africa's transition to democracy in 1994.

The careful and caring protocols around blood testing and the meticulous work of reading blood are productive as a parallel method for that of reading South African texts. These ethical and careful protocols include questions about why one might wish to break the skin to extract the blood in the first place, for whose benefit the blood is extracted, and where the bloods will go. The event of the blood test is necessarily time-sensitive: the record of a blood test includes reference to the date and time of the test. In addition, the blood itself contains in it other date stamps and histories beyond that moment of extraction. These meanings trouble, press on and complicate the moment of the blood's emergence above the skin – whether pulled into a syringe or smeared on to a test strip or microscope slide. Blood tests and blood samples can be used either as part of a care programme for the body from which the bloods were taken, or (as happens more frequently in some parts of the world than others) the blood can become part of biomedical databases that have little interest in the body from which the blood was extracted. This too is part of the work of this book: to trouble the routes of the circulation of knowledge about, and from, South Africa, and to document and log the routes of the blood readings.

I would like to thank in particular Semeneh Ayelew, Jacob Dlamini, Lindiwe Dovey and Grace Ahingula Musila, who were my first readers and patient interlocutors at various stages of the project. Jacques Coetzee and Harriet Armstrong read, often far too late in the night, and responded to each chapter. Ying Cheng, Dina Ligaga and Rebecca Jones were a constant inspiration, and it has been a comfort to imagine them at their parallel desks. I wish to thank the *Journal of African Cultural Studies* reading group for the sense of community and for creating and sustaining an intellectual bloodline. My thanks also to Mark Armstrong, Nomusa Makhubu, Beatrice Rubens, Kopano Ratele, Carmine Rustin, Ndirangu Wachanga, Silvia Elsner, Zanele Muholi, Kopano Matlwa Mabaso, Chege Githiora, Fanie Naude, Chielozona Eze, Daniel Roux, Susan Kiguli, Bwesigye Bwa Mwesigire, Litheko Modisane, Lindy Wilbraham, Barbara Fairhead, Rosalind Duignan-Pearson, Sarah Nuttall, Mignon Coetzee, Uniz Chuey, Eleni Coundouriotis, Ambreena Manji, Thomas Hendriks, Juliana Nfah-Abbenyi and Liese van der Watt, who read sections of the manuscript, or offered advice, comments or encouragement. My thanks go especially to Moradewun Adejunmobi, from whom I have learnt a great deal.

The 'Blood as Archive' workshop at Princeton (Jacob Dlamini, Luise White, Kopano Ratele, Grace Ahingula Musila, Victoria Collis-Buthelezi, Noah Tamarkin, Laura Murphy, Stephanie Selvick) offered a stimulating intellectual community alongside whom to think through the conceptual work of this project. My thanks to Princeton IIRS for funding the workshop that Jacob Dlamini and I hosted in February 2017. Thank you to Nikki Woolward, in particular, for care beyond what one can ever hope for. The members of the British Academy Funded 'Karin Barber Lab: Generation and Regeneration' have over the years provided another bloodline, and I thank the participants (Karin Barber, Stephanie Newell, Añulika Agina, Dina Ligaga, Caroline Mose, Alessandro Jedlowski, Katrien Pype, David Kerr, Paul Ugor, James Yékú, Joseph Oduro-Frimpong, Lynda Gichanda Spencer, Patrick Oloko, Insa Nolte, Rebecca Jones, Rotimi Fasan, Ying Cheng, Leslie James, Grace Ahingula Musila and Ceri Whatley) for their collegiality and friendship.

I am grateful to the staff at the John Radcliffe Hospital in Oxford, in particular to Paediatric Diabetes Specialist Nurse Diana Yardley and to Dr Taffy Makaya, who taught me how to read blood, and encouraged me to trust that I was a good enough reader. Thank you to Joseph Armstrong, who has never tired of drawing my attention to bloods of all kinds, and who was the first person with whom I discussed the idea for this book. Thank you also to Stephanie Newell, Ranka Primorac, Lynn Taylor and James Currey; and to the two anonymous reviewers for their generous and stimulating responses.

Parts of chapter 6 have appeared in *Africa* and in *Arts & Humanities in Higher Education*, in revised form. A version of the Introduction was presented at the 'Blood as Archive' workshop at Princeton in February 2017, and parts of chapter 4 were presented at the weekly seminar in the Department of African Studies and Anthropology at Birmingham University.

Introduction:
Piercing the Skin of the Present

This monograph uses the image of blood just under the skin to theorise and interpret understandings of the ever emergent present in South Africa. Blood just under the skin is a powerful image through which to imagine that which has not yet emerged clearly, but which is already there – like a bruise under the skin, or an undiagnosed symptom in the blood. Blood inside the body's circulatory system contains many secrets and is a rich source of potential information about the state of health or sickness of the body, as well as of its longer histories. Until the skin is pierced, these meanings remain undisclosed. Yet the heaviness of what might be revealed is not lessened. In fact, blood is at its most powerful the moment before the skin is broken and that which is already present in the blood becomes readable.

This moment before the blood becomes visible above the surface of the skin is invasive and potentially dangerous. The blood that becomes readable once it exits the body indexes and has encrypted in it the past, but the argument of this book is intent on the moment when the unbroken layer of skin still holds that blood inside the body. This book is attuned in particular (but not exclusively) to women's embodied experiences of blood, and one of the arguments running through the chapters is that women's experiences of blood are crucial to understanding and 'reading' the surging and ever emergent present in South Africa.

In the vast scholarship on blood, kinship relations and coming-of-age narratives dominate. A feature of this literature is the frequent division between men's blood and women's blood. The anthropological debates around blood catalogue and log the bloods of coming-of-age stories in ways that assign and confirm, but also trouble, gender roles. Women's blood has a distinctive literature attached to it, to do with reproductive and menstrual flows (Dahlqvist 2018; Delaney et al. 1988; Knight 1991), as well as the blood sharing and hosting of pregnancy (Rich 1986; Gallop 1988; Martin 1987). In addition, blood has associated with it a literature on secrecy and danger (Starr 1999), generosity and donation (Waldby and Mitchell 2006; Starr 1999; the 'Body Parts: Transfusion, Tissues, Transplants and the Commodification of the Body' research project under Catherine Burns's leadership at Wits University) as well as the more obvious associations with violence.

Two recent special issues of academic journals, on topics related to blood, are representative of the growing scholarship on bones, blood and other body tissue in medical humanities. The *Journal of the Royal Anthropological Institute* published a set of papers in 2013, under the theme 'Blood Will Out: Essays on Liquid Transfers and Flows'. In the editorial, Janet Carsten argues that, despite the fact that the meanings attributed to blood are 'neither self-evident nor stable across (or even within) historical locations', there is a continuity in 'the idea that blood reveals the truth' (2013: 2, 3). The essays collectively show that blood has multiple and sometimes contradictory meanings, and that blood promises to (but can never fully) 'encapsulate the truth' (2013: 4). As the title of that special issue indicates, it is the 'flows' and circulation of blood, as well as blood's 'propensity to travel within, between, and beyond' disciplinary boundaries, that are particularly emphasised (2013: 2). At the centre of this set of papers is the search for insights that allow the theorisation and analysis of the multiple kinds of truth attributed to blood.

Critical African Studies published, in the same year, a special issue entitled 'The Vitality and Efficacy of Human Substances', in which the editors (Joost Fontein and John Harries) observe that 'even as blood is evoked as the shared focus of this collection of papers, there is remarkably little blood and bleeding' (2013: 119). Blood, they write, has significance only as it 'becomes entangled in … cultural processes' and thereby acquires layers of symbolic resonance. The aim of that collection of essays was to respond to the question of how to imagine 'a more symmetrical anthropology of human substances' including blood, bone, flesh and skin (2013: 119). Human bodily substances, the editors argue provocatively, are at once subject and object; they exist on the very borders of personhood.

In the edited collection *Blood and Kinship: Matter for Metaphor from Ancient Rome to the Present* (Johnson et al. 2013), a range of scholars similarly historicise blood, and show how its meanings are constantly reconfigured. In another context, Luise White observes in her *Speaking with Vampires: Rumor and History in Colonial Africa* that, unlike English, 'many African languages distinguish between kinds of blood and the circumstances in which it leaves the body in ways that the scientific concept does not, so that the blood of childbirth and the blood of wounds are called by different names' (2000:14). Bloods, all of these writers agree, are diverse, and the meaning of blood highly contextual.

In addition to this anthropological literature on blood, blood is often invoked to describe scenes of extreme violence (rivers of blood, bloodbath, bloodthirsty), and the use of blood as an image relies on an excessive visual evocation. A well-known and often cited instance of South African blood in this sense is the phrase used by MK cadre (MK refers to uMkhonto we Sizwe, the paramilitary wing of the African National Congress) Solomon Kalushi Mhlangu, who said before his execution in 1979, on charges of terrorism against the *apartheid* state: 'Tell my people that I love them. My blood will nourish the tree that will bear the fruits of freedom.' Racial pseudo-sciences have developed a vocabulary to speak about the purity and contamination of blood (black blood, mixed blood, tainted blood), and this is a well-developed area of scholarship in South Africa. Shawn Salvant's *Blood Work: Imagining Race in American Literature, 1890–1940* is a recent example of scholarship that probes the ways in which blood has figured in the formation of racism in the USA, and his insights are relevant to South African discussions of racialised bloods and the blood of disease, violence and spectacular masculinities. While writing this book, I have been struck by how readily almost everyone to whom I spoke about the research was able to list interesting examples and pertinent references to blood in culture and literature. A different approach to the one I adopt here would be to catalogue and classify these bloods, developing typologies of blood as image and concept.

To 'read' blood is the phrase used in medicine to describe the work of logging, charting and interpreting the substances found in blood. When reading blood in a laboratory context, a phlebotomist opens the veins, extracts the blood, and labels and identifies the blood carefully, then sends it to a blood laboratory to be tested. Those doing the blood work need to have parameters for the reading, and to have contextualising knowledge: other bloods with which to compare the blood being read, other time-sensitive samples from the same body, checklists that have to be completed, and clearly calibrated scales for measuring the presence or absence of cellular elements and disease markers in the blood. The blood extracted will reveal intimate and sometimes unsettling information about the body from which it was taken, and the reading will determine the protocols of care required. In many cases, the reading will need to be repeated periodically or even, in extreme cases, several times a day.

This recording of the small changes in blood relies on testing and re-testing, on noticing patterns of repetition, and on careful and patient logging. The reader of the bloods needs to compare and calibrate minute changes, and needs to do so with extreme care, noting and interpreting the findings. For the phlebotomist, the needle that opens the vein is not an instrument intended to inflict pain; instead it is an instrument that invades the body with the aim of diagnosing what is hidden in the blood, in order to determine the treatment and care required. It is the double-sided nature of these needles (to break the skin with some violence, but to gather data for the purposes of diagnosis and with the intention of deciding how to heal and care for the body) that provides the trope for this book.

The blood in this book is history-rich and full of secrets that are as yet undisclosed; and in the analyses in the various chapters this blood is brought to the surface to be 'read'. The argument of this book is that ongoing debates will determine and challenge the parameters used for the readings of this metaphorical blood. To open the skin so that we can log the discrepancies and anomalies in the bloods is invasive, but it is also inevitable and necessary. The bloods are not simply collected and read (or readable); part of the blood work is to debate and to contest the terms and parameters through which this is to be done, and to pay attention to the protocols of testing as well as the ethical protocols of ongoing care.

Whereas some have wanted to insist on a post-racial lens for interpreting the South African present, there is, in particular among younger South Africans, agreement about the uselessness of this approach. It is precisely through the layered, conflicted and conflicting understandings of the racialised past that an understanding of the contested present can emerge: uncomfortable, difficult and invasive – like a blood test. Recent scientific discoveries have shown that much of our past and future is written (and readable) in our blood. Technology now exists to read a great deal in our blood, and we know that the world we live in (and that our direct ancestors lived in) has left traces in our DNA. To decipher these marks, scientists use the encrypted language of DNA sequences. One drop of blood can reveal one's sex and ethnic background, and is a strong predictor of hair, eye and skin colour. The epigenome – the patterning in the DNA of an individual – has been shown to correlate closely with socially patterned factors such as economic and social privilege. These correlations can even, it has been shown, relate to the more distant past. So, for example, the children of Holocaust survivors and the descendants of previously enslaved peoples have very different methylation patterns from those who have not experienced such trauma. Epigenetic marks remain much longer than do the physical scars visible on the surface, and this approach offers a generative way of thinking through the unevenly encrypted effects of *apartheid*'s pasts on South African lives and bodies.

The language used by scientists who study DNA and blood is drawn from the language of reading and writing, of inscription and encryption; this means that blood is itself a readable archive of the past ('Blood as Archive', 2017). The trauma associated with lives lived under and through *apartheid* is written in the blood that circulates under the skin, and blood's epigenomes hold inside them knowledge of the *apartheid* past: a past that has left unequal and oppositional scripts under the skins of our bodies. Gabriele Schwab, in her book *Haunting Legacies: Violent Histories and Transgenerational Trauma*, uses the term 'transgenerational haunting' to talk about the long reach of violent histories on individuals. In the book, she includes personal vignettes through which her own subject position as a German-born woman of a certain age, now living in the United States, is interrogated. Schwab's book is an exploration of the ways in which 'both victims and perpetrators pass on their ineradicable legacies of violent histories through generations' (2010: 1). This transmission, she writes, exceeds the passing on of narratives about the events. She quotes Nicolas Abraham's memorable description of a crypt for buried and disavowed memories of loss and injury (Schwab 2010: 1). Through not mourning, Schwab argues from within a psychoanalytical tradition, those who fail to mourn become like the living dead. Traumatic memories that remain silent are carried in and on the body, somatically writing the disavowed past. Schwab's method is to read texts alongside and through each other, to 'tap into experiences that were never fully known but nonetheless left their traces' (2010: 7).

Most useful is the attention Schwab pays to the ways in which the children of the survivors of trauma are the inheritors of their parents' lived memories, but also of their parents' somatised and disavowed memories. 'Children of a traumatized parental generation', she writes,

> become avid readers of silences and memory traces hidden in a face that is frozen in grief, a forced smile that does not quite feel right, an apparently unmotivated flare-up of rage, or chronic depression … without being fully aware of it, [second generation children] become skilled readers of the optical unconscious revealed in their parents' body language. (2010: 7)

This insight that the second (and third, and so on) generations are skilled readers offers us an alternative to the descriptor, near universally rejected now, of South Africans born after 1994 as 'born-free'. Instead, Schwab's method suggests that we think of this generation not as passively blank pages but as skilled readers of that which is written in the blood – of their parents' but also of their own bodies.

Schwab's work offers a further spur to my own argument, through the way she reads adjacent and oppositional legacies of second-generation victims as well as perpetrators. She uses the term 'entwined' (2010: 22) to describe the archives and memories of the children of perpetrators and the children of trauma sufferers. Sarah Nuttall's *Entanglement: Literary and Cultural Reflections on Post-Apartheid* has used similar phrasing to reflect on the intertwined nature of lives and experiences in South Africa: 'Entanglement is a condition of being twisted together or entwined, involved with; it speaks of intimacy gained, even if it was resisted, or ignored or uninvited' (2009: 1). What Schwab refers to here has a slightly different inflection. Her work, with its optimistic insistence on the possibility of (psychoanalytic) healing, is interested in how 'transgenerational memories and narratives of perpetrator nations can help create the conditions for the descendants of perpetrators to become allies in the struggle against violence and oppression' (2010: 27).

In Michael Rothberg's *Multidirectional Memory: Remembering the Holocaust in the Age of Decolonization*, memory is understood as a form of necessary labour, and his interest is in particular in cases of contested memory or what he terms 'multidirectional' memory. Contested and multidirectional sites of memory, he argues, have the potential to 'create new forms of solidarity and new visions of justice' (Rothberg 2009: 4–5) and through them we can draw attention to 'the dynamic transfers that take place between diverse places and times' (2009: 11). His last chapter, 'Hidden Children: The Ethics of Multigenerational Memory after 1961', is concerned with narratives of intergenerational conflict, and his argument reflects 'as much on the passing down of memory as [on] the histories being transmitted' (2009: 270). Rothberg's approach aims to account for the complex and contradictory ways in which shifting contemporary contexts can inflect and reshape memory, and how generational transfers affect this process. In his reading of three texts dealing with the October 1961 massacre of Algerians in Paris, he shows how the selected works foreground a haunting past and thus seem to *produce* conflict in the present. Yet, he argues, what the texts do is to uncover *already existing* unresolved conflicts and divisions, rather than producing something out of nothing (2009: 272). It is this labour of uncovering that which was already there, he writes, that constitutes the 'ethical dimension of multidirectional memory'. This insight is useful to help us understand the conflicts produced, voiced and staged in South Africa, through which a younger generation has been drawing attention to the existing and persistent unresolved conflicts and divisions running through society. Like those in the texts on the massacre in Paris, the #Fallists and their contemporaries have performed the difficult and costly labour of bringing multidirectional memories into the public sphere, drawing attention to what is already there in the 'overlooked or forgotten archive of the contemporary' (Rothberg 2009: 273).

The trope of a test allows us to think about blood as a richly historical archive as well as a predictive substance, allusive and meaningful with connection and belonging. What the blood test yields (in ways that the spectacular blood of wounds cannot) is precisely a contextualised and historical dimension. It is not simply that the metaphors of blood and blood readings happen to *remind* us of the way we talk about how to read texts, both literary and historical. The method of reading described in *Written under the Skin* requires that different bloods and readings be compared, and logged as a multidirectional and conflicting set, and – crucially – that the terms of the 'reading' be debated and contested. This does not mean that the method demands that the bloods be mixed up, but that the meanings of one blood reading event can only be interpreted when read alongside others. It is a method of reading that demands historical contextualisation, and that seeks out conflicted interpretations. It calls for comparative and intergenerational collaboration, even if this work is disturbing, unpleasant or troubling; and it is through this labour that the ethical implications of our memory labour can be made evident.

Blood's secret and intimate nature, and the necessity of opening up a vein in order for blood to flow out, have been used explicitly in recent scholarship and writings on South Africa's past (one is tempted immediately to say 'bloody past') to talk about the contested layeredness of the archives. In his book, *Askari: A Story of Collaboration and Betrayal in the Anti-Apartheid Struggle* (2014),

Jacob Dlamini urges an opening up in South African studies, and theorises a historical method that will place narratives into mutually interactive spaces, where perpetrators' stories are excavated next to, over and through the stories told by survivors of violence. Dlamini's history probes exactly the messiest and least comprehensible encounters in South Africa's recent history, finding in *askaris* who turn against their own people not marginal figures, but instead the mess at the very centre of our troubled past.

But the argument goes further than that, and Dlamini builds in fact a model for how to access the tainted and compromised archive of South Africa's past. A highly charged figure who enters Dlamini's book, and whom Dlamini arranged to meet in prison, is Eugene de Kock (who is also visited in one of my chapters). De Kock's bloody history, and his involvement in the death squads responsible for the death and torture of many, is well known to South Africans and beyond. In order to understand what the past's secrets mean today, argues Dlamini, we have to look again at de Kock; we are compelled to try to 'understand' him. Kopano Ratele has written on the nuances of the word 'understand' (in *There was this Goat: Investigating the Truth Commission Testimony of Notrose Nobomvu Konile*, Krog et al. 2009), which can mean a range of things – forgiveness being the most problematic one in this case. But Dlamini argues that to write histories of South Africa, we shall need, sometimes unwillingly, to access a range of archives, curated in hostile opposition to one another, and in some cases even bent on one another's annihilation. Interpreted using the terminology of *Written under the Skin*, Dlamini's method is that of the re-test, and the administering of multiple tests, run in parallel and logged alongside and over one another.

A concrete example of these hostile overlapping archives at work can be seen in recent reports of this same Eugene de Kock, who has had an extraordinary late career assisting those in search of the secret graves and burial sites of activists killed by the South African special police force. His knowledge has become extremely useful to those seeking to know the truth about their missing loved ones. It is no wonder that de Kock so fascinates and divides South Africans, but in this instance what I want to emphasise is the physicality of the intimate knowledge he has, of encrypted secrets under the surface. It is not that I want to bring him or his version of history into the light and to give it prominence; what Dlamini argues, and what I develop here, is that the past will keep unfolding and re-opening up in multiple and contradictory ways, and that 'the' truth is one that is made up of the messy, bloody and sometimes incoherent overlay of different competing versions.

Brian Rappert and Chandré Gould's inventive and surprising *The Dis-Eases of Secrecy: Tracing History, Memory & Justice* (2017) not only documents but actually performs uncertainty, and demands of the reader a willingness to be unsettled. The authors include, for example, a section called 'How to read this book', in which readers are shown multiple pathways through the text, either reading chronologically or thematically, following 'sewn threads' indicated in the text (2017: xv). The book is on one level a history of 'Project Coast', a top-secret chemical and biological warfare programme of the *apartheid* government. Yet despite the fact that the book is a distilled account of twenty years of investigation, the authors resist the notion that it should be read as an *exposé*. They want, they write, 'to call into question what is sought from the basic desire to offer a full picture of what took place' (2017: xiii). 'We hope that, between the traces and fragments of our accounts, readers will be able to question themselves and others about the purposes of history and the potential of memory' (2017: xiii).

This insistence on how much we still do not understand about the South African past informs and shapes my own project. Jacob Dlamini in *Askari* uses an embodied metaphor for his approach: I have a skeleton of facts, he writes, which I need to try and flesh out by drawing on many lives (2014: 17). Elsewhere he writes that *apartheid* corruption and inefficiency has seeped into our lives and poisoned us, like something that has entered our bloodstream (2014: 258), and that the histories of complicity run through current-day South Africa like veins and arteries (2014: 11). His book is in the first place a history of the *askaris* whose role in South African life is so complexly opaque. The human subject of his book about collaboration with the *apartheid* state, 'Mr X1', is not a reliable narrator, and is someone who can clearly not be trusted. The official *apartheid* archives, cited in the bibliography of his book, similarly cannot be trusted. Even his own historian voice, Dlamini writes, is not reliable – as someone writing about Mr X1, he is uncertain whether he can achieve a balance between explaining and understanding events. Dlamini places the South African secrets alongside those of Germany, Argentina and Chile, bringing scepticism and an insistence on murkiness to what has at times been the triumphalist discourse of the Truth and Reconciliation Commission (TRC) as a truth-producing machine.

Dlamini's project does not hope to place the four kinds of truth used by the TRC together to reveal a bigger truth; instead, he directs his gaze on to the messiness of compromised truths, to what it means that secrets still remain locked in the verbal and oral archives. The insistence on going back, going back over and going back in, to look again at what had *seemed* familiar stories, characterises Dlamini's approach – as it did also in his sometimes misunderstood *Native Nostalgia* (2009). What I take in particular from Dlamini is the insistence on multiple testings, repeated readings and a messily layered history that keeps unfolding. A further insight is that repeated testing is likely to reveal more secrets and a more bloodied past, rather than to yield a fuller and more straightforward account of the present as read through the past. Grace Ahingula Musila, in her book *A Death Retold in Truth and Rumour: Kenya,*

Britain and the Julie Ward Murder (2015) about the opposing archives through which to understand the murder of British tourist Julie Ward, makes a similar argument. Musila, like Dlamini, insists on the unknowability of her subject. Particularly generative is the argument that the various discursive frameworks around Ward's death do not provide us with *complementary* evidence that leads to a more complete picture. Instead, Musila shows, the different archives through which knowledge is produced and in which it circulates lead to a particular *lack* of focus and clarity.

It is worth being explicit about the advantages of talking about blood rather than skin. There is a well-established body of scholarship devoted to skin. This work is characterised by an interest in skin as a 'cultural border' between the self and the world, as the central metaphor of separateness (Benthien 2002: 1), as social interface and as boundary layer (Jablonski 2006: 2). Skin is theorised as the boundary between self and not-self, but also as a container of that which is inside the self. While skin can, in medical terms, be grafted or even grown, the scholarship on skin is particularly interested in containment and integrity, on the borders of the self. In the literature on skin, the skin *is* the threshold. My response to this body of work is that these meta-narratives are particularly limiting as frameworks for understanding South African everydays, and that they confirm rather than disrupt *apartheid* imaginaries.

Skin has long been the master signifier in South African thought (Nuttall and Michael 2000), promising to interpret even beyond the reach of *apartheid*'s legislated ending. South African histories are dominated by skin as explanatory category, and as principle through which to order and organise the world. Race (easily, *too* easily, read on and from the skin) is in South African everyday life an extremely visible category, even hyper-visible. Skin's very surface seems to insist on certainty, as if the meanings and possibilities of the body are inscribed on and can be read from the skin itself. In some Indo-European languages (such as Dutch and Afrikaans), the words for skin and paper are the same ('vel'), carrying the history of early forms of writing on animal skins with it, and remembering this historical link between the surfaces of bodies and of books. Skin and skin colour in South Africa (as elsewhere, but South Africa has a claim to special status in this regard) are a historical burden but also a spectacle, promising that meaning and value are immediately readable.

South African thought retains its obsessional interest with skin, and there is a widely held acceptance of skin (read as marker of 'race') as a useful analytical category. Kopano Ratele writes that we, South Africans, like 'skinning' each other (2013: 121). He means that we 'read' one another racially, but there is clearly also a reference to the visceral harm done by this 'skinning' work. Skin thus remains a structuring concept, and acts as a shorthand for a particular embodied history. In their introduction to the edited collection *Categories of Persons: Rethinking Ourselves and Others*, Megan Jones and Jacob Dlamini write that our (that is, South Africans') 'language for race is deeply rigid, and has settled into rehearsed grooves of accusation, polemic and defensiveness that remain insufficiently challenged' (2013: 3).

Steven Connor in *The Book of Skin* writes that skin is a container, a boundary between self and world, and that its function is to maintain the integrity of the body (2004: 22). 'For thousands of years, up until the beginning of modern medical science in the eighteenth century, the skin has provided most of the signs and symptoms of the diseases suffered by human beings' (2004: 95). Thus skin was seen as the body's 'script', as if symptoms could be read directly from it. Skin, Connor writes, was like a 'screen' (2004: 26) on which disease was projected and on (and from) which it could be seen, or read. Luise White makes a similar comment in the context of her research on African responses to the introduction of Western biomedical techniques that require penetrating the skin. These had profound and contradictory meanings for the Africans these doctors wanted to treat, she writes, as much African curing 'took place above the skin' (2000: 99).

Connor plays on the double meaning of skin as a screen which both covers and conceals, and on which an image can be projected and deeper insights thus revealed. Skin is not inside or outside, but complex and manifold, he writes (2004: 37). Connor's chapter on ruptures in the skin includes a discussion of scabs, a particularly interesting feature of the border between the open and closed body. Scabs reveal skin's inability to heal itself without blood flow:

> Since the scab is the mark of the injury, and not the injury itself, it transforms the injury *to* the skin into a mark left *on* the skin. A scab is a visual compromise between lesion and healing; it preserves the blemish or disfigurement to the smooth integrity of the skin's surface even as it affirms the skin's successful defence against puncturing or laceration. (2004: 51)

Scabs are scripts, then, of skin's double-sidedness: their function is to preserve the body's integrity, and to carry a memory (the scab itself) of this work, until the work is completed.

Not surprisingly, in an argument so interested in and alive to the meanings of writing on skin, Connor turns to the most interesting form of readable skin, namely tattooing. Tattooing, he writes, 'is a particularly complex form of this interchange between the injury and the mark, since here the marking of the skin takes place through a puncturing of its surface' (2004: 53). Whereas a tattoo is visible on the surface of the skin, the ink is in fact *beneath* the visible skin. The tattooist's needle inserts the ink below those layers of skin that are constantly being regenerated, otherwise the tattoo would simply be shed along with the upper layers of skin. This is a peculiar feature of skin, the fact that it is constantly regenerated since it is fed by blood supply; the epidermal layer is always being sloughed off and destroyed.

For a tattoo to be written on (or more accurately *under*) the skin, a needle needs to be inserted into a layer of skin that does *not* renew itself. The ink needs to be laid down on the reticular tissue of skin. Interestingly, this is also the part of skin that retains the memory of growth and change, and where stretch marks are formed and can be seen. What enables this layer of skin to retain memory is that it is here that the blood vessels are found – it is in fact in the blood and not on the skin that the 'memory' of a tattoo is laid down. It is worth mentioning too that the removal of a tattoo happens not on the level of skin but in the blood. Modern laser treatment can break up the ink under the skin, which is then carried away in the bloodstream. Newer inks carry fewer of the toxic elements that can be dangerous in older tattoo inks. Tattoos using older and now unregulated inks are not poisonous while in place, but can be very dangerous once the ink is dispersed into the bloodstream. Lasering a tattoo to remove it can cause permanent liver and kidney damage, in particular tattoos with a lot of the red pigment that contains mercuric oxide.

What is most distinctive about skin for my purposes is that the visible outer layer is always being regenerated and renewed. Skin layers and their constant regeneration are suggestive as a way of thinking about memory and intergenerational transfer, as skin speaks at once of permanence and inability to change (race or colour), but also always of renewal. Skin's hyper-visibility thus provides us with an archive that is both obvious *and* untrustworthy. In Zimitri Erasmus's recent monograph *Race Otherwise: Forging a New Humanism for South Africa*, she questions whether one can 'know' race 'with the eyes' and has argued for new ways of 'coming to know otherwise', of seeing the boundaries between racial identities as thresholds to be crossed through what she calls 'politically charged acts of imagination and love' that 'break open' the skin (2017: 139). In an argument with a slightly different investment, Sarah Nuttall has written about the artist Penny Siopis that her work 'explores the notion of skin surface as a place where meanings can be unmade' (2013: 432).

Skin understood in these ways is a screen which screens us from seeing more, and from seeing and knowing better. Skin's surface promises that it can seal in and preserve *apartheid* thinking about the classification and separation of bodies. When Connor and White write of how skin has, through the ages, been read as a script through which the body could be diagnosed, one might want to suggest that in South Africa skin itself *was* the disease, and that the 'readings' taken from the surface of skin continue to feed *apartheid*'s ways of knowing the body. It would also seem that *apartheid* thinking, like the skin on our bodies, has renewed itself and reinvented itself; and importantly has lost the memory of this process. What, then, does blood offer us as a way to think with, if skin's short memory and the way it seals off, and in, disappoints us and obscures so much? The argument of this book is not an attempt to escape or evade skin (by saying skin is dead), but instead to explore the meanings of the secrets and memories just under the surface of the skin, and circulating in the body. The time of skin and the time of blood are of different orders. If skin can be read (and misread) on the surface, blood is always encrypted.

Chapter overview

The first three chapters re-enter familiar prison cells (those of Nelson Mandela, Eugene de Kock and Ruth First) in a search for old traces and overlooked signs of blood. The cell that has stood at the centre of dominant ways of understanding South Africa's newness is that in which Nelson Mandela was imprisoned on Robben Island. Mandela's role as peace-loving mediator and understandings of him as the main creator of the 'Rainbow Nation', alongside questions of transition and the TRC's forgiveness agenda, have for the last twenty-five years provided some of the leading ways of understanding South Africa. These concepts have often been contested and challenged, yet in literary and cultural studies have guided approaches and shaped the ways in which South Africa is taught at home and in particular elsewhere. A concern with history and memory in South Africa in the 1990s seemed to herald a move towards greater historicity, but more recently a younger generation of South Africans have accused their parents instead of amnesia, and see the Rainbow Nation as a collective condition of forgetting rather than of resurgent remembrance. This chapter examines the ways in which certain understandings of Nelson Mandela have been central to the manufacturing of amnesia, and the creation of what I describe in this chapter as bloodless time. More importantly it argues that new approaches to the Mandela legacy are bringing out a Mandela for our times.

The next chapter again enters a prison cell, this time to examine the complex and contradictory discourses around blood as kinship. Eugene de Kock's name is associated with the bloodied histories of Vlakplaas, the farm close to Pretoria that served as the headquarters of the South African Police counter-insurgency unit and was home to the infamous death squads working on behalf of the *apartheid* government. Many accounts have been published of the atrocities authorised and performed at Vlakplaas, and de Kock's own testimony to the TRC has been the subject of much discussion, often interpreted as a form of truth-telling that exposed the horrors of *apartheid*. Why, when so much has already been told, do many journalists and the relatives of his victims still desire to meet the man himself and to spend time in close physical proximity with him? I discuss the accounts by two such visitors, both women, paying close attention to the ways in which they read kinship. I argue that, in each case, the author inscribes de Kock into a certain archive, and in particular an archive of kinship and belonging. The bloods of these two accounts of kinship systems are oppositional and contradictory (what Rothberg calls multidirectional), despite a recurrent discourse of shared humanity in both texts.

De Kock's release from prison in 2016, into a still undisclosed location, forms a strange coda to this chapter. The preparations made for this release into a domestic sphere outside prison reactivate discourses of home, intimacy and belonging in one of the accounts of a visit. In this chapter I scrutinise the circulation of the photographic archive of de Kock's life, arguing that the ways through which one enters (or resists) the kinship offered by his family photograph album reveal a great deal about how the 'blood' of de Kock's life will be interpreted. Many have read Pumla Gobodo-Madikizela's account of her visit to de Kock as an argument for a shared humanity; I find in her document a different, more resistant interpretation of the meaning of the visits and one that insists on the blood of violence rather than kinship.

In the following chapter, it is another prison cell that provides the scene of the test event. I show that the murdered activist Ruth First's layered revisiting of the prison cell in which she was held is a form of retrospective self-scrutiny. An overlooked reference to menstruation provides me with the lens through which to view the recurring references to seeping and leakage that run through her account, which is an account precisely of the careful work of *not* accounting. First's document of her imprisonment was written from exile in London in the 1960s, from where she re-enacted on paper and in a restaged documentary film her time spent in the prison cell. Going back into the prison cell in her memory is a way of making sure that she brought out all she took in with her, that she left no traces or marks, and that her statements and remarks made inside the prison are classified and interpreted within an archive she can control. First keeps imagining that the documents containing her words and her signature are now on deposit in the police archive, that her words have been used to offer a hostile interpretation of her own deeds and those of the other activists with whom she collaborated. It is First's reflections on the notion of a usable activist archive and her conception of a resistant library that provide us with a clear template for future ethical scholarship. Her account and her writings about libraries develop a model of scholarship as an absorbent (sanitary) pad, for what can enter and what must not enter, and for how archives and libraries determine what is known and can be known.

One of the most famous events to take place in South Africa was the first human-to-human heart transplant. International reception of this event has often inscribed the surgeon Christiaan Barnard within a certain modernity narrative, but there are rival interpretations such as the one articulated by Ali Mazrui, who wrote that the heart transplant was in fact made possible by *apartheid* understandings of the unequal worth of bodies, hearts and blood. Heart transplantation relies on donation, hosting and the extreme sharing of organs. Mazrui was quick to see how this mimicked the structure of *apartheid* society, which regarded black bodies as resource for the extraction of labour. A late and curious chapter in the heart transplant saga was the circulation of gossip that laboratory worker Hamilton Naki was in fact the surgeon who performed the operation. Naki was the subject of at least two documentary films, and of many web blogs and articles which championed the narrative of his belated recognition as a parable of the new South Africa. His reputation, it seemed, had been reinvigorated; more complex is the realisation that this narrative in fact served the interests of Barnard (a man who was always intent on revitalising his image). In this chapter, the gossip and rumours about Hamilton Naki lead us into multiple archives. The heart transplant can be contextualised and understood (as Barnard did) as evidence of the high flowering of medical science in ultra-modern *apartheid*-era South Africa; or it can be seen, through the gossip that circulated later, as evidence of the long extractive reach of *apartheid*. While Naki is enlisted as the enforced donor who revitalises Barnard's fame, his life's meanings continue to circulate in other, contested ways.

The second part of the book concerns archives of the emergent present, and the contemporary discourses around the activist labour of multidirectional memory as resource for the future. The first chapter in this section offers a reading of the recent student protests in South Africa, arguing that the protests were not coded through shit, as many have argued, but through blood. Accounts of the South African student movement typically locate the beginnings of the #RMF and the later #FMF (Rhodes Must Fall and Fees Must Fall) movements in the bucket of human excrement that Chumani Maxwele brought on to the campus of the University of Cape Town on 9 March 2015, and emptied on to the statue of Cecil John Rhodes. While origin narratives can never be trusted completely, it is nevertheless a powerful story, drawing attention to questions of dirt, cleansing and the often disjointed and disorienting journeys many students have to make between home and the university campus. In this chapter I make two linked arguments. The first is that thinking about discourses around cleaning, cleansing and dirt is a useful way of understanding some of the demands of the student movement. The chapter traces the life cycles of various forms of dirt and cleansing as part of the debate about the nature of the university and its historic and symbolic legacies. The second part of the argument is that these dirt discourses are informed by notions of blood and belonging. This chapter disputes the born-free descriptor of this generation of students through paying attention to the ways in which parents, ancestors and kin were invoked in their utterances and actions, and in particular through images and performances using blood.

A feature of South African fiction in the last two decades has been the interest in youth characters (in particular, but not exclusively, university students and school pupils), and this has reinforced an emphasis on themes of emergence and newness in the critical literature. Resisting this 'emergence' trope,

I read some influential novels not as works by new-blood born-frees, but instead as part of a trend in which writers turn their gaze to intimately configured scenes of care. The bloods in these novels, I argue, are not the bloods that mark emergence or rites of passage (despite the presence of circumcision and menstrual bloods that seem to confirm the emergence narrative) but instead are to be read as the bloods of intergenerational care. I link the novels and other writings to medical and literary forms of activism. The novels, if read not as symptoms but as crises, debate and configure rich contextual parameters for the way we should read. The bloods in the novels may be visible on the surface, but it is the histories of the bloods, and the careful reflection on what the best ways are to log, record and interpret them, that single out these novels as representative (and not emergent) works of our time. The novels are part of a trend in South African writing of constituting communities of care through literature, in particular through radical reinterpretations of self-care genres.

The final chapter uses as its focus a small prototype from visual artist Zanele Muholi's menstrual project *Isilumo Siyaluma*, the image that has been used on the cover of *Written under the Skin*. Muholi's thumbprint, from which she has created a series of kaleidoscope-like artworks, is a bloody record of identity rather than a forensic marker left at a crime scene. In Muholi's own reflections on her photographic and creative work, she describes her work as a form of activism: documenting lives, and remembering and marking where one has come from. But a crucial part of this project of documenting black women's lives is also documenting the violence done to black women's bodies. This final chapter's argument is that Muholi's powerful blood archive draws together bloods that have remained largely invisible and crucially unconnected – menstrual blood, the blood of rape and the blood of child-bearing. In her book *Rape: A South African Nightmare* (2015), academic and activist Pumla Dineo Gqola argues that rape is not peripheral but central to South Africa today. Gqola's book 'reads the blood' by showing the long histories that have shaped South Africa's rape nightmare, but also counts the costs not only of rape but of the work of caring for those who have been raped. While acknowledging the importance of the work, she also writes of her own wish *not* to have to write about this topic, in a passage that reflects on the ethics of scholarship as well as the costs of this bloodied knowledge.

It is part of the argument of my book that the younger generation of scholars and academics are taking up the hard and demanding labour of 'reading' the bloods – of our own times, and also of the past. Already in their thinking, their creative practices and their scholarly work, we see a recalibration of how we understand the South African present, as well as our shared, divided, multidirectional and oppositional pasts. Through the image of the blood under the surface, this monograph interrogates the existent archive and the accepted master narratives of the new South African order. The meanings of the blood, written under the skin, are to be understood in this way – as bloods that are taken from a body in order to determine the future care and improved health of that same body from which the blood was taken. This work is intimate, demanding and dangerous, and requires great care and respect. How the bloods are read elsewhere is often not the primary concern of this generation of scholars and writers. But anyone wishing to understand literature and culture from and about South Africa has a duty to be informed about these discussions, and to take note of the ethical protocols developed by the scholar activists reading the bloods.

Part I

Reading Mandela's Blood: The Transition, and the Cell as Portal into Bloodless Time

1

Nelson Mandela's death was not unexpected, as he had been ill and frail for some time, and absent from public life. Predictions of the confusion that would reign after his death, and the fears of lawlessness that would descend on the country, implied that it was Mandela himself who held the country together. Events around his death and funeral reinforced this sense of meaning being lost, the present becoming unreadable and the future uncertain. During the last months of his life, when he was already too ill to perform any public duties, striking mineworkers were shot at by security police at Marikana, who killed at least 34 and wounded a further 78 or more (see Alexander et al. 2012). The backdrop to the news of Mandela's death in December 2013 was the aftermath of these other deaths, and the struggles of families, mostly from the Eastern Cape Province, to pay for the burial of the men who had lost their lives. In the next months, South Africans witnessed the beginnings of what would come to be known as the #Fallist movement, the term Fallist being derived from the call for the statue of Cecil John Rhodes on the campus of the University of Cape Town to 'fall', and later for tuition fees to be adjusted for students who were unable to afford a university education. These events were seemingly unconnected to the 'transition' narrative of South Africa under Mandela, as if the present became – to many – unreadable.

The threat of meaninglessness was given form in a surprising way at Mandela's state funeral, when a sign language interpreter translated speakers' words into a language that other sign language users neither recognised nor understood. South African sign language communities have strong histories of activism and advocacy, and the inclusion of the sign language interpreter was a gesture in line with the ideals of the Rainbow Nation and the explicit and performed diversity associated with the celebrated constitution. The presence of an interpreter who was speaking a language that no one else could understand (he was speaking 'rubbish', other sign language speakers commented) caused embarrassment to the ANC and to the organisers of the funeral. Various representatives of the sign language community made statements such as the comment by Braam Jordaan, the 'Young Deaf Leader for the World Federation of the Deaf' (http://www.bbc.co.uk/news/world-africa-25330672), that 'deaf people had been excluded in South Africa long before apartheid happened', using the language of exclusion and marginality that is such a distinctive feature of South African discourses.

The nonsensical signing caused offence to many, leading the government to make a statement that it wished 'to assure South Africans that we are clear in defending the rights and dignity of people with disabilities'. Thamsanqa Jantjie, the 'fake' interpreter, made evident the crisis in representations of Mandela through his 'bad' translation. While his interpretation was not an accurate translation of what was being said, it was indicative in other ways of how Mandela's life (as well as his death) had come to be represented. Jantjie's hand signals and bodily actions were highly repetitive and used a limited repertoire. No matter what the speakers said, he made the same movements to interpret their words. Jantjie's inaccurate translation interpreted much of what is and has been written about Nelson Mandela, accurately reflecting the repetitive nature of the discourse.

In Sarah Nuttall and Achille Mbembe's contribution to *The Cambridge Companion to Nelson Mandela*, 'Mandela's Mortality' (an essay that was written before Mandela's death, but finalised after his passing), they comment on Mandela's own attitudes to death and the obligations of the living to the dead (2014: 267). They ask whether 'Mandela's death might reveal a void at the heart of a country that has already tried to mask such an emptiness at its centre' (2014: 268). Their chapter makes use of the memorable image of the cell as shroud, as if Mandela were already dead while incarcerated – or as if the cell prefigured his later absence as well as his grave. In my discussion of Mandela's death, I am less concerned with marking the void he left. The contribution of this chapter is instead to map the investment of a younger generation in excavating the revolutionary potential of Mandela's legacies, and regenerating these meanings for the present. The significance of the subsequent death of Winnie Madikizela-Mandela in April 2018 has brought a complicating perspective to the legacies of the Mandela name. Shortly after Madikizela-Mandela's death, former South African Police commissioner George Fivaz (who had been appointed in 1995 and served during the transitional period) admitted in an interview that there was in fact no evidence to link Madikizela-Mandela to the murder of Stompie Seipei, implying that there were more secrets yet to be revealed about her treatment at the hands of the *apartheid* government. For future scholars, the cell of prisoner 1323/69 might become a significant focus, and Madikizela-Mandela's autobiography *491 Days* (first published in 2013) will become a central text through which to excavate the past (Iqani 2015; Hassim 2014).

In his 'Theses on the Philosophy of History', Walter Benjamin writes that in every era the same threat hangs over us: 'that of becoming the tool of the ruling classes'. In order to prevent this from happening, every generation needs to reinvent anew the appropriate forms of resistance, so as to 'wrest tradition away from a conformism that is about to overpower it' (1973: 247). For Benjamin, the role of the historian is to fan the spark of hope from the past, because even the dead are not safe from those who desire that the working classes should forget their links to earlier struggles. Instead of keeping alive the revolutionary ideals from the past, these individuals are encouraged to invest all their energies in the vision of 'liberated grandchildren' (1973: 252). It is when the links to the past's activist agendas have been severed that the spark of hope dies down, opening instead the chasm that is the 'homogeneous empty time' devoid of hope (1973: 252). Benjamin's writings have a peculiar resonance for scholars of South Africa (Dlamini 2009; Dubow and Rosengarten 2004; Rothberg 2012), and his concern with the nature of redemptive memory and the urgent need to keep alive the spirit of messianic time speaks directly to many contemporary debates.

South African author and commentator Sisonke Msimang (2014) has written about the 'many Mandelas', dividing his life into blocks of time in which Mandela the 'teddy-bear' is just one phase alongside and against which the other phases and meanings can be mapped. To say, as I do here, that the significance of Mandela's legacies is in need of revision is not an original insight, and in the final section of this chapter I discuss some of the many projects that do exactly this: revising and complicating the narrative of Mandela as 'free' goods, free from historical time and freely available to anyone. The significance of one of the 'many Mandelas', Winnie Madikizela-Mandela, and her role as keeper of what Benjamin calls 'the spark', is likely to become a main strand in this unfolding narrative through which a younger generation is reinventing and repurposing the activism of previous times.

Temporality is an aspect of Mandela's image that has received a great deal of attention, especially the length of time he spent in prison. Prison time, and in particular the time spent in Robben Island high-security prison, is distorted and folded, cyclically and repetitively punctuated. The time of imprisonment was precisely intended to take the political prisoners outside of time; the isolation of prisoners has as its aim to break the prisoner's sense of his (or her) body as connected to the struggles outside. David Schalkwyk uses the phrase 'chronotopes of the self' in his analysis of the kind of self one can produce in prison (2001: 1). James Clifford glosses Mikhail Bakhtin's concept of the chronotope as 'a fictional setting where historically specific relations of power become visible and certain stories can "take place"' (1988: 236). Richard Vokes and Katrien Pype read this as drawing attention to the political possibilities of the concept (2018: 2), and write that chronotopes have allowed anthropologists to 'specify the entanglements of time and space in various social and political lifeworlds' (2018: 3) as they humanise time and space.

Mandela's cell as chronotope works in the opposite way, deleting time and space rather than making visible the particular mutual linkages between them.

It is not a chronotope of multiple chronologies and greater specificity, but instead one that creates a universal time-space that is 'free': freely available to anyone, anywhere, anytime. The cell as this space outside of history and time has become extremely familiar, and the dimensions and shape of it are known through the seemingly endless photographic records of the cell, and through the many biopics of Mandela in which the actors playing him re-enter this room or recreations of it. The many Mandelas on screen are different from the many Mandelas spoken of by Sisonke Msimang. Msimang's 'many Mandelas' argument is an attempt to disentangle and separate out the different, and at times contradictory, phases in Mandela's life and so to reinsert a date stamp and recuperate the activist agendas. The repetition of the many Mandelas on screen and in photographs confirms the substitutability of the same, universal, Mandela. They are, as Litheko Modisane puts it, 'signifier[s] of a signifier' (2014: 236).

Adding to this sense of a multitude of Mandelas is a familiar set of repetitions, the photographs of people (not only Mandela) looking out through the bars of what used to be his cell. Mandela himself was on many occasions tautologically pictured (as free man and president) looking through the window of the cell. The photographs of the cell's window are taken, at times, from outside the cell – the camera's viewfinder and the viewer gazing in on the restaging of the imprisoned body behind the bars. At other times, the camera lens is focused on the body inside the cell. In some pictures, Mandela is photographed from the viewpoint of someone standing in the doorway, the camera pointing at the window through which we can see yet more cameras pointing in the opposite direction into the room, thereby creating an infinite series of reproductions of the self-same image being captured. We see Mandela staring out of the barred window, a window that now does not so much represent imprisonment as the certainty of the freedom that came (for Mandela in the first place, though we are also encouraged to think of the transformative power of his 'long walk to freedom' for all – South Africans as well as more universally for anyone in the wider world).

In the visual memory of Mandela's life and presidency, the prison cell on Robben Island has played a central role, despite the fact that it is well known that this was neither the cell from which he walked free, nor the only cell in which he was kept imprisoned. Nonetheless, the Robben Island cell has taken on mythical proportions and in this way it has been emptied of its historically specific meanings and has entered the 'empty time' (that is, the time without activist agendas) that Benjamin identifies. Mandela was not the only prisoner to use that cell, but the time spent there by prisoner 46664 ('the President', as tour guides, who sometimes wear T-shirts with the number 46664 stencilled on them, would refer to him when he was in office) is what has been bracketed and is memorialised by the number on the door, freezing the room in mythological time.

The museum of the prison and the cell recreates, in the manner of the re-staged rooms of famous people, a particular moment in the life of prisoner 46664, and through it of the bloodless (violence-free) time of 'humanity'. The cell promises to be a portal into the significant and famous imprisonment, and to give the visitor access to the transformative presence/absence of prisoner 46664. In these recorded, photographed, staged visits to the cell, the effect is of a repetition of sameness. The images follow the protocols of the tourist photograph, a type of image that desires repetition, recognition and iconicity. The cell functions as the ideal space for a selfie, reliant as this genre is on a familiar and pre-determined set of locations, with which the self-portrait engages. The value of the image is precisely its acknowledgement and repetition of previous images, and its role as part of a series. Re-entering the cell (whether one is Mandela or someone else) offers a clean and bloodless entry into the timeless universal chronotope, a moment that has been packaged as part of a South African heritage tourism outing. Jesse Weaver Shipley has written of selfie photographs that while 'one aspect of selfieness is fixing in time and space an idea of the self, another, opposite aspect is capturing and conveying the idea of transformation' (2015: 409). The selfie taken in the cell of prisoner 46664 fixes the self in this time and space, but the space is at the same time emptied out of its own date stamp, in service to the transformative promise of the image-making process.

The official website of Robben Island contains the following description:

> Robben Island, the unique symbol of 'the triumph of the human spirit over adversity, suffering and injustice' with a rich 500 year old multi-layered history, is visited every year by thousands of people eager to understand and honour the important aspects of South Africa's history that the Island represents. (http://www.robben-island.org.za/tours)

The website includes graphics which seem to bring the viewer to the island by boat, changing suddenly to a bird's-eye view of the scene as we come closer. When we reach the island, the camera swoops away into blue sky before one reaches the prison building, as if to insist on freedom rather than imprisonment. Instead of the prison becoming visible, a banner appears in the cloudless sky, describing the island as 'a symbol of the triumph of the human spirit over adversity'. The meanings ascribed to the island prison universalise the incarceration of the prisoners held there, and the website urges the visitor to pay her ZAR 340 so as to be touched and illuminated by this transcendental place. On visiting the cell, the website promises us, we shall be impressed by prisoner 46664's 'human spirit', and be transformed by it. The photograph taken there proves that one has imagined *being* that transforming and transformative prisoner, and can exit cleansed and liberated from the guilt and burdens of historical time. The selfie inside the cell captures the moment of transfiguration, at the same time as it destroys the date stamp. This is the empty homogeneous time, according to Benjamin, that deprives us of hope that a more just future can be achieved.

The prison cell's function is thus to cleanse and to sanitise, and the incarceration is understood as a period that forged the human spirit, a spirit that Mandela is held to exemplify and embody. The incarceration itself becomes understood as a period of purification for Mandela, rather than as a time of resistance to or of oppression by *apartheid* laws. The cell and its inhabitant become recycled as universal and empty, a blank screen on to which anyone can project her desires. Re-entering the cell is to enter a timeless and universal space, and one that gives access to dehistoricised enlightenment with no reference to *apartheid* or to historical injustices: simply free. Here the cell functions as what Jessica Dubow and Ruth Rosengarten describe in reference to Benjamin as a 'dialectic at a standstill: that instant in which the sequential relation of past to present is exploded in a freeze-frame filled to the bursting point' (2004: 678).

This re-entry is in stark contrast with the difficult and bloody entries I theorised in the introduction, and which many interpreters of Mandela's life and political meaning have raised as alternatives. Entering the sanitised cell, with its unreadably universal date stamp, one cannot access any of the meaning-rich bloods through, and in, which we can read the ever emergent present of South Africa. What this re-entry does is merely to remix the meagre archive, without bringing new meanings to the surface, instead relying on the language of 'universal humanity' to provide a gloss that, like Jantjie's translation, drives Mandela's life into encrypted meaninglessness.

Litheko Modisane (2014) has made the illuminating observation that Mandela was always being adapted, always in translation. Adaptation and re-enactment offer us generative ways towards an understanding of Mandela's meanings. It is not only Mandela himself who was represented in repetition; there are many film adaptations of his life, and many Mandelas on screen. Vanessa Agnew, in a special issue of the journal *Rethinking History* devoted to the theme of re-enactment, argues that 'a concern with personal experience, social relations and everyday life, and with conjectural and provisional interpretations of the past' (2007: 300) is characteristic of re-enactment in recent times, an orientation Agnew ascribes to 'history's recent affective turn' (2007: 300). Agnew's insights about the temporality of re-enactment are particularly useful for understanding the ways in which Mandela's cell and body function on screen. She writes that 'reenactment's collapsing of temporalities and its privileging of experience over event or structure … raise questions about its capacity to further historical understanding and reconcile the past to the present' (2007: 301). Agnew also comments on televisual re-enactment as being reliant on a sense of history not in terms of narrating past events and large-scale processes, but as the substance of transformative experience and staging. Although reenactment often centers on the iconographic moment and presumes an understanding of the past 'as it really was', reenactment is, one might say, always a performance in search of a storyline. (2007: 303)

Pumla Dineo Gqola's *What is Slavery to Me? Postcolonial/Slave Memory in Post-Apartheid South Africa* includes an analysis of a 1999 SA television series called *Saints, Sinners and Settlers* (2010: 116), in which historical figures from South Africa's colonial past were put on trial. These trials were framed as history lessons, intended to teach not only the history of the figures put on trial but also the values and ideals of the constitution. In these staged trials, we see a public enactment of memory, and what has often been described as a 'coming to terms' with the past, as if the past can be laid to rest after it has been re-enacted and put on trial. Gqola points out that the televisual trials used the same format as the hearings of the Truth and Reconciliation Commission (TRC), reinforcing this sense of meaning-making from the present (2010: 117). Testing the past, Gqola shows, used presentist frames that were informed by and supported the spirit of the TRC's interest in reading the past through the present for the purposes of reconciliation. Re-enactment was seen as healing and transformative, part of the project of making the transition to a reconciled and healed future. In trauma theory, this belief in the power of re-enactment to reset the clock recurs. The settlement with the past, and coming to terms with the past, is often presented as a way of making a transition to a new start.

Trauma theory informs the way the TRC's project has been understood, as a definitive resetting of the clock. Such an approach rests on the belief that there can be a new beginning, reconciled and healed. Michael Rothberg argues that despite the fact that 'transitional eras are premised on a disruptive, qualitative break in political regime, liberal transitional narratives seek to install a more reassuring plot promising closure' (2012: 7). Nelson Mandela's cell, in particular as it has been represented on screen and in photographic images, has been constructed as a space outside historical time in which one can reset the clock, suspending time and gaining access to a reassuringly bloodless time. Film scholarship has provided us with ways of thinking about return, re-enactment and its effects. Robert A. Rosenstone's essay 'The Reel Joan of Arc: Reflections on the Theory and Practice of the Historical Film' (2003), on cinema and historical re-enactment, remains the standard theoretical intervention. Re-enactment in Rosenstone's analysis is not a form of therapy and healing, but is instead a troubling of history that provides us with useful ways of understanding the complexities of the date stamp, through paying attention to the historical contexts of the event re-enacted as well as of the moments and contexts of the re-enactment.

Lindiwe Dovey, in her work on film adaptation (2009), and Litheko Modisane, in his ongoing project about translations of Mandela for and on screen, have developed influential models in South African cinema studies. Modisane has paid sustained scholarly attention to Mandela on screen, complicating the bland version that cinema has done so much to perpetuate. He quotes Martha Evans's interesting observations about the fact that the first live broadcast on South African television was the release of Nelson Mandela from prison. This same 'live' event is endlessly repeated and quoted on screen (some examples include *Invictus*, *Otello Burning* and *Long Walk to Freedom*), emphasising the sense of Mandela's walk out of prison as a moment zero, a resetting of the clock (Modisane 2014: 225). What this 'live' broadcast, spooled over and over, does, instead of proving the specificity, is to re-enact that moment zero, another paradoxical chronotope of timelessness and universality.

Modisane does not test the accuracy of filmic portrayals of Mandela against actual historical events, but wants instead to 'inquire into how film has constructed Mandela and to assess the discursive implications of such constructions' (2014: 225). He shows, in his complex analyses of Mandela on screen, how Mandela poses an 'aesthetic and intellectual challenge' to film-makers (as well as to film viewers, one might add) precisely because he leaves so little to the imagination (2014: 225). Modisane's comments on the enduring appeal of the Clint Eastwood film *Invictus* are instructive: 'By moralizing and sanctifying the figure of Mandela, *Invictus* is able to install a dehistoricized version of the man, delinked from revolutionary connotations but available as a "post-racial" figure of unity' (2014: 234). The film Mandela who stands out in this category is undoubtedly Morgan Freeman in *Invictus*.

Invictus opens with the singing of a version of 'Shosoloza', an isiNdebele work song here interpreted by the overwhelmingly white South African boy band Overtone, and accented in the universalising sounds common to South Africa on screen. The soundscape of *Invictus* is representative of the diluted 'South Africa-lite' soundtracks on many films that use the country as backdrop and setting. The soundtrack is thus part of the project of translating South Africa to the world (and itself), and is a distinctive element of the interpretation of the transition miracle for an international audience. The film opens with news footage of then president F. W. de Klerk making the announcement of Mandela's imminent release. The film screen recreates the sense of an old 4:3 format television screen, the news footage taking up only a reduced rectangular space on the screen. This brackets the documentary aspect of the opening scene, emphasising the 'truth value' and recreating the moment of transmission. But it also creates the sense that we are about to see more, and get 'the story behind' the story seen on the smaller screen news report. 'South Africa seems to be on the verge of a civil war', we hear a white South African news reporter saying, interpreting the images on our screen inside a screen. The film cuts to Nelson Mandela/Morgan Freeman, who is shown asking a crowd of black men to give up arms, and the voice-over glosses the scene as depicting the 'threat of violence' (or as some news reporters liked to call it 'black on black violence') as the nation is poised on the verge of becoming. This is a heavily edited version of that moment, which deletes the historical contexts of *apartheid* and racialised violence, locating the threat of violence in black male bodies.

The screen opens up from the small-screen documentary version of events at around minute 4, when we see Morgan Freeman as Nelson Mandela waking up alone in his home. We are given many indications to help us understand that we are in the new time, and that he is 'free'. He rises and walks downstairs and out of an urban house's gate. 'Here he is like clockwork. That makes him such an easy target', one of his bodyguards says, interpreting the moment for us. The clockwork reference evokes Mandela's famous discipline and exercise regime, but for the bodyguards it is these very qualities that make him 'an easy target'. To describe Mandela as operating as if by mechanical clockwork has the extra effect of stressing again this man's ability to reset the clock, or to create what Benjamin calls the 'empty homogeneous time' of clocks and calendars through which the struggles of the past are laid to rest, devoid of their revolutionary spark, in the service of creating the unified nation.

This early morning walk creates one of a series of scenes of staged danger in the film, moments that are unconvincing because we know that the historical Mandela was *not* assassinated. What, then, is the purpose of these repeated moments of danger averted? They are there to teach us a lesson, and their didactic instruction is encoded using the language of film thrillers. We feel the tension, and the effect is to make us realise that it was Mandela who averted danger, and that this historical moment requires new genre conventions, new ways of 'reading'. As Mandela sets out very early, and starts walking out on to the street, we get our cue from his tense bodyguards. The film builds up this tension through a montage that layers Mandela's walk with sequences of a van racing dangerously around city corners, and seemingly coming closer to him all the time. The soundtrack prepares us for the fact that the van is coming, and that it holds a threat to 'Madiba'. As the tension reaches its peak, a man jumps out of the van to deliver a bundle of newspapers to a corner shop. Mandela looks at his guards accusingly: we should understand with them that there never was a threat. As if to confirm this interpretation, the next scene shows the sun coming up over peaceful daily life in a South African township, as a new day is metaphorically dawning.

The film develops this trope of averted danger through a series of instances where the viewer is given small didactic lessons about the need for a change in her attitude and a change in her genre expectations. The film is built around surprising and sometimes amusing juxtapositions that reveal to the viewer her prejudices. So, for example, we are sympathetic to the chief bodyguard (acted by Tony Kgoroge) who is unsettled by the presidential appointment of four *apartheid*-era Special Branch policemen as part of his team. Little dramas play themselves out in the newly formed 'team' of bodyguards, each member needing to unlearn the lessons of the past and to learn the new lessons of the 'Rainbow' moment. In time they are (as we are all meant to be) transformed by the special Madiba magic that unites them, and teaches us, and them, not to expect threat or danger and instead to learn the genre conventions of our new time.

An extended scene of danger averted concerns what the viewer is encouraged to interpret as a threatened terror attack on a rugby ground. The viewer is placed inside the cockpit of a plane, flown by two heavily Afrikaans-accented pilots (who nevertheless speak English to one another in yet another moment that translates South African voices and accents into a more universal filmic language). One of the pilots is heard to say: 'I take full responsibility for what happens from now on', his chiselled Aryan features chosen for maximum menace impact. These pilots are Hollywood baddies, and the viewer grasps the conventions through which to understand them. But at the same time we know this did not happen and that there was no terror attack on the stadium. Hence the suspense we are meant to feel is manufactured. We are being manipulated into feeling a fake sense of relief that Mandela survives, yet again. As the plane flies (without permission) over the stadium, the camera cuts from the menacing face of the (surely racist, we are meant to think) pilot to a view of the plane from below. The words 'GOOD LUCK BOKKE' are written on the bottom of the plane. The manufactured fear gives way to elation. Mandela is safe – and so are we.

In a scene that plays like an advertisement for Cape Town as the very location of the Rainbow Nation, we see the rugby team start running in Newlands, taking a route that ends at the Cape Town waterfront. Their rhythmic breathing is accompanied by the extra-diegetic soundtrack of the blandly inflected 'Shosoloza'. They run through Cape Town towards the docks where a boat will take them to Robben Island prison museum as part of a team-building exercise. We see them meet up with their girlfriends and wives for a rare group date, and set off on a tourist boat. The women are there as a reward, but we also see how they do the work of heightening the emotional register of the scene, and in particular how the captain's girlfriend provides a foil (a screen, one might say) to project and magnify his emotions. They depart from the Victoria and Alfred waterfront development, a shopping centre and playground that aims to create a safe leisure space characteristic of many cities. The trip to Robben Island is a team-building exercise, and the emphasis in the film is on collective identity, the team-building of the rugby team mirroring and echoing the team-building of the newly unified South African nation. The racist utterances of the locker room, we are led to expect, will be cleansed and laid to rest on this trip.

The gangway is familiar from many other films and documentaries where we see Robben Island prisoners upon release, walking in the opposite direction up the walkway towards freedom and away from their imprisonment. Here we see the row of (white) girlfriends and wives standing in a decorative honour guard all along the gangway. The ship sails in the wrong direction, not south but north towards Table Mountain for maximum iconic effect, folding Robben Island, the waterfront shopping complex and Table Mountain into one overly familiar tableau. As we approach Robben Island, the music shifts to a minor key, and a woman's voice wails a lament. The point of view of the camera swoops up and soars over the island as if we are in a helicopter, not a boat. A white warden in old South African Prison Services clothing shows the rugby team around: 'The cell is just as it was', he says in his authentically Afrikaans-accented voice. The rest of the group move on quickly, with the women who have been invited to accompany them. The soulful captain (Francois Pienaar, played by Matt Damon) stays behind and closes the door to the cell, as the others continue on their tour.

The realist conventions of the film are interrupted by this scene in which the ghost of Mandela appears to Pienaar, and the rugby captain locks his gaze on to the ghostly co-occupant of the prison cell. In the interaction between them, the viewer is invited to see that Mandela understands the task before Pienaar: to unite his team for victory. The film's extraordinary popularity can be ascribed to the way it sentimentalises Mandela, and its irresistible pull towards the double happy ending (for nation and team). Michael Rothberg singles it out as a film that 'emblematizes the transnational forces that are shaping the narrative of transitional justice today' (2012: 6). Its enduring appeal for film scholars and viewers is based also on the pleasurable ways in which the film teaches us new ways of watching, and instructs us that the language of danger is inappropriate, guiding us to be transformed and less suspicious.

During this scene in the cell, the camera grants Pienaar his moment of privacy, as the viewer is moved to a position slightly outside the cell and we watch the rugby captain staring out through the all-too-familiar barred window. We watch him looking at the inner courtyard, and spectral presences of prisoners appear, performing the repetitive work of breaking limestone. The white limestone and the dust covering the men are eerily evocative. What we are meant to feel is that this is the past, and that the time of incarceration is over and we are now in the colourful time of the 'Rainbow'. As the captain watches the prisoners working outside, he hears the voice of Mandela and turns around to find a ghostly Morgan Freeman reading the poem 'Invictus'.

Freeman/Mandela's voice is slightly modified to create an echoing sound, to acknowledge that this is a different time: it is the time of (false) memory, as Pienaar clearly cannot have a memory of Mandela in the cell. But it serves also to alert us to the transformative power of this room, and to the fact that the captain is about to attain the spiritual enlightenment that will make of him a great leader and a 'free' man. He stands quietly, watching the timeless time spool out in front of him. The film then cuts abruptly (timeless time could carry on forever, but we have understood our lesson and so can move on), and the introspective moment ends with the captain walking past the limestone quarry, but still hearing Mandela's extra-diegetic voice echoing in his and our ears. A further vision appears to him, as the rest of the rugby team moves on, and he stays behind to make eye contact with yet another ghostly Mandela. The wind rises and the white dust swirls, creating the transition needed for the time out of time to end, and for the enlightened captain to emerge transformed and ready to draw strength from his vision.

Mandela's paleness in this short segment of the film emphasises his otherworldly consciousness, and the sacrifices he made in prison in order to become the transformed and transforming presence. There is another layer of meaning, which is that Mandela seems in this scene to be losing life and blood as he donates power to the captain. In case we have not grasped this, the captain glosses the visit to his adoring and silent girlfriend: it is a narrative of 'incredible forgiveness'. In the next scene it is night, and we see a lifeless Mandela lying on the ground. He has collapsed from exhaustion, as if he has been depleted by all his spectral work and the labour of manufacturing timelessness and universality. The doctor warns that there is a danger to Mandela of working too hard, and the viewer understands: it is as if his life-force is being drained by all the transformative labour he performs.

While the Mandela of *Invictus* has become iconic, there have been other Mandelas on screen, and the list keeps growing. Two recent versions of Mandela attempt more en-blooded interpretations, both acted by South African actors, and in each case there are noteworthy issues related to the films' creation of a date stamp. *Drum*, directed by Zola Maseko (2004), was one of the first feature films directed by a black South African. It is a self-consciously black-centred (to borrow here the useful term coined by Litheko Modisane, 2013) project, and the Mandela we see on the screen is interesting in a number of ways. Maseko's film is set during what is called the '*Drum* era', the magazine acting as a dense chronotope of a particular time and place in South African history. The film recreates and restages many of the scenes so familiar from the *Drum* archive of photographs, and Maseko makes the inspired choice of thematising the camera by making many of his characters photographers who worked for *Drum*. This attention to documenting and capturing the moment creates a powerful meta-narrative about loss, archiving and alternatively imagined pasts as a way towards the future.

A notable minor character in *Drum* is Mr Mandela, acted by Lindane Nkosi. We hear him addressed as 'Mr Mandela' during the opening scene of the film, which is set against the backdrop of a boxing match, establishing for us a world of men, and in particular a world centred around muscular black masculinity. Similar scenes depicting the social world of boxing were included in the *Cry the Beloved Country* film version of 1995 (directed by Darrell Roodt), its presentist politics requiring a different kind of black man on screen than that found in the 1951 film version (directed by Zoltan Korda). Ironically the Reverend Khumalo in the earlier film was acted by Canada Lee, a man who really was a boxer, but whose body had to hide all signs of potential strength and violence. Lindiwe Dovey has written on the differences between the two versions, analysing in particular the nuances around the absence or presence of violence on screen (2009: 164–76).

In *Drum*, we do not see Nelson Mandela boxing, but we see him as part of the world associated with boxing in public life. The photographs of him by Bob Gosani, taken on a rooftop in Johannesburg, present him as a lone hero, shadow boxing and sparring with Jerry Moloi. These photographs are referenced in the famous images of an elderly and smiling Mandela wearing red boxing gloves. Here the point is not so much to remember his youthful vigour and anger, but to show Mandela smiling and jesting. His hands in these photographs resemble soft-toy hands in the register of the teddy-bear that Sisonke Msimang describes. In *Drum*'s opening frames we see Mandela in a social world, and this scene provides us with one of the most pleasurable experiences of viewing the many Mandelas on screen. There is not too much attention to his future singularity. He is 'quoted' here and absorbed in a world of newspaper men and boxing enthusiasts. Njabulo Ndebele's writings on the social life of boxing clubs, while centred on the Eastern Cape and not Johannesburg, build up a rich background of the role of boxing as part of black male sociality (http://stias.ac.za/news/2016/04/behind-sweaty-windows-reflections-on-the-boxing-mecca-of-south-africa/). Mandela's presence here is to situate us, and to help verify the date stamp of Maseko's film. He certainly does not appear in relation to his later imprisonment. Instead we are encouraged to see the young Mandela within a network of versions of black masculinity, and to imagine an alternative future that reinvigorates the activism of previous eras, reinterpreting the meaning of *Drum* for a new generation.

There is another more recent Mandela on screen who excavates other less bloodless meanings, the one played by Tumisho Masha (who took the role of Can Themba in *Drum*), in the film *Mandela's Gun* directed by British filmmaker John Irvin. The historical setting for this film is Mandela's African journeys, and the well-documented 'lost gun' is a trope for the film's attempt to find a Mandela before the lost time, the time that destroyed time, in prison. The gun is a connection with another possible timeline and other ways of thinking about Mandela's life. The buried and lost gun repeats a trope from Mandela's autobiography too, that of the buried and lost original. Mandela was himself aware of the metaphoric richness of the term 'underground':

> Living underground requires a seismic psychological shift. One has to plan every action, however small and seemingly insignificant. Nothing is innocent. Everything is questioned. You cannot be yourself; you must fully inhabit whatever role you have assumed. In some ways, this was not much of an adaptation for a black man in South Africa. Under apartheid, a black man lived a shadowy life between legality and illegality, between openness and concealment. To be a black man in South Africa meant not to trust anything, which was not unlike living underground for one's entire life. (Mandela 1994: 315)

In its attention to the African trip that Mandela made in 1962, the film encourages the viewer to imagine alternative histories that evade the universalising narratives of the many other Mandelas on screen.

Mandela's 'underground' identity has now, in this time after his death, taken on a literal meaning, with his physical body interred in a family grave in Qunu, his birthplace. From Mandela's frequently recycled life there is a reference to death and funerals that has now, after his burial, come to take on further significance. It is an anecdote about a play put on in prison, which concerns a burial and which asks questions about how to honour the dead. The anecdote about the play has been told many times, and is included in every biography. The descriptions are formulaic, and the recycled anecdote (like many origin narratives) is in fact based on a misidentification of the source. The misidentification reinforces the pattern of endless repetition and recycling; the original has been lost and over-inscribed with the incorrect anecdote, which takes over, and feeds into and perpetuates, the mythologised understanding of the event as part of the timeless bloodless story.

The play is often (even typically) ascribed to Sophocles, whereas it was based instead on an adaptation of Jean Anouilh's *Antigone*. In fact it was not even that: it was an English-language translation of the French-language play, a play that is itself an adaptation of the Greek original. The misattribution has been solidified in no small part by the play *The Island*, and by the international fame of Athol Fugard. But here too there is a mistake: the play is catalogued under Fugard's name, but was conceptualised in cooperation with John Kani and Winston Ntshona. This play, a two-hander, is set in a prison on an unnamed island (a clearly allegorical Robben Island) where prisoners are rehearsing for a production of Sophocles's *Antigone*. The themes of the play – tyrants and their unjust rule, and the recognition of the value of blood and community – are atmospherically and ideologically linked to the notion of island imprisonment.

Fugard's play within a play means to alert the audience to the allegorical and political significance of Antigone's revolt. The play is about burial, about the contested meanings of what should be above or below ground, what and who should be given access to a particular symbolic ritual, and who should be excluded and forgotten. In this textualised and staged adaptation of a (mis-identified) translation of an adaptation, we find a version of the encrypted meanings of Mandela's life. What seems to be a clear political allegory is, in fact, a much more complex palimpsest of fragments and incorrect facts.

In Mandela's *Long Walk to Freedom*, he provides what has become the definitive version, the version that most others copy and repeat: 'Our productions were what might now be called minimalist: no stage, no scenery, no costumes. All we had was the text of the play' (1994: 540). He continues: 'I performed in only a few dramas, but I had one memorable role: that of Creon, the king of Thebes, in Sophocles's *Antigone*. I had read some of the classic Greek plays in prison, and found them enormously elevating' (1994: 540). Mandela (or his ghost writer) offers this interpretation of the play:

> Creon deals with his enemies mercilessly. He has decreed that the body of Polynices, Antigone's brother, who had rebelled against the city, does not deserve a proper burial. Antigone rebels, on the grounds that there is a higher law than that of the state. Creon will not listen to Antigone, neither does he listen to anyone but his own inner demons. His inflexibility and blindness ill become a leader, for a leader must temper justice with mercy. It was Antigone who symbolized our struggle; she was, in her own way, a freedom fighter, for she defied the law on the ground that it was unjust. (1994: 541)

The description of this performance takes up little more than a paragraph. This incident is small in its autobiographical narration, but it has been projected on to the vast empty screen that is our collective understanding of Mandela. Striking in all the biographies of Mandela and of the collective experience on Robben Island is how rapidly the small anecdote takes on mythical proportions, and acts as a hook on which to hang large and allegorical interpretations. It is another instance of the production of universal, mythical time (Kathrada 2004: 259; Lodge 2006: 189; Sampson 2011: 234–5).

The play is clearly informed by narratives of life on Robben Island, handed down either through mythology or first-hand accounts by men who had returned to the world outside prison. Neville Alexander, in his book *Robben Island Dossier*, writes: 'It was an unspoken injunction understood by all prisoners who were released from the island that one of the most important contributions they could make to the well-being of those they left behind was to let in the light of public scrutiny on the goings-on in that prison' (1994: vii). In the notes to *The Island*, we read that the 'letters and reminiscences of imprisoned Serpent Players such as (mainly) Norman Ntshinga provided Fugard, Kani, and Ntshona with their inspiration, and the detail for most scenes' (Fugard 1993: 232). The play opens with a memorable enactment of two prisoners doing meaningless work, literally recycling matter endlessly, trapped in 'homogeneous empty time'. The stage notes describe the action as 'back-breaking and grotesquely futile labour'; each of the two men 'fills a wheelbarrow and then with great effort pushes it to where the other man is digging, and empties it. As a result, the piles of sand never diminish. Their labour is interminable' (Fugard 1993: 195). This description of meaningless labour is echoed in Mandela's *Long Walk to Freedom*, where it is made clear that the tasks assigned to prisoners were deliberately pointless to rob the men of any sense of meaning (1994: 458).

But this contextualisation and search for the origins of *The Island* only takes us part of the way. These contexts largely reinforce and confirm the understanding of Robben Island as a laboratory for creating the bloodless and violence-free time of the new nation. Instead I want to suggest a bloodier and more difficult reading of this play about a reburial, one that emphasises the themes of disputed legacy, and the weight of blood in relation to Mandela's (and Madikizela-Mandela's) funerals. Mandela's funeral and commemoration ceremonies were complex and disputed. Patrick Ebewo has attempted to reconcile some of these contested versions. He refers to 'the complex traditional mourning and funeral rituals of the AmaXhosa people', and his accounts of the various stages of Mandela's funeral 'as community performance' interpret these as a form of celebration that successfully balanced the needs for ritual burial with those of a secular state burial. He writes:

> In total, the celebrations during the funeral terminated Mandela's 'long walk', and ushered in the everlasting walk to eternal freedom. In this study, it has been established that ritual and entertainment, instead of acting in opposition to each other, reinforce their mutual complementarity. The rituals which surrounded the funeral were not only efficacious, but they also entertained and gave pleasure to both the performers and the audience, and this culminated in a celebration instead of mourning which is often associated with funerals. (2015: 254)

Ebewo's analysis of the funeral is intent on reconciling 'traditional' mourning practices with performance and entertainment. While such a reading of the funeral attempts to excavate bloodlines that are obscured by the universal narrative of Mandela, there is nevertheless a desire for oppositions to be reconciled and for peace to be made.

Rebekah Lee (2013b) has suggested that disputes about burials, what she calls 'mortuary politics', are part of everyday practices in South Africa. We should, she argues, see the struggles over Mandela's body as 'familiar and even ordinary'. Instead of the family disputes about the funeral being a sign of extraordinariness or disrespect, we might do well to understand these disputes in a more challenging register as a way forward for new scholarship on Mandela and on the current state of South Africa. What such an approach would include would be to re-enter the prison cell, on the lookout for blood and ways of exceeding the bloodless 'free' time. Instead, the disputed, multiple and contradictory meanings of Mandela's life can reverse the universal time's deleted date stamp. In addition, in order to avoid the flattening effects of presentism, we would do well to pay attention to the contexts of our own entry into the cell. I am not suggesting that there is one definitive Antigone-like act that will enable the final blood claim on Mandela. But the work of reading Mandela's bloods has begun, and the scholarship is bringing out a Mandela for the #Fallist generation.

One of the many striking characteristics of the #Fallist movement has been the performance art that has accompanied and interpreted the intellectual project. Frequent tropes in these performance artworks include re-enactments, and this has been a particular feature of the situated performance works of Sethembile Msezane (http://www.sethembile-msezane.com/). Her interpretation of the Zimbabwean bird rising as the statue of Rhodes fell ('Chapungu, the Day Rhodes Fell') captured a great deal of the symbolism of the moment and has been described as a 'poetics of remembrance as resistance' by Kopano Maroga (2017). In another artwork by Msezane, 'The Charter', the artist held across her shoulders a stick from which two scroll-like pieces of canvas hung suspended. On these canvases were printed the words of the 1955 Freedom Charter, and on the ground was a bucket containing red liquid. As she stood during performances in various locations in Cape Town, the red liquid gradually seeped into the canvas and seemed to spread upwards. The effect was ambiguous – was she washing the charter in a bucket of blood, or was the charter growing and being fed from the bucket of blood? In other performances, paint standing in for blood was smeared on faces, as a way of marking violence but also as a counter to the name 'born-free'. Instead, #Fallists were claiming, their births were marked by the blood of violent beginnings, and not washed clean with the blood of freedom. The recurrent accusation of the amnesia perpetrated by their elders, and claims about the absence of ancestors in symbolic spaces, has been a recurring part of the #Fallists' discourses, and I return to these discourses in greater detail in chapter 6.

Scholars associated with and supportive of the #Fallists' calls for the decolonising of the university and the curriculum have provided some challenging reflections on Mandela's meanings. Xolela Mangcu, biographer of Steve Bantu Biko, is writing a new life of Mandela. His project (provisionally called *Nelson Mandela: Romantic Hero, Tragic Figure*) is informed by and carries the date stamp of recent discussions about the transformation and decolonisation of the university. In a discussion of his approach to writing Mandela's life, he writes 'you can be an activist and an academic at the same time. It's very important for students to understand that' (Mangcu 2016). The biography will place Mandela in the context of black intellectual history and will respond to the one-dimensional versions of the early 'rural' chapters in Mandela's life, complicating the narrative of what his early political education brought to his life. The somewhat surprising title sets in opposition two ways of understanding

Mandela: as lone figure in the tradition of the hero as it emerged in the European Romantic tradition of the late eighteenth and nineteenth centuries, and as the tragic hero of Greek classical theatre. The tragic hero is flawed, but it is in particular the view of this figure as a member of a collective that draws Mangcu to the concept. A similar approach is followed by Sabelo J. Ndlovu-Gatsheni in his *The Decolonial Mandela: Peace, Justice and the Politics of Life* (2016), in which he argues that Mandela's life should be understood as an exemplar of decolonial humanism, and that his ideas about reconciliation and racial harmony are ways towards transcending colonial modes of thought.

In a recent special issue of the journal *The Black Scholar*, guest-edited by Litheko Modisane, Victoria J. Collis-Buthelezi and Christopher Ouma, the editors invited provocations under the rubric 'Black Studies, South Africa and the Mythology of Mandela' (2017). The special issue addresses the question of whether Mandela was the troublemaker that his birth name Rolihlahla predicted, or the 'peacemaker, the Father of the true (and reconciled) South African nation; his clan name, Madiba, conjuring up images of the iconic Mandela shuffle with a smile'? The articles collected here are presented as a 'stocktaking' of what Mandela's meanings can be and can become in future. Theirs is a Mandela for this generation, for the #Fallists and for a future Black Studies project in South Africa and beyond. Tshepo Masango Chéry's article describes something we do not read often enough, a teacher reflecting on the politics of the way she teaches 'South Africa'. Masango Chéry (2017) develops and documents some challenging pedagogical protocols for teaching Mandela. Her approach is to use Mandela as a way to disrupt and to trouble dominant narratives about South Africa and the wider continent, and to generate activist agendas in the classroom. Victoria Collis-Buthelezi maps a future Black Studies project for and in South Africa, and begins the work of imagining such a future and such a university. She argues that 'black studies [i]s wake work' (2017: 8), and that this wake can be an important component of the radical remaking of universities in contemporary South Africa. Her notion of the wake draws on Christina Sharpe's *In the Wake: On Blackness and Being*, a book that theorises the wake as the path behind a ship, and keeping watch with the dead – but also coming to consciousness. Collis-Buthelezi's contribution can be read as such a 'wake' for Nelson Mandela, re-entering the cell to pay respects but also to bring out something of value.

There is another grave that might do well as a comparison for Mandela's and that reactivates a certain date stamp and contains the sparks of previous generations' activism. The Natives' Land Act through which black South Africans were divested of rights to land was passed in 1913, five years before Mandela was born. In his famous account of the effects of the passing of the Act (*Native Life in South Africa*), Solomon Tshekiso Plaatje described the death of a child who must have been a close age mate to Mandela. In the chapter 'One Night with the Fugitives', Plaatje writes about the Kgobadi family's eviction from the land they had occupied. The death of their baby contributes to their sorrows and sense of loss, but there is an additional dilemma: the child is not allowed to be buried. Under cover of darkness, the parents bury the baby and have to leave him behind on land that will not claim him, and in ground in which it is illegal for his remains to be interred. Placing Mandela's death (and life) next to that baby's death is suggestive of new ways of understanding the burial within the fullness of Benjamin's messianic time. The links between Mandela and the Kgobadi baby make it possible to draw the bloodlines from the Kgobadi baby and Mandela through to the #Fallist movement and the ideals and projects of those misnamed the 'born-frees'. Reading Mandela's bloods historically troubles the notion of a moment zero that broke these bloodlines and shows ways forward that will excavate and reinvent the activisms and struggles from the past, reinvigorating these meanings for the future.

He Must Not Circulate: Eugene de Kock's Blood Relations and his Prison Visitors   2

The Truth and Reconciliation Commission's promise to uncover the truth about life under *apartheid* provided us with a template through which to understand the South African present. The TRC's findings are archived in recordings and transcripts, and the Commission has been debated in scholarly literature and in the media, and interpreted, transformed and adapted on screen and on stage, as well as in literature. The reckoning with the past brought many secrets to light, although as Jacob Dlamini argues in *Askari*, and as Brian Rappert and Chandré Gould show in *The Dis-Eases of Secrecy*, the many secrets that were *not* told structure the present still, and run like veins under the skin of the current order. Eugene de Kock's testimony to the TRC has been the subject of much discussion, newly reactivated after his release from prison after having served only twenty years of what was meant to be a prison term of 212 years plus two life sentences.

Since his release, de Kock has appeared, incongruously, at two literary events, in both cases attending with his biographer Anemari Jansen. He was asked to leave the *Sunday Times* literary awards shortlist function (Malecowna 2016), as his presence offended many of those attending the event. He was also photographed, thinly disguised as an ordinary civilian, with Jansen at the Franschhoek Literary Festival (Gqirina 2016). He remains recognisable despite the fact that he no longer wears the distinctive thick-lensed glasses so familiar from his photographs, and that his build is much heavier. To see him drinking a glass of Porcupine Ridge wine at a public event, celebrating a book about himself, has angered many South Africans.

Even before his release he had been photographed outside prison, and his name appeared from time to time in sensational newspaper articles, reporting on the help and advice he has given to forensic teams looking for the physical remains of people killed by *apartheid* special forces. His complex role as special advisor came about because of his intimate knowledge of the violence (the word journalists often like to use is 'encyclopaedic', as if praising de Kock for remembering so much); this tainted knowledge is used to locate and return the remains to families who have been unable to bury their dead. His work is a form of decryption, revealing *apartheid*'s secrets and opening the forgotten and hidden crypts. Antjie Krog, whose *Country of my Skull* is widely regarded as one of the important journalistic accounts of the TRC, wrote a more recent piece on de Kock in the *New York Times* in which she reported that de Kock has been described as a 'treasure trove' of information about the secrets of the *apartheid* death squads (Krog 2015). This image is disturbing, as if the graves simultaneously reveal de Kock's worth, and his knowledge of violence is a jewel cache.

The work of finding the bodies is clean: there is no blood left on the bones and physical remains of those disinterred. The blood that de Kock claims to smell, still, on his body (Gobodo-Madikizela 2003: 51) does not hamper this work and in fact has functioned to cleanse him. Louise Green and Noëleen Murray in 'Notes for a Guide to the Ossuary' write that

> [s]eparated from proper names and institutional recognition, human bones unearthed outside the formal spaces of interment present an ethical, as well as an organisational challenge. They are human but also detached from the social networks and institutions whose work it is to recuperate the material trace of the body for human society. Free of the disturbingly organic quality of the newly-dead body, which makes it the object of such careful management, the bones of the long dead are vulnerable to being reinscribed as relic and artefact. (2009: 371)

The bones of the dead that are located using de Kock's intelligence are in this sense 'clean', and the work of locating them is part of de Kock's self-cleansing project.

Madeleine Fullard is the leader of the team of investigators and forensic anthropologists searching for the human remains of *apartheid*'s victims. Their work started in 2013, and Fullard has said of de Kock that his greatest value is his many connections. When Fullard first visited de Kock in prison, she was placed on the other side of a protective glass pane. Initially de Kock was unwilling to assist the Missing Persons Task Team, and during the first meetings with Fullard he was dressed in his orange prison jumpsuit and his hands and feet were chained. Fullard's team were granted permission to take de Kock outside prison, and in an extraordinary act of social excavation and kinship re-enactment, they arranged for de Kock and some of his old colleagues to meet at a private home around a *braai* (the Afrikaans term for a barbecue). The consumption of meat and alcohol is a staple of photographs and descriptions of life at Vlakplaas, and in recreating such scenes Fullard hoped that networks would be unearthed and re-enacted, and old bonds re-established. The purpose of this fabricated sociality is to elicit information that can bring to the surface those buried in forgotten and secret graves; but the point I am underlining here is that the social ties of kinship were themselves reconstituted, and that *this* is what can bring the secret knowledge to the surface.

Journalist Jacques Pauw, the man who broke the Vlakplaas story in the national media, has described how in his early meetings with Dirk Coetzee (the founder of Vlakplaas), he would ply Coetzee with 'more booze and what have you so that I could get this story' (2013b). In Jansen's book on (and partly by) de Kock, his intimate social world is reconstituted through documents, interviews and family photograph albums, and through shared food and drink. While the book has been praised for this excavatory work, I regard this other aspect of it, the kinship networks that are reconstituted through the research for the book, as even more crucial. *This* is the treasure trove that needs to be opened, for the old networks of knowledge about torture and killing to become visible, and to allow the bloods to be logged.

While the promise of *full disclosure* was what underpinned the TRC's relationship to 'truth', in practice perpetrators often revealed *as little as possible*. During the hearings, the testimony of Eugene de Kock was singled out as deserving of a jail sentence, as punishment for his role as commander of Vlakplaas, the *apartheid* death squad headquarters. The 'truth' about Vlakplaas has been exposed in countless books, newspaper articles and television special reports (notably the work of Pauw, du Preez and Dlamini), and de Kock received the name 'Prime Evil', singling him out as the one individual more responsible than anyone else for the murders committed under *apartheid*. De Kock's own testimony to the TRC has been the subject of much comment, and has been read as a form of truth-telling that shocked and exposed the horrors of *apartheid*, leading South Africans into what has sensationally been described as 'The Heart of the Whore', 'The Heart of Darkness' and 'Dances with Devils' (all titles of books about the activities at Vlakplaas).

Anemari Jansen's version of this 'work' presents de Kock's assistance to the Missing Persons Task Force as an apology for the crimes he committed (2015: 303) and as 'help' that he generously provides (2015: 305). This work enabled de Kock (and she claims the same for herself) to look the past in the eye and to move forwards without a sense of guilt. These are extraordinary words, and the 'eyes' into which de Kock looks (to disenchant for a moment her metaphor) are the empty eye sockets in the dried skulls of his victims. The work of identifying the graves is seen not only as clean work but as actually *cleansing*; it is work that makes it possible to enter the future without any sense of having done wrong. Jansen goes even further and talks about her own book as an '*Afrikanerfado*', claiming thereby that what is mourned here is something that Afrikaners have lost. She describes the pain in her 'Afrikaner heart', and as if the point has not been made clearly enough, there comes a final reflection on blood: the blood of 'war veterans' (and we know she means a particular kind, namely Afrikaner war veterans who fought for and in the name of the *apartheid* state) is the same as the blood in her own veins (2015: 309). This identification of what is faced when the grave is opened is shocking, and instructive.

The work of the Missing Persons Task Force is clearly to bring secrets to light; but it is the persistence of other secrets and networks of affiliation that is the more powerful secret unwittingly documented in Jansen's book, and which is revealed also in the book's circulation and how it is discussed in internet chat rooms and on Afrikaans-language news pages. Marjorie Jobson, who assisted families of the missing and dead who wished to meet de Kock, describes how these mourners would be in his presence for more than two hours, during which time he would tell them 'in the finest details exactly what happened' to their murdered loved ones. An important part of this 'treasure' was his willingness to tell the families of victims what happened to the bodies; his intimacy with the bodies is offered to their relatives as a gift. How different would the history of *apartheid* be, Jacob Dlamini asks, if it was told not as a racial war but as a story of fatal intimacies (2014: 2)? Dlamini uses the image of a skeleton coming out of a grave (clearly an image densely informed by the work of the Missing Persons Task Force) and asks us to put flesh back on it. Fleshing out these skeletons will take us back to the moments when the blood was freshly spilt, in close intimacy with the bodies of the killers and torturers such as de Kock. De Kock describes to Jansen the strict and precise protocols followed by the forensic archaeologists of the Task Force, who are able to determine with great accuracy which blows were dealt to a body and what was the cause of death (2015: 305).

Prison writing scholar Daniel Roux writes about 'the demise of prison writing' in the post-*apartheid* era (2014a: 250). He remarks that prison narratives, once a staple of South African autobiographical writing, became nearly invisible after the demise of *apartheid*. In the classic prison writing tradition he has analysed in his work (2006, 2009, 2014a), the archive of prison writing overlaps to a remarkable extent with the archive of resistance writing. In this resistance tradition, individual experience was often used to illustrate or record a collective experience (2006: 22), making many of these autobiographical accounts documents that blurred the boundaries between the self and the community inside, as well as outside, prison. Eugene de Kock's own autobiographical writings, published in the form of interviews with him or directly quoted in Jansen's book, clearly do not fit this model of anti-*apartheid* resistance and in fact belong to the archive of *apartheid* itself. Yet there are some ways in which de Kock's writings (and the sympathetic account of him in Jansen's book) do create a community and make the argument that de Kock is not singular, but representative, and therefore not accountable. In his own writings, de Kock makes this argument repeatedly, claiming that his deeds were not singular and personal, but performed on behalf of a collective.

Roux writes of the new trend in post-1994 prison writing towards 'more collaborative, interview-driven memoirs' (2009: 239) and mentions Pumla Gobodo-Madikizela's *A Human Being Died that Night* as part of this tradition, which he sees as linked to the work of the TRC and through which journalists became the 'editors of and commentators on the life stories they were recording' (2009: 240). Reading the many accounts of visits to de Kock in prison as edited versions of the meanings of his actions is suggestive and helpful. If we read Jansen's book in this way, we see the author at work redacting the material to best serve her readership (and the subject of her biography), and shaping the narrative precisely in search of such a representative voice. The social and intertextual fields of reference that Jansen draws on determine the parameters of the interpretation we give to the text, and the ways in which a text, after publication, circulates in public spaces (at literary festivals, at social events around a *braai*, in discussion forums and in newspaper discussions) and provides a rich set of calibrations through which we can read the social worlds built in, and through, the text.

Related to this is Roux's analysis of new texts in the evolving prison genre, namely the many collaborative prison memoirs that 'tend to adopt an anthropological and therapeutic approach, and are often the products of creative writing workshops for prisoners or ex-prisoners: in other words, they derive from reform and training programmes driven by the prison itself' (2014a: 250). De Kock's biography is not explicitly a self-help text, but if we use some of the protocols Roux outlines for reading this emergent genre, it is possible to plot the theme of self-redemption through narrative (and, crucially, in collaboration with the editor-ethnographer), making de Kock's new biography a surprising and complex continuation of the genre of prison writing. The interweaving of many voices, which was a feature of many of the classics of the South African prison-writing tradition, provides us with a protocol for reading this newly edited version of de Kock's career. And, like the collaborative self-help tradition, this new book includes different contextualising voices – prison psychologist reports, gossip from ex-colleagues and friends, historical writings by de Kock himself, as well as a to-do list written by de Kock in which he projects himself into a future as a free man. Prison writing is often marked by a sense of isolation and its own sense of time. Yet, Roux argues, prisons are also peculiarly responsive to national history and places where we 'discover the deformation of the old still entangled with the inchoate emergence of the new' (2009: 248).

De Kock's biography, of which he is an unnamed co-author, can then be read as a challengingly representative text in the tradition of South African prison writings. Roux points out that the heterogeneity of prison literature has often been muted or forgotten in the service of new hegemonic narratives. He writes:

> The South African prison provides a forceful case study of the complicated way in which history works, the way in which notions of 'periodicity' unfold in social practice, and the messy ways in which time, day-to-day sociability, relations of power and political change can be entangled. It seems to me that if the prison affords many opportunities to talk about the relation between space and power,

there has been surprisingly little work on the complexities of the prison's relation to historical change. (2014a: 249)

The complex archive of de Kock's prison stay provides an ideal subject for such an exploration of prison writing as what Roux calls 'a space of contradictions and multiple temporal points of reference' (2014a: 258).

A further useful set of insights from the existing literature on prison writings concerns understandings of the relationship between the prisoner and his or her interrogator. Roux writes that, for the prisoner in solitary confinement, the only interlocutor was often the interrogator (2006: 25). Barbara Harlow writes in *Barred* about texts by and about women political prisoners, and about their first readers: their interrogators and torturers (1992: x). In the prison writings of political prisoners under *apartheid*, there is often a tension between different versions of writing – that which the interrogator wishes (or sometimes forces) the prisoner to write (a confession, a list of names, an account of secret operations) and the resistant account which is often forbidden and needs to be kept hidden or written in code.

This oppositional, private archive is expressive of resistance to *apartheid* and in defiance of prison censorship, and written as a defence against the prison's denial of selfhood. In many prison narratives, we read of how these records were concealed, buried or smuggled out of prison – the most famous example is probably that of Nelson Mandela writing about the lost and fragmented manuscript that became his famous biography (Mandela 1994; Lodge 2006: 243). Harlow, responding to the numerous accounts of writing on toilet paper, goes so far as to describe prison culture as toilet paper culture (1992: 14). Toilet paper as the surface on which many of these accounts of prison experience are said to have been written is suggestive – toilet paper (in particular the poor and rough variety to which only some would be fortunate enough to even have access in a prison) is not a strong medium, and also is not durable. In addition to the flat surface providing space on which to write, the shape of the roll is mimetic of prison time and its cyclicality, and makes it impossible to read or write more than a small section at a time.

Journalists visiting political prisoners under *apartheid* were typically witnesses, bringing narratives from prison to the outside world as part of a project of seeking justice. In these accounts written in prison, authors were careful not to betray loved ones and others involved in the political struggle. De Kock's prison writings have a rather different impulse behind them: to show that he was part of a collective and acted as the 'assassin of the state', and was thus not individually culpable. His revelations are of two kinds, the first of which is the revelation of where the graves are – a revelation that purports to be in search of salvation. The second set of imperatives is to re-establish contact with networks outside prison, and to prepare for his eventual exit – which coincided roughly with the publication of this collaborative biography.

In the case of de Kock's imprisonment, there is no restriction of his access to writing materials such as we read about in the resistance tradition, and in Jansen's biography we read transcriptions of many of his own writings composed during his prison time, alongside older contextual reports and legal documents and texts. De Kock as prisoner was, under correctional law, not allowed to publish his own version of events without permission; Jansen quotes these words, often in full, and the reader has to be particularly vigilant to notice the seams between her words and de Kock's; the editing blends the voices together into a collective voice. In an interview with the journalist Herman Scholtz, and repeated tirelessly in many of her promotional interviews, Jansen emphasised that de Kock did not receive any financial reward from the sales of the book, as this would have been a contravention of the terms of his sentence. Jansen's biography functions as an envelope through which to smuggle out de Kock's words in plain sight. In this way, her book's relationship to its subject reveals a blurring of boundaries, with the interlocutor's accommodating and sympathetic containment of the prisoner's words. De Kock finds in Jansen someone willing to take out, and bring in, messages. The fragments and texts he is allowed to hand over to her are incorporated into the archive of her biography, which contains them and absorbs them. Writing the biography, she is also rebuilding for him his life outside prison through the network of people she contacts and interviews.

Roux's point that South African prison writing has always been heterogeneous is well taken. There are overlaps and continuities with the hostile *apartheid* archive – continuities that have at times been driven into invisibility. In addition, the new prison literature draws on and is shaped by the protocols of the interrogation and torture practices of the previous time. The intimacy and embodiedness on which it draws for its grammar is bloody, and is informed by the 'dirty' wars of the *apartheid* government. Gabriele Schwab's description of conflicting stories in mutually interactive public circulation (2010) is useful here as a way of understanding the nature of the new prison writings such as this smuggled out and edited (one might want to say disinfected) version by de Kock. In Dlamini's *Askari*, we find a method for reading interstitial archives, and Dlamini writes of the work of historians as readers of the past in search of small spaces in between the archives we think we know. The messy intimacies in accounts of prison visits to de Kock encourage us to pay attention to the protocols of the interrogation room and the intimacies of blood and torture, even when (perhaps especially when) what we are shown seems to be intimacy that has nothing to do with the blood of violence, and all to do with the blood of forgiveness and a shared humanity.

While he was in prison, de Kock was visited by many journalists and writers, and by lawyers and psychologists working for the state, as well as those who took up his cause and campaigned for his release. Near incomprehensible are the visits from family members of those whose deaths he caused directly or indirectly, who came to interview him in search of information about their lost family members – in search, one might say, precisely of any traces of their blood kin (Krog 2015; Gobodo-Madikizela 2003). Many of these relatives speak of wanting to gain access to the last moments of their dead loved ones, and hoping that contact with de Kock might give this (Krog 2015). It is as if de Kock's presence and his very skin promises to hold a trace of the last moments, through his intimate contact with the bodies of those he tortured and killed. He has 'given' (and there is a heavy emphasis on this 'generosity') his expertise and intimate knowledge of where dead bodies were buried, leading the investigators and families backwards along a trail of blood to the unmarked graves where the decomposing bodies have long turned to dusty bones. In accounts of interviews with relatives of people he murdered, we read of de Kock creating shocking intimacy. When the daughter of one of his victims, Candice Mama, asked to meet him, it was widely reported that the meeting ended with de Kock apologising to Mama that she had grown up without a father; then he whispered in her ear how proud her father would be of her as he hugged her. This intimate and invasive physical contact is read by his sympathetic biographer, Jansen, as evidence of what a changed man he is. The relatives come to seek the smell of the blood of their lost ones, and Jansen accepts that what de Kock gives them is enough to atone for his deeds. In particular she emphasises his willingness – eagerness even – to touch and embrace these visitors. In contrast, I want to argue that de Kock's embrace, skin to skin, is not so much a sign of his newly tender self but instead a repetition and continuation of the 'fatal intimacy' he has known with the deceased loved ones.

So much is already known about de Kock and his and his colleagues' actions; what is it that a prison visitor might gain from an interview, or even a series of interviews, with him? It is precisely the proximity and embodiedness of the visit that generate the new insights, and enable the readings under the skin. Janet Malcolm, in her book *The Journalist and the Murderer* (1997), writes about how the promise of negotiating special and confidential access makes a prisoner (a murderer in particular) an exciting subject for journalists and biographers. De Kock, singled out as the most evil of prisoners, cultivated his role as host (and the meetings as romantic and sexualised encounters, as I show later) during many of these prison visits. Skilled as an interrogator and torturer, he seems to have brought to the interviews in the prison's confined spaces the techniques of interrogation and torture, and an acute ability to unsettle and destabilise his conversation partners. De Kock's method as interview subject was to regulate carefully how much he revealed at each visit, and to control the flow of intimacy. Typical in the language used by his interviewers is the belief that a 'breakthrough' has been made. This language is also reminiscent of that used in a psychoanalytic context, with de Kock often creating a sense of such a 'breakthrough' just as the visiting time runs out. His masterful control over how much information he allows to 'break through' is not unrelated to his skill as torturer. De Kock creates a hunger for the next encounter through his promise of revealing more, going deeper and creating ever greater intimacy.

On his part, this technique – so similar to the 'fatal intimacy' (Ndebele in Jones and Dlamini 2013) created between torturer and victim – creates moments of closeness and identification that he can use to his advantage. In Jacob Dlamini's account of visiting de Kock in prison (2014: 40), we see little of this. Dlamini instead shows de Kock as unable to control the terms of their encounter. Dlamini applies for permission to see de Kock, and during the visit asks him if he knows what an *askari* is. Dlamini's version of the conversation shows de Kock discussing the meaning of the term (what distinguishes an *askari* from an 'officer'), but certainly not encouraging (nor allowing – although this is not what Dlamini has come searching for) intimacy. Dlamini asks the question about the meaning of the word, knowing full well that de Kock knows the answer, but the intention of the meeting is not so much to gain knowledge from de Kock as to show him how much he, Dlamini, knows. Luise White has written that gossip is often a way to test how much a conversation partner knows, rather than a response to an impulse to share information (2000: 79). Dlamini does not enter the cell hoping for a breakthrough, he is there to show how much he already knows and to assert his presence.

One might think of each entry into the prison visiting room as a test event, after which the result has to be brought out and interpreted, to decide how to decode and categorise what has been learnt. What are the protocols for understanding the accounts of prison visits to de Kock? How do we understand the intimacy of the 'breakthroughs' in the visiting cell? The prison visiting room is a place of seepage and leakage, of blood under the thin skin; but it is also a place where bodies come so close together that the blood traces on top of the skin, slippery and slimy, can be smelt. The prison visiting room is where the interviewers come so close to de Kock that his body can be seen and touched, the soft white skin on his hands and under his eyes seen close up. This room itself is like a skin between the outside world and the world of prison's confinement, and it is in this interstitial space between outside and inside that the meanings of the visit and the knowledge shared during it are negotiated, contextualised and edited.

The physicality of the archive of torture and killings on behalf of the *apartheid* state is well documented. The TRC record contains many reports of family members holding recovered body parts. In one edition of Antjie Krog's

Country of my Skull, the cover showed a woman, Joyce Mtimkulu, holding the hair of her son Siphiwo (the famous photograph was taken by Jillian Edelstein). The TRC brought stories of suffering and victimhood to the surface alongside confessions of bloody deeds, and the broken surface of bodies was a common strand in the narratives, the TRC archive acting as a documenting crypt to the bodies maimed and killed. How to listen to, and document, such stories of visceral suffering was the topic of these commentaries (Krog 1998). The TRC's archive contains, in many media forms, documents of these narratives.

In *There was this Goat* (2009) we read how translator and academic Nosisi Mpolweni decided to go in search of a recording of a certain Mrs Konile, suspecting that the interview with the TRC had been poorly translated and transcribed. Mpolweni decides to check the transcript against the recording, rummaging through boxes of taped interviews and recordings of hearings to find the original tape. The book *There was this Goat* (which I discussed in greater detail in *Accented Futures*, 2013) documents the many things deleted and lost when Mrs Konile's words were transcribed, and is an attempt to reconstitute her words. In *There was this Goat*, one of the central research questions that occupies the team is how to 'understand' Mrs Konile, and what the different meanings are of the term 'understand' (for a sustained discussion, see Coetzee 2013b: chapter 2). It is even more complex when we ask this question in relation to understanding the deeds and motivations of de Kock. What does it mean to listen to his words and to 'understand'? How does this 'understanding' relate to the bloods under the skin and the memory of the slippery and smelly blood on the skin of his hands? In the intimate encounters that take place in the prison visiting room, the nature of this understanding and the intimacy that makes it possible are negotiated and tested, yielding oppositional archives hostile to one another. Hannah Arendt famously said of Adolf Eichmann that 'no-one should be expected to want to share this earth' with him (Arendt 2006: 279); Pumla Gobodo-Madikizela's account of her visits to de Kock asks this question of herself, whether (and why) she would choose to share the intimate space of the prison visiting cell with him.

Entering the prisoner's space, the two writers whose ethnographic accounts of the visit I discuss in this chapter bring along various recording devices to compile their impressions and record their conversations. We read of their notebooks, pens, tape recorders, extra batteries for the tape recorder and (rather ridiculously in Jansen's account) notes written on to the skin of the body itself. Before they enter the visiting cell, their bodies are searched and their bags X-rayed (Gobodo-Madikizela 2003: 48) to make sure they bring nothing unauthorised into the meeting. It is not evident whose safety these checks are meant to secure, and it is also clear that the two authors have a different understanding of the potential risks posed by being with de Kock.

This controlled membrane (the security check, the forms to be signed, the private property inspected, the many doors leading to the prisoner) is like a skin that is broken. This insight is confirmed by the language of 'breakthroughs' that is repeated in the narratives, and the recurrent commentary on de Kock's own (thin) skin. The two accounts could not be more different from one another. The ways in which skin and blood figure (on as well as under the skin) are starkly oppositional. Yet both accounts document extraordinary intimacy with de Kock, and we are allowed to see the markings and tracings left on the bodies of the interviewers. Reports about de Kock during his prison years comment almost without exception on his soft pale skin, his soft hands, the tender skin around his eyes (the references are too many to cite and constitute a near universal element in descriptors of him). In these accounts, it is as if de Kock, in prison, has grown a new skin and shed the skin on which the blood of his victims could be smelled. His vulnerability is offered as evidence of the possibility of uncovering deeper truths about him, truths that can be accessed when seeing him in person. But it is also the thin, fragile skin that becomes described as the skin of a more forgiving and, crucially, more forgivable version. It is the documentation of this new vulnerable self, parading remorse (real or feigned), that secures his early release.

In *The Journalist and the Murderer*, Janet Malcolm writes about the identification and betrayal that characterises the relationship between a journalist and her imprisoned subject, even referring to it as a love affair (1997: 59). In the accounts of Gobodo-Madikizela's and Jansen's series of prison visits, we read many passages describing how the writers get ever closer to de Kock, even to the 'real' de Kock. It is in search of extra information and 'deeper' intimacy that they apply for permission to interview him. Gobodo-Madikizela met de Kock for 46 hours over a period of months, but the relationship between de Kock and Jansen lasted for three years, and since his release it has clearly continued and even developed. What both projects are in search of is something that goes deeper, goes under the skin, of the countless already known versions of de Kock's life and histories. This 'deeper' insight is made possible by sharing the intimate space with him, by being physically close to him – so close as to be able to touch him, the knees touching his under the table in the visiting room. The physical proximity creates a heightened sense of intimacy, as if the closeness of their bodies (their skins even) can reveal and bring to the surface what cannot otherwise be known. Jansen describes how getting to know de Kock has made her come alive again and given meaning to her life (2015). The meanings of the meetings for Gobodo-Madikizela are much more complex and at times contradictory. In the reception of her book, the themes of reconciliation and forgiveness, and a shared humanity, have come to dominate. The foreword by Nelson Mandela is partly responsible for fostering this interpretation. While there are many moments in the text that contradict this reading,

Gobodo-Madikizela's own subsequent comments confirm this interpretation of the book as part of a reconciliation project – as if she has been won over by this reading of her work. My interpretation emphasises instead those moments in the text that draw out a different, and less conciliatory, relationship.

I follow the two ethnographers into the visiting room, to see how the protocols of the intimate encounter and the knowledge gained generate 'readings under the skin'. It is not a room I would have liked to enter. I log the two antagonistic accounts of the visit to de Kock alongside, against and over one another. In the accounts, the two authors read their notes into very different archives. Through attention to the audiences thus evoked, the archives thus constituted, and the self that is brought into being in the encounter with de Kock, his prison sentence and his freedom are interpreted in violently different ways. The prison visit is a peculiarly constituted conversation, and in the two accounts I discuss here there is a great deal of attention to protocols of listening, recording and writing; but it is the intimacy that de Kock clearly welcomes that is the most shocking part of this ethnographic archive.

Striking in discussions of nearly all his interviews with women is a recurring theme of sexual attraction and intimacy, and repeated references to his body. On an Afrikaans-language news website, *netwerk24*, a report appeared with the title *Eugene se stem het haar bekoor* ('She fell in love with Eugene's voice', http://www.netwerk24.com/Nuus/Misdaad/Eugene-se-stem-het-haar-bekoor-20150322). When I accessed the story in March 2015, the advertisements in the sidebar seemed to underline the sexualised nature of the relationship: a sponsored set of advertisements from a dating service called '*komonskliek*' ('Let's get together') listed dating profiles, all about and by white Afrikaner men, describing themselves as friendly, well brought up, honest and loving. When I went back to the site to read the article again, however, access had been closed unless I registered as a user. I declined to sign up for more news (and possibly even alerts to '*komonskliek*' advertisements). All that remained readable of the article was a quote from Jansen, describing de Kock as '*'n outydse jintelman wat eers die bankie vir 'n mens afstof*' ('an old-fashioned gentleman who always brushes the dust away for one'; implied is that this labour is gallantly performed for a woman). One comment to the story read, possibly enviously: '*Lyk my vroue het maar 'n sagte plekkie vir die Eugenes en hulle stemme*' ('It seems as though women have a soft spot for the Eugenes and their voices'). These insinuations proliferate whenever women report on or meet with de Kock.

The capacity of the torturer's body for extraordinary intimacy with others is often interpreted in terms of sexual attraction. This taint of sexualisation is not uncommon in the literature on prison visits (Malcolm 1997), but the repetition of the trope around de Kock raises interesting questions with regard to someone whose body has experienced unimaginable intimacy with the bodies of people on whom he was inflicting intense pain, or whom he executed. De Kock seems to be very aware of the strange attraction he has for (some) women. At the end of an interview with Anemari Jansen, he is reported to have asked her 'How was that for you?' (Jansen 2015: 148), as if they had just had a sexual encounter. Pumla Gobodo-Madikizela writes about how many people assumed she was in love with or at least sexually attracted to de Kock (2003: 122–3). In the literature on political prisoners in South Africa, we see women prisoners subjected to ambiguous and sexually loaded conversations and interrogation (some of this is documented in the TRC's reports, although many have commented on how much gendered violence was silent or silenced; see, for example, Ross 2003; Driver 2005; Goldblatt and Meintjies 1997). De Kock initiates and seeks out a transgressive closeness. The intimacy that he manages to manufacture and elicit in the prison visiting room negotiates for de Kock access to his old police and special forces networks outside prison, and his eventual freedom. The prison visits and the record of them taken out, transcribed and edited reveal the intimacy created by the proximity of skin and blood. Through her research work, Jansen in fact reconstitutes for him a community of his 'blood brothers'. De Kock is, through his skilful management of the membrane of the prison visit, reconnected with old networks and absorbed into communities of care that enclose him, again, in familial ties of blood. We read, shockingly, in the last pages that the biographer goes to buy de Kock fine sheets for the home he will live in when he leaves prison, revealing a disturbing domesticated intimacy (2015: 310). At moments when de Kock seems to 'open up' and create for his visitors a sense of his vulnerability and 'soft' touch, and in particular during the moments when his skin touches the skin of those whose loved ones he killed or harmed, we see him negotiating this other opening – into freedom outside prison. The prison visiting room is thus an interstitial space where de Kock negotiates his exit and where the meanings of his life and work are recalibrated and retranslated, and slowly and carefully regulated. The prison waiting room is a space where de Kock cleanses himself of the dirty and smelly blood that was on his hands. He leaves this blood behind (one imagines him taking off his orange prison jumpsuit, which covers him like a flayed skin), to step across a threshold into a free domestic sphere.

The architecture of the prison structures both accounts, and references to the prison building confirm a sense of the visit as a search for greater and deeper knowledge. As the many prison doors are unlocked, it is as if we are entering the interior of de Kock's mind, entering under his skin even. The many locked doors and the security protocols are suggestive, too, of secrets that remain locked away, and that will be revealed as the writer enters the maze that is de Kock's intimate space. In this next section, I move between the two texts, mapping and logging the intimacies (at times deeply desired, at others violently feared) that they describe and acknowledge. The reason for reading the two books over and adjacent to one another is to highlight the confusing overlaps in the ways de Kock creates intimacy with the two women who enter the cell, with such different relationships to the bloody history of racialised violence and to de Kock's own 'blood' and ethnic identification as an Afrikaner. The chapter moves between the bloodlines, intent on how the discourse of blood circulates and who is included as kin. This method allows me to log the very different readings under the skin that are taken in the intimate encounters with de Kock.

The first pages of Gobodo-Madikizela's account are written as if in flight from a scene of torture, her body anticipating that the intimacy of a shared space with de Kock can only lead to violence. In a harrowing description we read of her despair as she arrives at the prison and remains seated in her car, feeling as if her head might explode with anxiety (2003: 1). This is a powerful image, which shows her archiving her proximity to de Kock through the accounts of activists assassinated using car bombs and parcels, letters and Walkman tape players exploding. Perhaps the most famous case is that of Bheki Mlangeni, who was killed by a parcel bomb containing a Walkman and headphones, which exploded when he put the headphones over his ears and pressed the play button. When Gobodo-Madikizela arrives at the prison reception and has to spell her name, the scene plays out like one of countless such moments when black South Africans have had to spell their names to hostile white police officers. Throughout this opening scene, the text reads as if Gobodo-Madikizela is being brought to de Kock in order to be interrogated and tortured, as if this is the only relation a body like hers can have to him. Having passed through the security check (which makes her feel as if *she* is in danger, rather than visiting a high-security prisoner), she finally meets de Kock and writes: 'I knew the face' (2003: 5). Seeing his face, so familiar from countless journalistic reports of his deeds, leads to a paragraph written in the collective voice of 'every black South African' (2003: 6). Seeing de Kock's face, she calls on this collective 'we', as if her identity is at risk of being deleted. This is a curious inversion of the prison-writing tradition in which it is the prisoner who, in the face of the interrogator, is at risk of disappearing.

Before they even enter the visiting cell, we read of the protocols to be followed related to sharing the intimate space with de Kock. In the case of Gobodo-Madikizela, the protocols confirm her sense of possible danger, and anxieties about the fact that the interview risks becoming more like the violently intimate encounters that de Kock has described. To some extent the feared and anticipated violence is also self-persecutory, as the author questions her own motivations for wanting to share an intimate space with this man. In her briefing from the prison director (2003: 18), she is given a demonstration of how to kick the special chair on wheels they have provided away from de Kock if he should become violent. The assumption is that their relationship might pose a danger to her, and this briefing confirms the sense of peril.

The doors that open and the corridors that take Gobodo-Madikizela to de Kock lead her into versions of South African history where she might have been his victim and in some sense is still being tortured by him. Sharing the small space of the visiting cell with de Kock is described as if it were an assault. Instead of returning to Cape Town directly after a particularly harrowing visit, she decides to spend the night with a friend to experience the smells of home. The time with de Kock is not an extension of home, but instead poses a threat to it. The descriptions of the maze that is Pretoria (a city marked by *apartheid*'s symbolism) highlights this sense of entering a world that has not recognised her as a 'human being'. The text contains a description of her ride through these streets, which feel hostile still to her as a black South African, destabilised and brutalised by the intimacy with de Kock.

What is it that Gobodo-Madikizela wants from de Kock? The text provides us with one option, her hope that the meeting with a criminal can restore a victim's humanity (2003: 127). Yet we see that this is not what in fact happens. Perhaps Jacob Dlamini's visit to state the name of his book and his project, to insert himself confidently in the intimate space, provides us with a clue to another possible motivation. Gobodo-Madikizela is not in search of a deeper truth that will allow her to see de Kock as a human being. Instead, she is searching for a version of the encounter in which he will acknowledge that she, and the many killed and tortured, are human beings (*A Human Being Died that Night*, the title reminds us, if we need reminding).

Anemari Jansen's account of driving through Pretoria (2015: 11) and entering the many doors of the prison is strikingly different. For her there is not the introductory self-defence demonstration. She is accompanied on her first visit by Piet Croucamp, political scientist and more recently the presenter of a television programme called *Megaboere* ('Mega Farmers', http://www.agrisa.co.za/inspiration-of-the-megaboere/), and a consistent champion of de Kock. From the earliest encounter she calls the prisoner 'Eugene' (bullying the reader into seeing him more intimately), and through her account we see how she and de Kock 'open doors' for one another. He puts his friends in charge of her (2015: 41, 43), and opens doors for her to his inner circle ('*binnekring*', 2015: 43, 50, 51). She even writes proudly that she has become a member of the police 'family' (2015: 69) and includes photographs of herself on outings with various of these connections: sky-diving, swimming, standing outside the gate to Vlakplaas, wearing sunglasses and flip-flops (what in Afrikaans are called *plakkies*). De Kock as a topic and as a life-affirming project is introduced over a meal with friends. The book is full of descriptions of meals and drinks shared with his friends, ex-colleagues and her handlers. Congenial moments are repeated throughout the narrative.

Jansen also finds ways of smuggling food into prison to de Kock – presumably her bag was not searched as well as Gobodo-Madikizela's was. She brings him home-cooked food, buys him treats from the prison canteen, and shares her own Kit Kat and juice with him in one of their earliest interviews, accentuating the sense of this as a romantic date rather than a professional interview (2015: 193). We read how, from the first visit, physical intimacy between Jansen and de Kock is not only lacking in danger, but characterised by a natural and empathic warmth. The often taciturn de Kock's garrulous style is described as bubbling (*borrel*), to underline for us the intimacy and private and homely self to which she has negotiated access, and the special nature of the bond between them. This choice of the word '*borrel*' creates a visual image of blood, but we soon realise this is not the tainted blood of violence but instead the blood of a protective community. De Kock opens doors to Jansen that lead her back into his private spaces outside prison: to his brother, his school and his Koevoet colleagues, collecting together a 'car-load' of pictures and stories (2015: 16). The networks that the interviews unlock for her in turn open doors for de Kock. They reconnect him with the many professional networks he had outside prison, and from which he has been isolated. Jansen is able to carry messages to men with whom de Kock worked in what was then Rhodesia, as well as in the special forces and at Vlakplaas (2015: 36), and through mapping these networks for her research, also re-establishing them.

The growing intimacy between her and de Kock is described using an architectural metaphor: 'A door opens in my head', she writes (2015: 160). What is this door, what is the intimate knowledge that 'opens up'? The insight is that the connections between her and de Kock are all about blood. What she brings out of the prison cell documents the histories of the networks in which de Kock was involved, and also reconnects the flows of blood in these networks. Included in her book are many documents, quoted in the original Afrikaans. These documents include reports by a psychologist and documents written by de Kock himself. The text ends with a memorandum by de Kock in which he imagines his life outside prison, as if Jansen's book becomes explicitly a document that negotiates the opening of this particular door into a liberated future. Jansen has repeatedly made the sensational claim in interviews that 'I am Eugene de Kock', and that she and he have entered one another's skins and it is shared blood that unites them. Malcolm (1997: 149) writes of the biographer that you know your adversary/subject more intimately than you know most real people, as you put so much of yourself into that person. She uses the metaphor of a house for the writing of biographical non-fiction (1997: 15). The home that is shared and co-created in Jansen's book is the house of shared blood, the blood that is protected by de Kock – Afrikaner blood.

Gobodo-Madikizela's narrative draws attention to a collective history of skin, so dominant in how South Africans understand themselves and are understood (although Jacob Dlamini in *Askari* and Zimitri Erasmus in *Race Otherwise* argue that skin can lie, and that the histories of *apartheid* are not as sealed as we might like to think). If we are to read the skin here through Sara Ahmed's useful terminology in *The Cultural Politics of Emotion*, Gobodo-Madikizela is aware of how her skin's histories have been shaped by histories of contact with Eugene de Kock's skin. The most dangerous moment is one when de Kock's (performed) vulnerability manages to persuade her to turn around and face him again, just as she is about to leave the prison visiting room. In a gesture of humanity (and one that many readers of the book want to hold as a central image, symbolising forgiveness and reconciliation), Gobodo-Madikizela reaches out to touch de Kock's hand to comfort him (2003: 32). She describes fleeing from this encounter, as if pursued by something life-threatening (2003: 33). Gobodo-Madikizela feels, she writes, as if something has been taken from her. The loss, we realise, is that the 'skin barrier' has been compromised (2003: 42). Her having touched the skin of de Kock's hand, the very hand that used to smell of blood, becomes even more dangerously charged when, on a later occasion, de Kock is brought out of prison to testify before the TRC. A messenger comes to where Gobodo-Madikizela is working as a TRC officer to say that de Kock wants to see her. When she meets de Kock, the meaning of the sinister encounter becomes clear. He wants to torture her by asking whether she was aware that the hand she touched was his trigger hand (2003: 40). The information is unsettling, but more disturbing is the fact that de Kock calls her out of a professional setting to recreate an intimate encounter and to reveal to her the sinister interpretation he has given to her compassionate gesture.

Gobodo-Madikizela tells, in the opening pages of her account, three linked stories from her own life, all of them to do with violence and threat, as if mapping the ways in which her life has intersected with the projects of de Kock. The aim of the intimacy she seeks out with de Kock is complex, and too often the complexity and resistance in this book's understanding of forgiveness is deleted in favour of discourses of salvation. The last pages of the book in particular encourage such a reading. Yet I want to argue against this interpretation of the book, even though the author herself has often presented the work in this way. I want to excavate those other meanings, less conciliatory and more invasive, by paying attention to the moments of terror, and to the moment Gobodo-Madikizela describes as the 'breakthrough' (as if she penetrates the skin and reaches a deeper meaning). She realises that what she wants to achieve in her meetings with de Kock is not to forgive him and recognise his humanity, but instead for *him* to recognise *her* humanity. The human being whose death is referenced in the title was someone like Gobodo-Madikizela. To say that this is an argument that wants to assert that we are all the same under the skin, we are all humans, is to miss the point of the demand for respect and recognition from de Kock.

Both Gobodo-Madikizela's and Jansen's accounts emphasise the physicality of that which is brought out of the interview space. All items taken into the room with de Kock have to be made known at the security check, which means that the only permitted materials are those used to record the conversation. Gobodo-Madikizela refers to her notebooks and pens as a form of armour, and as proof of her professional and scholarly credentials (2003: 50). She also brings with her a tape recording device on to which she records some of the 46 hours of conversation with de Kock. The recordings are archived, but not used; we read that it is six months before she plays them, and that she waits until she is far away in Boston (2003: 114) before she presses the button that will allow her to listen to her conversation with de Kock. She does not mention it, but reading how she presses the play button evokes the narratives of tape recorder bombs, and the danger of playing and listening to his words. The distance, of time elapsed (2003: 169) and geographical space, provides another version of the protection she needs (like the chair on wheels with which she was provided in case de Kock became dangerous).

The relations between what is brought out of the visiting room and her physical body has none of these meanings for Jansen. In one particularly striking scene, she returns to her car after a visit and writes her notes about the conversation directly on to her skin. The bodily scribbling is described and performed as a way of proving the intimacy between her and de Kock. She writes on the skin of the inner arm, skin which must be uncovered in order for this strange writing to take place, as a form of self-marking that ritualistically records the intimacy of her connection with de Kock. There is no reason why, in her car, she would not have access to paper – the intimacy of writing on the body is artfully chosen and deliberate. The border between her own body and de Kock's words is here literalised; his words have the same shape as her body. Writing on her body becomes the (faked, staged) mnemonic for reconstructing the conversation between them, as if she remembers it on her very skin. This tattooing theme has a curious echo when Jansen brings a friend along to visit de Kock, and her friend lifts her shirt to compare tattoos with one of de Kock's fellow inmates in the shared visiting room. The flirtatious tone of this scene is disturbing, and the two women's delight in the intimacy they create in this all-male prison is weirdly pornographic.

Eugene de Kock himself is revealed to be a busy and prolific writer. A recurring theme in the earlier resistance period of prison writing is the restricted access to writing and reading materials. In contrast, de Kock produces and consumes writing – and his biographer gives us access to what he writes by quoting him and ventriloquising his notes. His writings are not only contemporaneous; he claims that he was always an archivist of sorts during his time in what was then Rhodesia, that he kept notebooks and took photographs (Jansen 2015: 63, 92, 97). There is no way to verify what he recorded, nor even that he did so. De Kock's intention with this version of what is often described as his extraordinary memory is to focus our attention on the agency of the deletion – to show how he was always making notes, always documenting. It is, claims de Kock, the commanders and generals (2015: 170, 212) who have deleted his careful accounts of what happened. It is easy to see how this self-serving anecdote works to absolve him of guilt and to prove that he was imprisoned by those intent on hiding the truth (the truth he documented so carefully, but which was unfortunately destroyed). It is in this same spirit and in an attempt to absolve himself that he opens the many doors to Jansen, giving her access to photographs and family archives (2015: 139).

Jansen develops this theme of the deleted truth, writing about how the paper trail of Vlakplaas was destroyed (2015: 171). This destruction of the documents (2015: 212) is contrasted with her and de Kock's careful work of reconstruction (2015: 212), and extraordinarily also with de Kock's intelligence about the location of bodies in the final sections of Jansen's own words. Thus the book, Jansen's text and the texts it takes up under its skin, functions as evidence of de Kock's willingness to bring secrets to the surface, as if this urge to truth telling absolves him and cleanses him of the deeds.

Jansen's book includes many documents, including the photographs that are familiar from the many accounts of Vlakplaas. What is striking though is how we read these photographs in her book, alongside the 'exclusive, never seen before' photographs from de Kock's family albums and the intimate and introspective documents written by de Kock himself. We read of how these pictures and documents are accessed and reconnected through the contacts Jansen establishes with de Kock's intimate networks, and we see reproductions of his school magazine covers, of military memorabilia, and photographs of school camps. The pictures build up for the viewer an intimate archive (some of them border on the inappropriate, such as photographs of scenes of small humiliations at school camps), and the shaping of a certain kind of violently racialised white boyhood. The photographs are taken from de Kock's family albums, an inclusion that forces us to look at them with different eyes. Marianne Hirsch, in her book *Family Frames: Photography, Narrative and Postmemory*, writes about the ways in which we 'read' family albums, and how the album functions to record but also to constitute the group (1997: 7). Because a photograph gives the illusion of being a simple 'transcription of the real', it has the effect of 'naturalizing cultural practices and of disguising their stereotyped and coded characteristics' (1997: 7).

What is naturalised in these family photographs is a certain kind of militarised manhood, and an archive of whiteness that has often been driven underground (see Jansen's chapter 'Brothers in Arms'). Nicky Falkoff and Christo Doherty have written about the nostalgia industry surrounding the SA Defence Force and in particular the 'border' experiences. Antjie Krog is another ethnographer who has brought out some of these stories about nostalgia for the border wars (for example, Krog 2013; a concern with the 'men of [her] race' runs throughout her work; see Coetzee 2001), and where this is visible in popular cultural forms. Many readers may prefer to look away and not pore over the family album of the de Kock family (he describes as 'family' both his blood kin and the various counter-insurgency and military groups). But recent scholarship on the uses of photography in Abu Ghraib (Schwab 2010; Apel 2014; Kinney 2016) and photography's complex relationship to the historical archives of South Africa (Farber 2015; see also the other contributions in this special issue of *Critical Arts* on archival addresses) have shown that photographs are a rich source for historical research. Christo Doherty's film *Klaaglied* engages in complex ways with the visual grammars of Vlakplaas. In the film, Doherty recreates scenes from the *apartheid* archives, with model figures of soldiers in SADF uniforms torturing and killing captured black figures. The camera pans slowly over the model landscape and takes in a picnic scene, where little female figures are shown relaxing alongside their men. The choice of toy-sized figures in these re-enacted scenes emphasises the ordinariness of the events, and the intimate ways in which the insistence on securing the white family's safety are linked to violence.

In the photographs that Anemari Jansen gathers and reassembles we see the scattered archive of Eugene de Kock's life put together again, and a new family created to make up for the family he lost when his wife and two sons emigrated and broke contact with him. We see the photographs from de Kock's childhood (shooting, hunting, on school trips) alongside photographs of acts of violence in which the bodies of victims are clearly displayed. In some of the photographs, faces have been smudged or pixelated – presumably to protect the identities of persons who have not been named in the TRC hearings. The inclusion of the photographs emphasises the many secrets about Vlakplaas that remain hidden. But there is something else – the faces that are clearly visible, on the many photographs of social events at Vlakplaas and during de Kock's days in Koevoet, reconstitute for the reader and viewer an excavated social world from which de Kock came, and which is reformed as he leaves prison and re-establishes links.

These photographs do not merely record scenes of violence, but also work in the same way as do family photographs, to reassert connections and reinforce bonds (Hirsch 1997). What is particularly shocking about these photographs is how the violence is domesticated. This is evident from the photographs of de Kock's youth, which show various forms of militarisation and brutalisation. On one particularly disturbing photograph, a naked boy is seen trying to escape from the photographer's camera, a small act of brutality that prepares the chronicler (the new role de Kock has given himself) for the many other acts of violence. The childhood photographs reveal a culture that sees violence not as a rupture with family life, but as a continuation of it.

Jacob Dlamini has written about the photograph albums used by the *apartheid* police in interrogation sessions. In *Askari*, Dlamini reproduces some of these pictures. He is quoting from and referencing a different archive from the intimate one that Jansen uses. Among the photographs printed in *Askari*, glossily reflecting the light shining on the plastic sheets that cover the pictures in the police album, are three from security police files that show men pointing. In all three pictures, the men (Mandla Maseko and Simon Dladla) are pointing at something. The picture is clearly meant to be evidence – not only of the place pointed out, but regarding the man who is giving this information. The photographic evidence of the revelation of information is meant to incriminate the men, whose faces stare blankly at the photographer who is recording not only the information but the moment when it is shared.

In the snapshots in de Kock's family album, the photographer's relationship to those being recorded is different. The photographs give the reader access to the 'family' of men who were members of Koevoet, part of the networks of Rhodesian and anti-Mau Mau special forces. We see a world almost entirely peopled by men (although two pictures of de Kock next to women are included, recording moments with his first girlfriend and his wife). A third 'partner' to de Kock appears on many photographs – the author herself. We often see her sharing a meal with some of de Kock's contacts, or at social events as a member of the 'team' or family of informants and connections. What the archive (the car full of documents and photographs) does is to bring these networks into view – and this is the great contribution of Jansen's book. Her research, and the many doors opened by de Kock himself, let the reader into the 'family' of men who were members of Koevoet or worked at Vlakplaas. Through the photographs and anecdotes she brings together, we can map the many links between various military groups which will allow us to understand how these networks structured and continue to structure the world (see, for example, the work of Luise White, Miles Larmer and Caroline Elkins).

There is one photograph in Jansen's book that is striking for its difference from the others. It shows three women in a restaurant somewhere in South Africa on a sunny day. The woman on the left is Candice Mama, the daughter of one of de Kock's victims and the young woman in whose ear he whispered how proud her father would have been of her. In the middle is Pumla Gobodo-Madikizela, on her right Anemari Jansen. The photograph is included here as a badge, proof that Jansen's book has been endorsed by Gobodo-Madikizela and Candice Mama. They are photographed to prove that they were there, that they met Jansen and shared a meal with her. I keep scanning this picture, to see if it will reveal more about the complexities of the 'family' convened and staged here. Am I imagining it, or does Gobodo-Madikizela lean away from Jansen and towards Mama? Jansen's hand hovers near her mobile phone, perhaps hoping that she will receive a message or even a call from Eugene de Kock while they are all there together, or excited about the prospect of sharing news of this family reunion with him.

All three of the women in the picture have been touched by de Kock, their skins touching the skin on which the smell of blood remained after torturing and killing. Behind them sits another woman, leaning back on a chair, perhaps nursing a backache – she is heavily pregnant and unaware that she is being included here. Jansen's arm around Gobodo-Madikizela and the uneaten food in front of them on the table evokes all the meals shared with de Kock, and the preparations Jansen has made for his comfort in his safe house. While Jansen was accompanied by de Kock to promote her book about him, Pumla Gobodo-Madikizela writes that she did not give de Kock a copy of her book (2003: 169). Even when she agrees at times with readers who find in her work a willingness to forgive, this was a gift she was not willing to make.

Ruth First's Red Suitcase: In and Out of the Strongroom of Memory   3

Ruth First died a violent and bloody death at the hands of the South African security police in August 1982, when she opened a letter bomb addressed to her at her office at Eduardo Mondlane University in Maputo, Mozambique (Frankel 1999: 303; Pinnock 2012: 24; Wieder 2013: 251). Her murderers' identities are common knowledge. They were Roger Jerry Raven, Johann Coetzee and Craig Williamson, one of the *apartheid*-era police spies and a man at the centre of many rumours and the acknowledged agent of countless crimes (Ancer 2017; Frankel 1999: 316; Slovo 1997: 321–40; Harlow 2009: 26). After he made what he presented as a full confession of First's murder, the TRC granted Williamson amnesty for this and for the many other crimes that he had committed. He remains a free man. The force of the explosion that killed Ruth First was such that her blood and body fragments were dispersed throughout the office she shared at the university (Wieder 2013: 251). Descriptions of the murder scene linger on the details of First's dismembered body in the space where she used to work, write and read.

First's relationship to the *apartheid* security archive is one that haunted her, and her own work is best understood as that of a counter-archivist. Her praxis as meticulous editor of the work of others is suggestive of her writing method in *117 Days*, a book typically read as a documentary report of her time in prison (Frankel 1999: 2), and as representative of the ethnographic tradition of South African resistance writing (Roux 2005, 2009, 2014a). Instead I argue that the writing method approximates more that of careful editorial practice, reading and rereading the events, redacting what the author might have left behind as part of the hostile archive that did in the end fatally seek her out. Barbara Harlow has suggested that First's work as librarian, archivist and researcher provides us with ethical protocols for the work of reconstructing the past as legacy for the future (1996: 116–17). In a subsequent commentary on First, Harlow wrote that First's life and what she calls her 'bio-bibliography' are in their own ways 'instructive … in reconsidering the contemporary issues facing the "humanities" as both academic discipline and intellectual tradition' (2009: 29).

This chapter files the deadly letter addressed to Ruth First alongside the other hostile texts that the *apartheid* state collected and archived about her and her colleagues and co-workers. The letter bomb was sent from, and was supported by, this hostile archive and its associated paper trail. Williamson justified his actions to the TRC through reference to the *apartheid* archive that documented First's 'terrorist' activities. This chapter resists entering the hostile archive from which the letter was sent, and instead rehearses a re-entry into what First called the 'strongroom' of her memory. In *117 Days* she writes: 'I was packing my mind into a strongroom' (2010: 130). This strongroom is, in the first instance, the prison cells in which First was detained and which she revisits in various forms and through different media. In the second place, this strongroom is also the threshold First wanted, repeatedly, to prove that she had *not* crossed. Through her creation of a strongroom of memory, she wanted to seal in and seal off any crossings into the hostile archive from where her death sentence was later issued. First reads, and rereads, her own documents and those of others, going over again and again to see if she had missed something, or let something leak.

In an attempt to create such a sealed counter-archive, First wrote an account of her incarceration by the *apartheid* government in 1964 (published in 1965 as *117 Days*). It is a text that stands as a centre-piece of the histories of the activists connected to First (see Wieder 2013; Frankel 1999). Living and working in careful evasion of the official state paper trail, the written evidence of First's private life does not constitute a large archive, although many entries are catalogued under her name – the scholarly and journalistic texts that she produced and edited (Pinnock 2010; Harlow 1996: 147). *117 Days* has been widely referenced, and has been adapted and recreated numerous times on screen and in novels. In this chapter I argue that the text constitutes a particular kind of archive, or to use First's own evocative term, a 'strongroom', self-consciously sealed against the state and police archive. In it, First provides a resistant chronicle and asserts her non-inclusion into the official archives of her jailers and eventual murderers. Barbara Harlow calls First's activist practices 'strategies of active discursive disengagement' (1996: 149). Contrary to the way it is typically read, I argue that the text is not simply a documentary account of her time in prison. It is a text that does much more (and less) than merely *document*: it obfuscates and encodes, creating a strongroom impermeable to the gaze of her interrogators. Alongside this reading of the text of *117 Days*, I suggest that Ruth First's red suitcase has been mis-classified in the archive of scholarship on her. The cotton wool in the suitcase, in particular, misfiled as part of a bourgeois beauty regime, offers a revealing clue to the complexly bloody encryption of *117 Days*.

Prison writing has attracted a great deal of scholarly attention, in particular in South African contexts where the prisoners who wrote accounts of their prison time tended to be associated with oppositional political movements. Typically, these, prison diaries have been read as modes of resistant testimony (Roux 2009; Schalkwyk 2001). Many of these accounts are described as examples of 'prison ethnography', emphasising a critical distance and an attempt at controlling (through narration) the hostile prison environment. Ruth First's *117 Days* is often described as a typical example of prison ethnography (representative discussions are Schalkwyk 2001; Wieder 2013: 135). Its documentary status was underlined and confirmed by a 1966 BBC film, *90 Days*, based on the account, in which First acted herself and which provided, for a UK audience, a key to understanding the events.

In *117 Days*, we read of the many other, hostile documents recording First's prison stay. Most crucial is the 'statement' that First makes to the police but never signs – thus not attaching her signature to it to authenticate it. Even without the incriminating signature (which would have proven and marked her cooperation in the making of this statement), First becomes obsessed with the dangers posed by this document and how it might circulate ('cyclostyled and in many dossiers', 2010: 146). Herself a journalist interested in the reproduction of texts through mechanical copying (2010: 132; Frankel 1999: 41), she imagines a nightmarish version of the statement multiplying and circulating widely. Another dangerous document in need of containment is a suicide note she writes when she realises that the way in which her 'statement' can be used against her has possibly compromised her. This suicide note, addressed to her husband Joe Slovo, is written on the inside cover of a crossword puzzle book (2010: 143), which First claims to tear out and flush down the toilet (2010: 150; also in Frankel 1999: 43) but which surfaces again in ways I analyse below. A further hostile document is the official release form from prison, handed to First in 'duplicated' form, confirming again that there is another version of her arrest and imprisonment filed in ledgers and folders held by her interrogators (2010: 130–1; Wieder 2013: 138).

When First is released from prison, she leaves behind the unsigned statement, but is unable to retract or delete it. Her release form, too, is a compromised and compromising document. The 90 days' detention had as its express aim the extraction of information from those held under it; to be released was to raise suspicion that one had colluded in the production of statements and given information that had resulted in securing one's freedom at the cost of incriminating others. When First, after her release from prison, applied for a passport to allow her and her daughters to travel to the UK for a time, she was denied official permission and was instead issued with an exit permit (Smith 1964); her departure from South Africa in March 1964 was to prove her final exit from the country, to which she never returned. Her file remained open, however, and it is this archive that was used in justification of Williamson's murder of her.

Documents related to First's prison stay, alongside the counterfoils for the exit permit that was handed to her instead of a passport that would allow her to re-enter South Africa, must exist in a number of state depositories. In the prison service's archive, there are ledgers and folders in which her name and prison movements were documented, and into which – on her insistence – her complaints about her treatment were entered. First and her circle avoided paper trails, and notes and records of meetings and agendas were kept to a minimum to protect identities and plans. In a life lived in avoidance of the official archivist of the state, First left behind little that is not part of the official and hostile archive. When she left prison and later exited South Africa, she was aware of leaving behind this tainted and hostile archive. In his testimony to the TRC, her murderer Craig Williamson weakly repeated that what he did was legal and official, sanctioned by the archives and documents of the then government's secret murder squads (Wieder 2013: 251).

Ruth First started writing *117 Days* while she was already living in the UK. The grey autumn and winter of 1964 was a time of challenging transition. Ronald Segal, we read in accounts of her early days in London, persuaded her to write a narrative of her prison time as an *exposé* of prison conditions (First 2010: ix; see also Wieder 2013: 146; Frankel 1999: 280). The book is also an account of and testimony to her own role as 'master of the ambiguous and evasive reply' (2010: 13). In the remembered cell, we see First checking and rechecking that she left nothing behind that could be used as part of the hostile archive. In order to do this, she returns to the cell in her memory, scrutinising it for any taint or stain it could leave on her character. Tony Judt, in the title essay in his book *The Memory Chalet*, described the method he developed for organising memories, after being affected by amyotrophic lateral sclerosis, a disabling disease that rapidly led to his death in 2010. Losing his ability to move meant the loss of what he calls 'the yellow pad, with its now useless pencil' (2010: 5), and of interactions with others. Judt returns in memory to a chalet he used to live in as a child:

> Each night, for days, weeks, months, and now well over a year, I have returned to that chalet. I have passed through its familiar short corridors with their worn steps and settled into one of two or perhaps three armchairs – conveniently unoccupied by others. And thence, the wish fathering the thought with reasonably unerring reliability, I have conjured up, sorted out, and ordered a story or an argument that I plan to use in something I shall write the following day. (2010: 7)

In Judt's memory chalet the atmosphere is one of cosy return to a beloved building, starkly opposite to the ways in which First revisits her prison rooms. But in other ways this architectural metaphor is suggestive of a space that is revisited repeatedly as a way of reorganising memory, editing and redacting the events, and fearfully imagining what has been overlooked or not remembered.

Obfuscation and subterfuge are dominant themes in the literature on the group of which Ruth First and Joe Slovo were part in the 1960s, as countless references and incidents in the biographies of the group (sometimes called 'Rivonia's children') document (Slovo 1997; Wieder 2013; Frankel 1999).

Deliberate opacity was part of the daily lives of this group, in order to evade surveillance and minimise the risk of exposure. Such a group does not leave a written archive, and typical of the reference sections in biographies are lists of oral sources and interviews conducted with those who remember and lived through the events (Wieder 2013: 24). In her family autobiography *Every Secret Thing*, First's daughter Gillian Slovo comments explicitly on the paucity of a written archive, explaining why she had to rely instead on interviews – which in turn reunite and continually reconstitute the group of people about whom we read (Slovo 1997). Ruth First's biographers do not enter the *apartheid* archive either, relying instead on the oral and written sources produced by and circulated in the anti-*apartheid* movement. *117 Days* forms a key text in this archive, is often read as the primary documentary source of information about the times, and is heavily used in most biographies and histories of the period.

In piecing together and re-editing these pasts, the biographers of this circle have had to create and sometimes even invent an archive. This threshold between documented fact and remembered invention runs as a submerged theme through *117 Days*, which is an extended reflection on the nature of remembering without written notes as aid to memory. In a revealing description of Ruth First's working method as journalist and writer, she is described as literally pinning scraps of paper with sentences on them together, as if building up a text through splicing other texts, using the domestic machinery of sewing and mending (Slovo 2010: x). First's energy and skill as editor (of newspapers, academic journals and the writings of others) is often remarked upon, as is her industriousness. We know also that she was a noisy worker, her writing often accompanied by the seemingly ceaseless clatter of her Hermes typewriter (Frankel 1999: 318; Pinnock 2012: 25). In her account of her time in prison, denied not only a typewriter but even a pencil, First makes a surprising observation, especially for someone whose personal archive has turned out to be largely an oral one, based on memories and reminiscences. She writes about how poor her memory is, and how she always needs a pencil and sources to construct her writing (2010: 78–9; also xi). This is a challenging comment to integrate into one's reading of the text, which we know to be reconstructed *from memory*, without a pencil at hand to make notes. If the author acknowledges her poor memory, what we are holding cannot be read in an uncomplicated way as a documentary record of a remembered experience. Instead, it becomes a text about sealing up the archive and reinforcing the strongroom of memory.

In the narrative of *117 Days*, there are a number of self-referential comments to the process of recording information and gathering data, but it is crucial that these are *remembered* scenes. The record is of the memory of the *desire* to record, not a record of the event itself. Perhaps one way of reading *117 Days* then is to read it alongside First's editorial comments on Oginga Odinga's *Not yet Uhuru*, which First was editing at the same time as she was writing (but importantly not when she lived through the events narrated in) *117 Days*. In this interpretation, *117 Days* is an edited version of the memories of the experience, rather than a documentary or diary. The editing happens in retrospect, and against the background of the otherwise (and hostilely) edited versions of the prison time.

Ruth First's work as journalist and editor forms a mainstay of accounts of the meanings of her life (Pinnock 2012; Marks 1983). More opaque for the meanings it has for her political work is the time she spent training to be a librarian (First 2010: 3–5; Frankel 1999: 118). At the time of her arrest First was prevented by a banning order from working as a journalist. For someone whose political work consisted of writing and trying to read documents that were either banned or restricted, there is a certain irony in her training to be a librarian. In the account of her arrest, we read that First was sorting atlases, making a list of what was needed in the library (First 2010: 3). Barbara Harlow, First's most astute reader, glosses this scene in her account of the arrest, interpreting the choosing of atlases as an act of revolutionary preparation. Harlow died recently, before completing the intellectual biography of First that she was writing, but her colleague Professor Toyin Falola reported in an obituary that it will be published. Once Harlow raises the possibility of the librarian being someone who smuggles knowledge out of the official archive and library (1996: 119), the potentially explosive meanings of this activity proliferate. The revolutionary who is pretending to be a librarian, and indeed working *as* a librarian, learns what the official archive contains in order better to evade her inclusion in it. This approach is echoed in First's repeated insistence that in prison, she would watch to see what 'they' knew before she planned how to evade their questions. First's famous comment that in prison you only see the enemy's moves (2010: 44) takes on another meaning too: her own moves must remain invisible and illegible *to them* while she must learn the shape of their archive, the better to build her strongroom against their attempted intrusion. She writes about her relationship to her interrogators: 'I was packing my mind. Into a strongroom section labelled "Never to be divulged"' (2010: 130).

The relationship between confession, testimony and secrets informed Barbara Harlow's writings. Her legacy has been to plot the intimate connections between resistance traditions of writing and the work we do in the academy, reminding us, again and again, that our desks are not neutral spaces. In *After Lives: Legacies of Revolutionary Writing* (1996) her subject was the work of writers who put themselves at risk through their words. In this early and insightful response to the TRC, she wrote:

> The subsequent work of librarians, archivists and researchers must in turn encounter new methodological and professional challenges. The reconstruction of the past

as legacy for the 'new South Africa', as for new and critical geographies of the history of the struggle, must eventually develop alternative directions and directives, contending with the 'broken chains', covered tracks and interrupted narratives. (1996: 117)

Harlow was always astutely aware of the relationship between our academic practices and the work done by writers in resistance organisations, and how reading prison writings could, and does, bring our disciplines into crisis.

The archivist and librarian working inside the official library that contains only unbanned texts is someone who learns how to evade the enemy's moves. It was in a library that First was arrested, and in the version of her arrest contained in *117 Days* she recounts slipping an incriminating note out of her bag (2010: 4). This note possibly remains in the library, undiscovered; but it was in her home that the police discovered a copy of the banned magazine *Fighting Talk* which First had carelessly neglected to file with objects that needed to be hidden from the enemy who was potentially searching for them (2010: 5). There are repeated self-flagellating references to her carelessness in having mis-filed this document, in a house which has to be ready to go on display at any moment as its own legal counterfeit, containing only items that one might also find in the depository that contains legal books. The discovery of this journal provided the arresting officers with a motivation for First's imprisonment, and it is to this untidiness that First often returns in her thoughts (2010: 5, 9).

One of the most frequently repeated anecdotes around First's arrest and imprisonment relates to the packing of her suitcase under the gaze of her captors (First 2010: 6, 12: 'I had supplies', she writes). The red suitcase itself has a literature attached to it, with many interpreters pointing out the gendered as well as racialised contents of First's luggage (Frankel 1999: 119; Schalkwyk 2001: 12–13; Harlow 2009: 35). In the introduction to *117 Days*, written by her daughter Gillian Slovo, we find references to a loved and remembered mother's elegance, itemised through her perfume and lingerie (Slovo 2010: viii). The contents of the suitcase are carefully catalogued (repacked again in, and from, memory) for the reader of *117 Days*. The case was packed, First says, 'with experience' (First 2010: 11); it contained the comforts one might need in prison. In this way of describing the suitcase, the presentation catalogues the suitcase as an instance of a genre that binds First to other political prisoners. The packing of the suitcase is done according to knowledge that circulated among those expecting to be detained and thus inserts her into a community (2010: 86). The documentary film version broadcast by the BBC in 1966 is in black and white, so the suitcase remains grey (a greyness I discuss in greater detail below); and in *A World Apart*, wardrobe supplied Barbara Hershey (playing a thinly disguised Ruth First) with a powder-blue suitcase instead of a red one. Here it is as if the suitcase itself has become encrypted and disguised; although it is more likely that the colour of the suitcase was not regarded as significant in a film otherwise near obsessively interested in period details.

There is one item, in particular, from the suitcase as archive that no one has commented on in the extensive writings: the large amount of cotton wool it contained. David Schalkwyk, in a censorious discussion of what he describes as First's bourgeois identity, glosses the suitcase as containing 'unlikely, but characteristic, items such as silk underwear, makeup, eyebrow tweezers, a mirror' (2001: 9). Schalkwyk judges First harshly, comparing her relative comfort to the conditions suffered by other woman prisoners not protected by their middle-class, white identities. I want to lift this one item from the suitcase, the roll of cotton wool; I do this to mark how crucial it is where this cotton wool is archived. For most readers cotton wool would be catalogued under make-up and cosmetics, and simply glossed over as one of the less interesting items in this category, further proof that First was preoccupied with her appearance. First describes, in *117 Days*, how the policeman disgorged the cotton wool: he 'pounced on the cotton wool and sprawled it on the counter like the innards of some hygienic caterpillar' (2010: 6). The account of the invasive and hostile unpacking of the intimate contents of the suitcase is followed immediately by a series of paranoid questions: 'What did They know? Had someone talked? Would their questions give me any clue? How could I parry the interrogation sessions to find out what *I* wanted to know, without giving them the impression that I was resolutely determined to tell them nothing?' (2010: 7; also Slovo 1997: 113). The uncoiling of the cotton wool, as if it were a live creature being cut open, seems to conjure up the fear of other documents and secrets being opened up. We read that her books, pencil, necklace and nail scissors are removed, but we are not told whether she is allowed to keep the cotton wool.

In a later scene in the narrative, a fellow inmate who is to be there for one night only (and who turns out to be an acquaintance of First, Anne Marie Wolpe, who describes the moment in her autobiography *The Long Way Home*, 1994: 197), asks in 'a high fastidious voice' (First 2010: 14) for cotton wool as she is about to have her period. For the reader who knows how to read the archive of cotton wool and menstruation, *this* is the function of the hygienic caterpillar, rather than as part of the beauty archive. During a prison stay of 90 days, a woman of First's age would expect to menstruate three times. Apart from the reference to someone else being unprepared and needing to have some cotton wool, there is no direct mention made of menstruation, nor to the uses made of the cotton wool to absorb menstrual flow. Yet the language of barriers and prevention, leaks and seepage, saturates the text (2010: 57, 128, 129).

First's insistence on her dignity and her personal care is a central part of the narrative, and is to be understood – as she intended it to be – as a form of resistance to the dehumanising effect of her solitary confinement. To write about menstruation is not part of First's activist programme. In the 1970s menstrual activists in the US feminist movement would encourage women to speak out about the secret world of menstruation, and the indignities suffered by women deprived of sanitary products while menstruating in prison has recently become something of a *cause célèbre*. One might also wish to contrast this hygienic caterpillar (and perhaps this is part of Schalkwyk's impatience with First) to the harrowing descriptions of torture and excessive menstrual bleeding in Winnie Madikizela-Mandela's *491 Days: Prisoner 1323/69*, or to the many references to menstruation in the TRC hearings (Graybill 2001). A history of menstruation and its racialised archives in South Africa would be a useful and important project; but it is not what I want to pursue here.

In one of the most famous early artworks to reference menstruation, Judy Chicago's *Menstruation Bathroom* (1972), a white, cell-like room littered with the paraphernalia of used and unused products to staunch and absorb menstrual blood speaks eloquently of privacy and secrecy, exhibiting in clear view that which women often chose, and still choose, not to speak of in public. *Menstruation Bathroom* is an archive that makes visible the work needed in order to keep menstrual flow invisible (Chicago 1996: 33). Unmentioned, and uninteresting except to the reader who files cotton wool under 'sanitary and menstrual products' rather than 'make-up', the cotton wool is, to me, by far the *most* interesting item in the suitcase. Its purpose is to absorb, to contain, and to staunch a 'leak'. First's *117 Days* uses the language of the 'leak' several times; it is the event she most fears. *117 Days* is, in fact, a document compiled to prove that there was not a leak (2010: 61). The narrative is an account of a mind acting as an impermeable barrier, containing and absorbing any leaks so that nothing becomes visible to the enemy. The book, written after release, from outside prison but also from outside South Africa, is an account of this active and activist work of staunching any outflow; a redacting in memory to make sure nothing was left behind.

Menstruation has a peculiar place in narratives of secrecy. The most obvious connection is the well-documented history of menstruation itself as a secret (Dahlqvist 2018; Delaney et al. 1988; Martin 1987). In histories of menstruation in literature, Anne Frank's name appears on every list. Living in a hideout, Frank's day-book mentions with breathless excitement the anticipation of her first menses. While the changes in her body seem to Frank a reminder and promise of her future life outside, there is to the reader (as there must have been to the adult women sharing the hideout) the reality of concealing any materials to do with menses while living in secret and confined spaces. In scholarly work on Frank's diary, the discussion typically revolves around her father's desire to censor matters to do with sexuality when he edited it (Houppert 1999: 122–36). Hence the theme of embodied secrecy is brought to the level of the domestic and familial, rather than in relation to the larger themes of secrecy and subterfuge. A related incident of menstrual flow and the need for secrecy, also from a resistance literary tradition, is found in Elsa Morante's *History: A Novel*, in which Mariulina, a young Italian woman at gunpoint while enemy soldiers demand to know from her the whereabouts of her lover and his comrades in the underground resistance, feels the first signs of the onset of her menses (2001: 338), and finds herself telling everything she knows. Here, menstruation is linked metaphorically but also physically to a 'leak'. First does not make explicit links between menstrual blood and leaks, but other bodily outflows are mentioned. These include her bladder endurance test (2010: 71) and the attack of diarrhoea she suffers after making the statements that lead to her crisis (2010: 147). In the case of her control over her bladder, her endurance proves to her that she is victorious and will not be broken. The outpouring of diarrhoea, however, speaks of a darker threshold that has been crossed.

When First is interviewed by her jailers, she prides herself on her ability to lock the strongroom of her memory. One of the ways in which her interrogators seek to break down this strongroom is to deprive her of reading and writing materials. The suitcase, as it is packed in First's home (although we know she is not allowed to *unpack* all these items once she arrives in prison), contains at least one novel (she mentions *The Charterhouse of Parma*) and a pencil, although we do not read that it contains writing paper. Given First's working methods (her 'poor' memory, her work as an investigative journalist, her use of interviews as the basis of her journalism, her editorial work in which she responded to the work of others), it is not clear what she would have written in her prison cell, other than letters. The restriction of access to writing and reading materials is a mainstay of her period in solitary confinement. It is repeatedly justified as part of a programme to make her uncomfortable, and to give her time to think about her interrogators' questions. Reading and writing, they suspect, will protect her against their interrogations.

Yet First finds, and remembers, many instances of reading material, in her cell as well as in the two different prisons that are her home for the 117 days. To readers of a literary bent, *117 Days* has much to offer. The text contains references to other literary works (*Chess* on page 78, *The Charterhouse of Parma* on page 158); the narrative breaks off to include in italics the narratives of others, making of the text a redacted and retrospective collective account (2010: 15–19, 47–51, 83–8, 99–114, 123–7); it catalogues and inventories references to writing on and in prison, as well as glimpsed through a window, and it is a companion to and refutation of another document – the purloined 'statement' that her interrogators fabricate. First finds an archive of the resistance movement in the prison ledgers that document the names of the other jail inhabitants (she likens this find to a reunion, 2010: 43), and also in graffiti on the walls (2010: 39). Further texts include the book into which her complaints about her treatment are entered (2010: 45) and the official visitor book (2010: 119). All of these entries leave a trail that can potentially be used against First.

Many readers have commented on the scraps of paper and newsprint she finds (2010: 40, 77, 78), and most accounts mention the chewing gum wrappers given by her daughters during a rare prison visit (2010: 51; Wieder 2013: 135). Hauntingly described, and undiscussed in any commentaries, is the written archive of Afrikaans name tags that she finds when walking across the prison courtyard and coming across laundry hung on washing lines. 'Each item was marked with a number and a well-known Afrikaans name. I wandered between rows of dresses, shirts, vests, blouses, shorts, and jeans marked Van der Merwe, Kemp, Prinsloo, Erasmus, Van Wyk, Buitenkamp, Rossouw, Potgieter, Coetzee, Van Zyl, and Du Plessis' (2010: 73). The archive of garments, underpants and sheets is described in a hauntingly evocative passage. This reading of the names on the washing line is not only glossed by First for the names it includes, but she develops from it a short historical analysis. This isolated reading exercise is an example of what Barbara Harlow describes as First's 'transgressive, if still hypothetical, counter-narrative of resistance' (1992: 150).

Since its publication, *117 Days* (itself a kind of counterfeit text, as it is a narrative in which First recounts telling the interrogators only what they already know) has been taken up in many other texts and accounts. First's daughters have all in some way responded to and entextualised this account. The clearest version is that provided in the script written by her daughter Shawn Slovo and filmed as *A World Apart* (Harlow 1992: 151; Slovo 1988). In the film, First is given a different name (Diana Roth), a fitting acknowledgement of a life lived so much in secret. The film draws on the diary and on the documentary film *90 Days* for its iconography. In the novel by Gillian Slovo, *Ties of Blood*, the prison period is strikingly absent from the account of the life, which in many other ways closely resembles that of Ruth First. In *Catch a Fire*, Robyn Slovo plays her mother in a non-speaking part, in a film written by her sister Shawn and produced by Robyn. The most striking reflection comes from the biography of their parents by Gillian Slovo, in which she sets out to investigate what she calls *Every Secret Thing*, her book making the claim that secrets were what shaped her family and her childhood. Written from a post-1990s point of view, Slovo recreates the archive of her family against the background of the TRC, at a time when the confession of political secrets had become the master narrative of the new dispensation. First's children are thus seen continuing the work started by their mother, revisiting and revising the archive of their life.

First writes in the most famous line from *117 Days*, 'In prison you see only the moves of the enemy' (2010: 44). This can be reinterpreted through the lens of the hostile archive that I have theorised above. When First makes her statement, she sees her words lose the meaning she intended them to have, and become part of the hostile archive bent on her destruction. After making her statement, which First initially thinks of as a non-statement, she is asked to return the next day to sign and authenticate it. It is this evidence, the signature on the statement, which will not prove her agency and control of the situation as she had hoped, but will instead be evidence of the fact that her words have entered (and are used in support of) the official and hostile archive.

This threatened signature is what leads (in the version of events stored up in the strongroom of memory) to the crisis, a crisis that is not entirely legible. Gillian Slovo in *Every Secret Thing* writes of reading a sentence in *117 Days* over and over, trying to make sense of it:

> She thought her friends would judge her and they/some did … If Ruth had not written her book, no one would have known that she had said anything, however trivial. Yet, once the book was published, instead of applauding her courage, some of her closest comrades judged her for her weakness. She must have known, before the book came out, that this was bound to happen and yet she let it ride. She was a brave woman, my mother. // She began imagining the rumours that must be circulating. (1997: 115)

This passage makes apparent the seepage between bravery/cowardice, and frames bravery as in fact the ability to withstand accusations of weakness. In this version, then, suicide becomes proof of bravery, an attempt at redacting an act of perceived cowardice through overwriting it with a 'brave' act.

In First's own account (remembered, written in an attempt to reseal the strongroom), the meaning of her suicide attempt is rather opaque. Deciding to commit suicide, she writes 'there was only one way out' (2010: 149), but the logic of this statement remains unclear. Does she mean it is the only way out of signing the statement? Or that the only way to exit prison is to die, since leaving alive would be compromising? First writes of needing to send a sign to the outside world, and the sign she uses to encrypt her message is her own suicide (2010: 149). The planned suicide, then, seems a way of *in-authenticating* the document, of drawing attention to the *absence* of her signature. She encrypts the deed in another way too, by writing a suicide note in the form of an apology to her children (2010: 149). The suicide note is written, using an 'indelible pencil' with the words 'PROPERTY OF THE SOUTH AFRICAN ADMINISTRATION' written on it (2010: 144), into a crossword book – the tools used to write the note admitting that her words are constrained by her jailers, but also that she has encrypted a message, a message that is not what it seems. The suicide note is intended as a cancellation of the 'statement'. Yet the sleeping tablets she takes turn out to be counterfeit too, too weak to have much effect (2010: 151).

In First's version, she rips the suicide note from the book and flushes it down the toilet (2010: 150); the note now seems to become evidence of cowardice rather than an encrypted message about the strongroom's intactness

– because she failed to commit suicide, or because it is now revealed why she tried to commit suicide? Here again the meanings double back on themselves, the point to which the cowardice attaches itself is not clear (2010: 166). 'Detention had not given them what they wanted'; the longer she remained in prison, she reasoned, the more proof there was that she had not betrayed them (2010: 151). The interrogator in the documentary film version shouts: 'You've told us nothing.' In a voice-over the viewer hears First say: 'Devastated with guilt that I had begun to make a statement, and they could use the statement to demoralize others as they had used Jan's statement to break me down.'

In one of the many reinterpretations and adaptations of First's *117 Days*, the film version of her daughter's script *A World Apart*, the note rises to the surface again. Of course this film is not in a simple way biographical (the changes in names alert us to this fact), yet the events follow closely the events of the lives of First and her daughters. Their lives are encrypted here in a way that speaks, in the nature of documentary evidence, of a life lived under the sign of subterfuge – as another daughter phrases it, where 'every secret thing' was the ruling principle. In the film version, the note is written in a Bible, which contains markings claiming it to be the property of the prison services, but which has mysteriously made its way home with First. The scene in the film does not convince – it is unclear, for example, how and why First would smuggle a Bible *out* of prison, let alone a Bible with a stamp claiming it as the property of the prison services. In the adaptation of the suicide note, the note itself is smuggled out to be brought into view. This resurfacing is yet another attempt to read this illegible, incomprehensible and contradictorily encrypted moment. After the end of the first 90 days, when First was re-arrested for a possible second period of 90 days, a number of things had shifted. She was allowed a Bible, an aggressively inappropriate book to give to an atheist Jew. A second text she was handed after many weeks was the already mentioned book of crossword puzzles (2010: 159), with her name already written on the cover, an insidious version of the statement she was tricked into making. The crossword book is an example of a text that helps one pass the time, making empty and meaningless time bearable. For my reading of the account, however, its implications of encryption are richly suggestive.

When First leaves prison, she does not bring the suicide note with her (she destroys it as another piece of potentially incriminating evidence against her), nor does she bring the text of what will become *117 Days* in her red suitcase. She walks out with one document only, the carbon copy of her release – the original filed no doubt alongside other documents about her in a file about her activities. Here it will join the incomplete, unauthenticated yet darkly dangerous 'statement'. The carbon copy is not a copy of the statement that First regrets having made, never sees again, yet often imagines. But it is a reminder of the incriminating document held in the official archives.

After First left prison she spent some time recovering at her home in Johannesburg, during this time applying for a passport so as to join her husband and father who were already living in London (Frankel 1999: 217). The South African authorities did not grant her a passport – which would have implied that she was free to return – but instead issued her with exit papers, closing, as it were, her identity files. The exit from prison and the exit from South Africa are sources of anxiety. The very motivation for the 90 days' detention was to extract information. To have left prison, First feared, implied (in the circulation of gossip and rumours about her) that she had cooperated. She writes in her account that she would have preferred to stay in prison longer (2010: 151), as this would have been proof of her non-collaboration. The memory strongroom has this layer, then, of a desire to return. The prolonged or returned stay is an attempt at completing the work of proving her non-collaboration, of checking again that nothing had seeped or leaked.

The text contains a number of passages that record this desire to double back, as if to edit and redact a document. 'I could now see unravelled the campaign of attack against me' (2010: 151), she writes, the 'now' positioning her both inside back then and outside, now, during the writing process, remembering her way back in. References to plots and 'secrets, top secrets' (2010: 54) multiply, and during her remembered account of the interrogation session she notes with some pride the sheet full of evasive answers that she provided (2010: 55). During the course of this scene, however, the ground shifts as First recalls being told that there has *already* been a 'leak' from elsewhere. The existent leak exposes her (and others) and makes it unclear whether she herself has leaked something by mistake. Even the evasive answer, read with the knowledge provided by the leak, can become readable as a new leak (2010: 55–60).

Leaving South Africa with her two younger daughters (the eldest was travelling to Europe by sea with friends), First arrived in London, unsure how she was to make a living, or what kind of meaningful work she would find. It was in the grey of a London autumn that she began to write the document that was published as *117 Days*. It is best read as an account written to overwrite the 'statement' and to counter the suspicions that may have become attached to it. *117 Days* is therefore an account of non-disclosure, an attempt to edit and check the events by going over them in memory. The paranoid language about the need for tidiness and careful vigilance is striking. Yet this self-supervision is not an act that takes place at the time of her imprisonment; it is written from London, in order to document and archive her own version – to put her signature to what she hopes will become *the* definitive statement that will seal the strongroom once again. The text is intent on checking and confirming, to herself, that nothing was left behind, nothing was leaked, no stain was left that could incriminate others or herself.

Soon after completing *117 Days*, First was invited by the BBC to collaborate on a documentary film for which she wrote the script, as well as making a radio programme and a radio play (Wieder 2013: 147). This rarely seen film, entitled *90 Days*, was made by Jack Gold with First's collaboration (Harlow 1992: 120). It is an extraordinary parallel text, in which First recreates and re-enacts her own imprisonment. The film's authenticating palette of greys speaks also, evocatively, of the isolation of her new life in London. There is not much written on the making of the film, but from the few anecdotal sources and the account in Barbara Harlow's book, it is evident that it was made in London and in a decommissioned prison building close to Oxford, thinly and unconvincingly disguised as South African locales (Harlow 1992: 121). The film is presented as a documentary, but is better viewed as one in a series of revisitings and re-enactments of the events narrated in *117 Days*, versions in and through which First reimagines the scene and tidies up the memory prison. The film is experimental in form and unsettling in its stylishly stilted acting. The title was changed to *90 Days*, for viewers to whom the phrase would be more easily understood as referring to the South African detention laws. Yet the change of name is resonant for this text, which thematises *noms de guerre* and the subterfuge involved in the writing and political activism of First's circle of comrades and friends.

The final scene of the film shows Ruth First walking out of prison, her suitcase (quite possibly the very same red suitcase she packed in South Africa) in her hand. As her footsteps echo down the re-enacted prison passage, we hear the voice of the male narrator glossing the scene: 'She left prison and South Africa.' In the conflation of the two scenes of exit, the viewer is meant to understand that First left South Africa because there was no other option. The film's narrated events end with her walking out of the prison, yet this is also where the written narrative begins, as the author of the document, First, starts writing the account of her imprisonment. The red suitcase contains (as well as represents) the remembered events. The version we see, like the suitcase itself, is and is *not*, accurate. The red colour is leached out on screen, as if First's own memories are themselves being deleted while she attempts to record them.

The film goes over the same events, but as re-enactment, and re-enactment that deviates from the original events in significant ways. There were practical reasons for this deviation. First's exit visa meant that she could not return to South Africa; the film was made on a small budget; it was made in the genre of the didactic news documentary; and First might have wanted to protect her children's privacy. But the re-enactment's differences from the text on which it is based are more than practical. They in fact reveal the urge to re-enactment and redaction already present in the original text. In the act of writing the text, First revisits the scene of the prison cell in which she was held, sealing the strongroom and attempting not to reveal any information to her interrogators, even in retrospect. They had declared that she would not be set free until she had told them what they wanted to know. The leaving of the prison cell became, for First, a moment of testing. It was the moment when suspicion settled on her, and in her book and in the film she reinhabits the prison to go over again her attempts to reveal nothing, playing out and re-enacting the fact that she *had* said nothing. Overlaid with the leaving of the prison (and her country) is the fact that the film was made and the book published in London, removed from the engaged activist work in South Africa. Revisiting the memory prison is painful and traumatic, but there is also comfort in that revisited scene and the community of comrades to whom she was connected by the shared if not communal imprisonment. Remembering the prison cell, and reconstituting it, it is as if she reinhabits that remembered place. Book and film in this reading become evidence of, and in fact documentaries about, her non-inclusion in the hostile archive that wanted to use her words as a trap for others.

In *90 Days*, the re-enactment is a counterfeit, self-consciously so. The film depicts the effects of solitary confinement in a cool cinematic style, reminiscent of the European *avant-garde* cinema that First knew well and loved. I do not mean by this to suggest that the film is artful and therefore not truthful. Instead, what I mean is that this counterfeit South Africa is precisely to be understood as that: in a staged prison the real Ruth First is visited by counterfeit children, revealing to us the estrangement brought not only by solitary confinement, but also life in exile. It is worth going over the ways in which Gold's extraordinary film can be viewed as a document of forgery and an account of successfully resisting a 'leak'. The children who re-enact First's children are members of a counterfeit (and uncredited) family, and the house in which the red (or grey, in this case) suitcase is packed is clearly an English suburban one. Behind the children and their grandmother, we see not Elsie – the black woman so prominent in histories as housekeeper and carer to the Slovo girls (Slovo 1997: 85) – but instead an English garden (possibly the garden of the house on Lyme Street in Camden Town that they had bought; Frankel 1999: 280), with a greenhouse and a wooden bird-feeder. Another counterfeit house, filmed in the 'plush white suburbs' of Bulawayo, is described in the 'Extracts of a Diary' in Shawn Slovo's *A World Apart* as 'modest' (1988: 3) compared to the house it is acting. Here Elsie does appear, although Slovo writes that she had great 'trouble finding an Elsie' (1988: 10). They eventually cast an ambivalent Linda Mvusi as Elsie – she was authentically South African (which Slovo regarded as crucial); but in an unpleasant exchange with a local white Zimbabwean man, who remarks that they could have simply used 'his' maid to play the part, Slovo relishes being able to tell him 'that Linda's an architect actually' (1988: 19).

In the language available to cinema, the documentary film *90 Days* picks up on and reinterprets the book's paranoidly embodied descriptions of prison life.

The book brings to the surface the themes of surveillance and self-surveillance through narration and the many written texts used to document and control the versions of events (First 2010: 1). In the film, the visual language of cinema reinforces this paranoid sense, but by using the camera as an eye. We hear First's voice make this theme explicit: 'I try to make time pass with the activities of others, but the figures I see could be on celluloid. They are not part of my world.' The black-and-white documentary images from the South African resistance archive replace the italicised twinning narratives included in *117 Days*, creating both proximity and distance for First, who is re-enacting her imprisonment far away in London. In a further complication of the re-enacted archive, it is worth noting that these images circulated outside South Africa in ways very different from the censored news environment inside the country.

The accented speech in the film is striking, providing us with yet another instance of distancing and encoding, and of how inauthenticity and forgery are used to make a truthful and accurate testimony. The film opens with First in a library in north London (Camden Library as a counterfeit Cullen Library at Wits University), in front of a shelf of books on political resistance (Murphy 2015). First is shown dressed in the kind of outfit that is iconic of her style, holding in front of her a black folder into which she seems to be entering data – as if the accuracy of the film is proven by the careful note-taking from documentary sources. The camera then follows her as she descends the stairs in a mid-century modernist building of the kind we know First admired. She does not make eye contact with the viewer of the film (as if we are spying on her, or as if we are watching her while she knows we are spying on her but pretends not to be aware), and is met by two men speaking in what is meant to be Afrikaans-accented English. The poor acting and unconvincing accents of all of First's interrogators can be understood in the tradition of the stock Afrikaner villain in cinema, a perennial favourite still. Yet these counterfeit accents are significant in another way, and can be brought in relation to the stylised and wooden acting of white people who were in fact part of the resistance movement, but who played characters with whom they did not share a vision of the world. An excellent example is Myrtle Berman, a friend of Ruth First, who played an unspeakable 'madam' in Lionel Rogosin's *Come Back Africa* (Rogosin 2004: 99). In scenes that are hard to decode without the knowledge that all the actors taking part in such a project would by definition be sympathetic to the aims of the film, one sees the protagonist Zachariah in conversation with the gratingly racist white 'madam' and her passive husband. The woodenness of the acting is an encrypted defence, since the poor acting is more than an act; it is a counterfeit and is meant to be understood as such. Only progressive white South Africans were trusted to take part in Rogosin's project, as he writes in a section called 'Casting Whites' in his book documenting the making of the film (2004: 98–103). The same constraints are visible in the casting for *90 Days*.

The accented speech of the interrogators and guards is meant to evoke and record a particular South African reality, and this is the world that is being exposed by the writing of the book and the making of the film. Yet, at the same time, the counterfeit accents remind the viewer (at least the viewer who can hear and correctly categorise them) that this account is being compiled from the other side. First is 'free' and out of prison, in a London where South Africa is accessible to her only through black-and white newsprint and the re-enactment of a counterfeit. This same 'outside' conflates painfully with her exit from South Africa, and the loss and isolation that brings. The counterfeit Afrikaners re-enact the scene as her interrogators, but also from the outside – the actors are neither security branch policemen, nor are they representatives sent from there. When First is shown being arrested and driven away from her workplace, instead of the car driving through Johannesburg we see English streets and countryside through the windows; the re-enactment faithfully records, but translates the recording into this other register, one that speaks eloquently of the many losses experienced by those who left on exit permits to make lives elsewhere. The greyness of the world seen on the black-and-white screen adds to this sense of the past receding as the journey unfolds.

Gillian Slovo writes in the Acknowledgments at the end of her book *Every Secret Thing*: 'Although my parents' history was enacted not written down and the raw materials of their past were often destroyed the truth of what happened was lodged in the memories of their friends and comrades' (1997: 365). The use of the word 'enacted' draws the reader's attention and is an unusual choice. Slovo is making a point about the absence of a written record, but we see also here the extra meaning of a life edited against hostile surveillance. There exists a set of images of First leaving South Africa and arriving in London to be united again with her husband Joe Slovo. Looking at these images, so often invoked in accounts of First's departure, one's eye becomes unusually attuned to what might be an 'act' and what the photographs have been edited to conceal. The child Gillian, her adult self recalls, is shown carrying a *Tintin* book as she climbs the stairs into the plane (1997: 133; this picture, or one from the same day, is included in the Virago edition of *117 Days*). On the famous photograph the book is not actually visible. It is clearly seen, though, on the picture taken after their arrival in London. Here we see her clutching her *Tintin* book, *Tintin and the Prisoners of the Sun*. The book is held upside down, as its owner looks up into her mother's face. First herself does not return the gaze; and what is most striking in this family portrait is the fact that both Joe Slovo and Gillian are looking at Ruth First, whose arm is protectively around her younger daughter. The eye settles on the parallel position of the arms, Gillian's enfolding her upside-down book while her mother enfolds her sister, and the meanings of a family under siege proliferate. The photograph may well have been taken in the BBC studios, and above their heads we read a sign that says 'No Entry' (Slovo 1997: 134).

On the cover of my copy of *117 Days* is a photograph of Ruth First, an awkward image that shows her face held between two hands that look, because of the angle of the camera, too large to be her own. Her face is tilted slightly downwards, her lips a tight line, and her hands press her face on both sides – as if what is inside her head needs to be contained. The last words in *117 Days* refer to the fact that her release from prison felt as if it was not the end, and that 'they' were not done with her. Barbara Harlow writes in *Barred* that nineteen years after her release from the women's cells in Marshall Square, 'the Pretoria government apparently sentenced [First] to death' (1992: 146).

Gillian Slovo's *Every Secret Thing* includes a description of a letter, and through it some imagined conversations between her parents:

> When she [Ruth First] spoke to Joe on the phone, she must have told him something of the way she felt. She must have told him, as she wrote eventually from England, to a nameless friend inside the country, 'I found myself very nervous when I came out about intruders and hearing walls … My spell [in gaol] brought all kinds of things closer to the skin and some popped uncomfortably out.' (1997: 128)

This sentence evokes the bodily metaphor of blood and the threshold of skin that contains it; and it also reinforces the dangers inherent in the moment the skin ruptures, when meanings leak out. It is a passage from the mother's correspondence, written from outside the country, to a 'nameless' friend, the address of the letter illegible, and the words providing the daughter with an imagined script for a conversation between her parents.

First's body is described as having lost the ability to read, with any certainty, itself as well as its environment: are the walls overhearing her, has someone intruded into the home to spy on her, or worse? This disorientation is described as something that has come closer to the skin, lurking just underneath and ready to 'pop'. To pursue this explosive metaphor in terms of First's death is too grisly, although Slovo comes close to it when she writes: 'The risks our parents took had meant that we were always on the look-out for that terrible event which would break through the fragile skin of everyday life' (1997: 23). Instead one can read this metaphor as one that describes the reading, editing, mentoring and archiving practices (reading under the skin) whose protocols include going over, going over the lines again, re-testing and re-editing the events and the documents we think we already know.

A Life Transplanted and Deleted: Hamilton Naki and his Archivists   4

The first successful human-to-human heart transplant, performed in Groote Schuur Hospital in Cape Town on 3 December 1967, has received a great deal of scholarly and popular attention. The year 2017, when I was finalising this chapter, marked the 50th anniversary of the operation, and with the opening of a museum called the Heart of Cape Town, housed in the very same hospital space where the operation took place, yet a new context has been created for understanding these events. The museum lovingly recreates, with a mixture of archival materials (such as letters, telegrams of congratulations and items that belonged to Christiaan Barnard), the events of 3 December 1967. Barnard's white rubber theatre boots were recently brought to the museum by a nurse who had kept them since the operation (Makwabe 2013). News reports covered this story (on television as well as in the press), the return of the boots emphasising the completeness and veracity of the archive, but also illustrating the emotional weight of the museum, with each donation reactivating the life of the museum in the public eye (and heart, one is tempted to add).

The museum's accuracy and truthfulness is stressed by guides and its website (http://www.heartofcapetown.co.za/), as well as by the labels and information that guide one through the rooms. The most fascinating aspect of the museum is the fake moments in the truthful reconstruction. There are two significant anomalies, both of which disturb the careful date stamp of the recreation. The first interruption in the date stamp is the way that the bedroom of Denise Darvall (the donor of the historic heart) has been recreated. The bedroom includes elements from an imagined future moment, extending beyond the death of the young woman, and creating for us a space that she *might* have inhabited had she not died. Descriptions of Darvall typically linger on her beauty and her youth, emphasising also the smallness of the heart inside her girlish body. The reconstruction of her bedroom in the museum is faithful in its period details, but nevertheless creates the bedroom not as it was, but as it might have become, extending her life beyond the premature death. Darvall had made some rather child-like drawings of dresses (the drawings are on display), and these have been interpreted by a tailor and made up into dresses that we see in the bedroom. In this way her memory is 'kept alive', as the guide informed me, using the language of second chances that permeates heart transplant discourses.

The second disturbance of the time capsule's careful date stamp happens when one enters through the heavy doors into the museum. The first space one walks through contains a dog anaesthetised on an operating table (although, of course, this is a model), its thorax clamped open and its waxwork heart clearly visible. Dogs were, self-evidently, never patients in the human wards. This introductory tableau takes us back in time (whereas Darvall's imagined bedroom takes us forward), to events that took place before the historic events of 3 December. The waxwork dog lies here to teach us that initial experiments were conducted on animals, before the operation was attempted on humans. The histories of experiments on dogs and discoveries about blood are intertwined (Starr 1999: 10–13), and the border between humans and animals is likely to be a topic in scholarship in the future (Harraway 2003, 2006, 2016 has mapped some directions). Dogs have received much scholarly attention in South African studies over the last years (Gqola 2009; Baderoon 2016; Green 2016; Woodward 2008). They were not the only animals to be used in Groote Schuur (McRae 1997: 160-9), but the waxwork dog serves another function here. It invokes (stands in for, transplants even), the body of the man who has become famous for his surgical work on, as well as the daily care of, the dogs that were experimented on in the animal research laboratories connected to the heart unit. His name is not mentioned in the labels in the room, but his spectral absence haunts the exhibition. All the wax figures are white (though Denise Darvall appears only as an absence), apart from the dog, whose fur on the exposed throat and head is black and white, its body covered by the same surgical sheets as we see later in the museum.

The man whose presence is so confusingly implied, but then deleted, is Hamilton Naki. A large literature exists on Naki, which I discuss below, although I do not bring new archival research to his case. Instead this chapter explores the various archives into which his life has been read, and for whose benefit these readings have been taken. The conflicting archives into which and through which we read Naki's life are coded through the language of transplants, organ donation and blood. Unlike Darvall, Naki did not die in order for the historic heart transplant to take place, and so his absence has to be understood differently. The absence of a reconstructed model of him (such as the ones we find of the medical team and of multiple Barnards elsewhere in the museum) is a more complex acknowledgement of his role in this museum, and in the events it commemorates.

Naki's contribution as part of the narrative of the heart transplant operation is a later (re)insertion, and in the museum he is a figure at once referenced and visibly deleted by this scene of the dog on the operating table. His reputation and contribution to the heart transplant became for a time a *cause célèbre*. It is his absent presence that I trace in this chapter, reading Naki's insertion and deletion using the trope of the heart transplant, and suggesting that Naki is the donor who makes possible this museum's evocation of the events. While it is now accepted that he was not the 'skilled surgeon' who actually performed the first heart transplant while Christiaan Barnard looked on, the rumours around his role in the operation remain alive. Luise White writes in *Speaking with Vampires* that rumours are not just a way of debating change; they are a way to debate the very terms in which these changes are to be described (2000: 209). It is this approach to the rumours around Hamilton Naki that informs my chapter. I do not aim to uncover a new 'truth'; I look instead at how competing rumours circulate like blood, and how the trope of donation and revival provides us with a possible way of understanding his present absence.

In this chapter I trace the ever-changing self-representation by and of the surgeon at the centre of these events, Christiaan Barnard (the 'celebrity surgeon' as Chris Logan, one of his biographers, calls him). I show that in his writings (which have not received much scholarly attention apart from being read neutrally as archival documents and sources) we see a particularly revealing instance of the enforced donation of Hamilton Naki, in order to bolster Barnard's fame. Themes running through Barnard's writings include the need for his own regeneration and constant renewal, as well as an enduring interest in his own fame. During the early 1990s, this autobiographical project (like so many others by white South Africans) retrospectively wished to edit the earlier accounts of his life, and to revise earlier moments from his career. The insertion of Naki sought to absolve Barnard, and the medical establishment generally, of accusations of perpetuating white privilege – or indeed of ever having had a part in it.

The heart transplant captured the imagination of the world, and there is a large medical as well as popular literature devoted to the events leading up to the operation, as well as documenting the day itself. Barnard devoted himself to keeping alive the memory of the day (and this trope of repeated resuscitation will recur in the discussion below). The human heart is an organ with powerful symbolic and religious connotations, and in South Africa, with its pervasive racial discourses that reference the body and blood in particular, the metaphoric meanings proliferated. In countless reflections on heart transplants, one sees the recurring question of whether one's 'race' could be changed by changing the 'race' of the heart. The heart is regarded as at once the most private and intimate part of the self, but also a place that harbours secrets and violent urges. These ideas are explored in the popular book by Rian Malan, *My Traitor's Heart* (1990). Malan is not alone in pursuing the meanings of the heart transplant as metaphor; it seems almost impossible to resist, and nearly all writers on the event make use of metaphorical language that often verges on sentimental *cliché*, sealing up the meanings with too neat stitches.

The operation has been discussed in countless medical histories, with typically sensational titles, often exaggerating a sense of time running out (a representative example is *Every Second Counts: The Extraordinary Race to Transplant the Human Heart*). This was also a common theme in Barnard's own utterances. In the growing medical humanities literature, the heart transplant's relation to research on the histories of blood donation (in particular the links between blood donation and race discourses; see, for example, Waldby and Mitchell 2006) remains a common theme. Douglass Starr's *Blood: An Epic History of Medicine and Commerce* contains fascinating discussions of the blood donation industry, and shows how the value of blood can be measured economically (blood is one of the most expensive liquid commodities; 1999: xi), but that the meanings attached to blood and blood donation are highly contextual, an argument also made in a special issue of the *Journal of the Royal Anthropological Institute* on blood transfers (Carsten 2013). Histories of the links between scientific knowledge and *apartheid* typically include the heart transplant operation, as the issues around race and the benefits of medicine are so dominant in the discourses. The scholarly literature on the ethics of medical research on animals returns to the early cases for evidence of our changing understandings of the body, as well as of interspecies responsibility.

A further area of scholarship related to the first heart transplant is the analysis of media histories and the links between the early heart operations and emerging media discourses around medical ethics (for example, Ayesha Nathoo's excellent *Hearts Exposed: Transplants and the Media in 1960s Britain*). The case is fascinating not only because of South Africa's pariah status in world media at the time, but also for the fact that South Africans had no television until the 1970s, and so South African consumption of the events was peculiarly distorted in relation to the rest of the world. South Africans learnt about the international reception through newspapers and radio, and thus the reception of the heart transplant became bound up also with the ways in which South Africa and *apartheid* were perceived on an international stage.

In Barnard's own writings and in interviews he returns obsessively to the problems posed by the international media reception. He blames the breakdown of his first marriage on 'the media', and writes about how unprepared he was for the effect of media coverage of his private life. The international media reception of the news, as well as of the young and handsome heart surgeon at the centre of the events, contrasts with the local reception – and the museum includes seemingly endless archives of celebratory press responses and letters and telegrams of congratulation. Barnard's autobiographies are preoccupied with gossip and the international press, and his concerns are typically about his inability to manage and direct their attention, rather than wishing it were absent. The conflation of the heart transplant and media reportage of South Africa reached a surreal high point when Barnard worked for the national intelligence agency, acting as a rather naïve ambassador for South Africa (Logan 2003: 232–62). I discuss in a later section of this chapter the strangely uneven book, *Sharp Dissection*, which was (at least in part) ghost written but published under his name.

In international discussions and reception of the news story, the heart transplant was from the outset closely associated with the *apartheid* project. South Africa's increasing militarisation and the stigma of *apartheid* meant that there was a great deal of international suspicion around the ethics of the operation. The earliest questions by international observers were about *apartheid* and race, and there is a large literature on the early BBC documentaries and newspaper reports, which Ayesha Nathoo's fine study (2009) discusses.

A further context, as yet largely unexplored, is the way in which modernity was debated elsewhere in Africa at the time that the Afrikaner Nationalist party was propagating its own version of *apartheid* as a well-meaning and hyper-modern project (Giliomee 2003: 666). One thinks for example of Wole Soyinka writing less than a decade later: 'My African world … embraces precision machinery, oil rigs, hydro-electricity, my typewriter, railway trains … machine guns, bronze sculpture' (1975: 38). The meanings of modernity were debated in newly independent Africa, in ways that offer an adjacent archive to South Africa's continental isolation. The African reception of the events surrounding the heart transplant have not been researched, although there is an interesting reference in an essay called 'The Poetics of a Transplanted Heart' published in 1968 by Ali Mazrui, in which he quotes the Deputy Foreign Minister of Uganda, Mr Rwamaro, in a piece written a month after the first transplant, and prophetic of the economic and social inequalities surrounding organ harvesting, cautioning that in future 'an African might be dragged from his house to a hospital and have his heart pulled out to save a dying man', and so black bodies could become 'spare parts for whites' (quoted in Mazrui 1968: 55). In South Africa, Mr Rwamaro wrote, black bodies are not regarded as human beings, yet their organs can be donated to white bodies. Hence, he argued, white South Africans may 'value the hearts of coloured people precisely because they hated coloured people'.

Mazrui explores the metaphoric meanings of hearts and heart transplants, and asks the reader to imagine 'Beethoven's Fifth Symphony blaring away on its own in the midst of the vast desolation of Antarctica'. The symphony is an example of an artwork created by a human (in contrast to the natural beauty of, say, the Ngorongoro crater, which he also references). 'A poetic heart must reside both in the person who writes the poetry and in the person who can listen to it with justice' (1968: 53), he writes. This sympathy between 'hearts' and the drama of the transplanted heart, Mazrui shows, makes use of a poetics of mutuality and sharing, of love and benevolence. The literal transplantation and donation of hearts, however, is characterised by 'a supreme impersonality' (1968: 55). A recurring theme in the early discussions of the heart transplant procedure was to question the mutuality of giving and receiving circumscribed by *apartheid* understandings of the body. Mazrui here suggests that the rhetoric of donation is in fact integral to the grammar of *apartheid*. He concludes his response piece by asking readers to contemplate the transplant 'in connection with aspects of African traditional religion and with *négritude* as a literary movement' (1968: 56), suggesting that the different values ascribed to bodies by *apartheid* is not the only way of calibrating our understanding of the events; there are, he argues, other cultural matters that need to be considered.

Mazrui's concerns, and those of the Ugandan dignitary, can be usefully read alongside recent work on the prevalence of zombies in popular imagination as well as scholarly and other writings on and from South Africa. Jean and John Comaroff have written of zombies as 'spectral floating signifiers' (2002: 781) who create value for the benefit of someone else who appropriates and consumes their energies. It would be too easy to suggest that Naki in his absent presence is one of these bloodless zombies who labour for the benefit of others, although one can imagine such an argument. I do, however, wish to build on the insights of Mazrui and the Comaroffs to explore the ways in which Naki has been co-opted into a project where his labour is extracted for someone else's gain. This case is emblematic, I argue, of the ways in which some revisionist projects attempt to insert and acknowledge black lives but without wishing to disturb the existing white-centred version of history. The museum devoted to the heart transplant operation, housed in the very same operating theatre where it was performed, stages a re-enactment with waxwork figures, their whiteness spectrally emphasising the exclusively white space of the 1960s hospital corridors. The museum is open to all (all who are willing to pay the entry price, an amount undisclosed on the website), but the way it solves the problem of Hamilton Naki's absent presence is revealing and significant.

The suspicions about the 'value' of Naki in the museum inform my discussion. In heart transplants, a heart from a foreign body is placed in the new context of the recipient's body, thus reviving the ailing body. Naki is brought in to revive the ailing 'body' of Barnard's fame and Barnard's place in public memory, and by extension the Afrikaner *apartheid*-inflected modernity of the 1960s. Naki's late insertion into the narrative is intended to rescue the ailing body of white settler entitlement and this moment of white privilege; in the museum his presence is acknowledged just enough to extract this labour from him, before he is again awkwardly deleted.

In 2017 celebrations marked fifty years since this medical breakthrough, and there were a number of initiatives to mark the event, including the museum I discuss in this chapter. In present-day South Africa, remembering and commemorating this event involves re-enacting and remembering a context in which white racial superiority and white privilege informed and animated the events. The time capsule created in the museum is reached by pushing open two heavy doors to enter the hospital ward. The heavy doors also seem to seal in the events that are here contained and frozen. When one enters the ward, the moments before and during the operation and the celebratory day after the operation are lovingly recreated. The styling of the exhibition (and the strikingly retro look) invites and creates nostalgia and retrospective pride. Yet there are complications, since this nostalgically recreated hospital ward is not equally accessible to all; while anyone can now enter the ward, this would not have been the case in 1967 when Groote Schuur was a racially segregated hospital. The desegregated entrance now is, and is not, the same entrance that was there in 1967. There is no 'whites only' sign; this is assumed and naturalised but also self-forgivingly deleted.

Missing from the display and the imagination of the museum's creators is any desire to show parallel lives and contexts other than that of celebratory scientific progress. So, for example, 1967 was the year when uMkhonto we Sizwe members conducted the first military actions in what was then north-western Rhodesia. It was also the year that military conscription became compulsory for all white men of school-leaving age. A year before, in 1966, H. F. Verwoerd had been rushed to this same hospital after he was attacked by Dimitri Tsafendas, and this was the hospital where he died. It is important to see that the heart transplant was not a rupture with this political background, but that the scientific experimentation and risk-taking that enabled the transplant was a continuation of the spirit of defensive experimentation of the Verwoerd era.

A final set of meanings that are informed by the racial discourses of the high *apartheid* era then, but translated into the idioms of the post-transition time now, are comments to do with rootedness and indigeneity. Barnard's autobiographical self-representation has always stressed his provincial, 'barefoot Karoo boy' upbringing. But a strand to this discourse, more in keeping with a time when a white-dominated and white-centred historical consciousness is no longer taken for granted but is in fact under question, gives rise to a new set of interpretations. In these uses of the metaphor of transplantation, Afrikaners become the heart itself, and the story of medical innovation is taken up as evidence of Afrikaners having earned their transplantation from Europe into Africa (see McRae 1997: 45–8). Here white South Africans are no longer merely the saviours, a common theme in early responses such as statements by Verwoerd himself (McRae 1997: 63); Afrikaners now become the very heart of the newly formed nation, having 'earned' this position. McRae builds up the metaphor even more (and these tightly wrought metaphors are typical of writing on Barnard) to take in the use of immunosuppressive drugs that prevent the foreign heart's rejection by the body as a way of talking about the entrenched and legitimated role of whites in the future South Africa.

While in this narrative white South Africans (Barnard in particular) thus become the saviours once again, this time using a more intimate metaphor that places the white destiny inside the body, my argument pursues a different set of metaphoric possibilities. In my reading, it is instead Hamilton Naki who comes to be the donor, in an attempt to keep alive and rescue the heroic moment, ensuring that it be retained and preserved. Naki's invisible supporting presence is perhaps, to adopt the overly metaphoric readings of writings on the transplant, that of the donor who has to die for the recipient to live. In this reading of the metaphor, the terminal patient who is kept alive by the donation from Naki is the 'whites-only' moment so lovingly recreated in the museum.

The rhetorically dense use of metaphors is characteristic of Barnard's style of speech, and also the writings that have appeared under his name. The son of a missionary, it is tempting to see this religiously inflected discourse as the origin of his clumsily portentous style. His autobiographies are striking in their constant revisiting of the transplant. From the outset he can be seen editing and reinterpreting the narrative, in *The Second Life* even revisiting the process of writing *One Life*, thus editing and revising the first autobiography in and through the second. His writings are prolific, almost all of them in collaboration (one is tempted to use the metaphor of the piggy-back heart transplant he named and performed), which adds to the sense of language straining towards metaphors that will capture all. Barnard was a vain man, and in one unkind obituary (now removed from the internet) it was even claimed that he died reading one of his own autobiographies. Not much attention has been paid to his novels and autobiographies as texts, perhaps partly because they are all co-authored. Collaborations of this kind sometimes lead readers to see a work's authenticity as discredited, yet co-authored works can also provide us with more, not less, information, as they reveal traces of a life already being edited for a listener.

The metaphor of revitalisation (or more literally of a heart transplant) is apt for Barnard's perpetual reinvigorating of his own identity. Unfortunately for a surgeon, he started experiencing debilitating arthritis pain in his hands rather early in his career, and the deterioration of his own body no doubt fuelled his obsessive interest in the earlier glorious moment, and archiving his career became a dominant preoccupation. Barnard's interest in and for women is a theme that runs through his biographical and autobiographical writings too, and his second and third marriages, to women not yet twenty years old, is a rather obvious expression of a desire to be associated with youth. The last project to which he devoted his time before his death in 2001 was the underwriting and promoting of Glycel, a supposed rejuvenation cream, and his role was to lend some medical authority to a treatment universally held to be fake.

A significant repackaging of his career took place in the 1990s, when many white South Africans sought to reposition themselves and to recuperate what could be saved of the past. Part of this reinvention was to bring his supposedly secret anti-*apartheid* beliefs finally into public view, a common and unremarkable enough opportunistic strand in white writing from the time. But there was one extraordinary statement among his own claims to heroic (and secret) resistance to *apartheid*, and that was his confession that his work had been shared and made possible by a highly skilled black surgeon, a certain Hamilton Naki. These sensational statements were rapidly taken up by international newspapers, eager for good news stories about the rise of a new South Africa, and Barnard tirelessly gave interviews and promoted this version of events.

Donald McRae traces the beginning of the gossip to a film made by a 'couple of ambitious South African filmmakers [who] began to peddle a bogus story that Naki had actually led the team of surgeons who excised the heart of Louis Washkansky in December 1967' (1997: 307). He devotes nearly four pages of closely printed footnotes to documenting the rumours, showing that it was in 2003 that the extraordinary story started to circulate widely, of a black surgeon who had been a member of the original team, but whose role had had to remain secret. This was the kind of narrative that rhymed beautifully with the new order – here was a story of a life lived under the shadow of *apartheid*, and of a man whose work was finally being recognised. The spectacular revelation was all too soon followed by humiliating (for Naki) refutations of the story. Yet the version that holds Naki as a man denied his rightful fame and recognition because of his race has remained a presence on the internet, and in popular memory.

While Naki's contribution was not that which Barnard had claimed in those interviews, his work in the animal laboratory certainly supported and in many ways made possible what Barnard and his team did in the famous operation. But it is the story of these 'hidden figures' (to use a phrase from Margot Lee Shetterly's book, now a film, on the African American women whose mathematical work at NASA was instrumental to the success of the US space programme) which revealed so much about the *apartheid* past. In 1990s South Africa, the rumours about Naki's involvement were more compelling and more revealing than the denial of those rumours could ever be. Naki's name remains associated with the operation, and he has received honours and had scholarships named after him, and a square and streets carry his name. He remains celebrated on various websites. The internet is a particular kind of rumour machine that keeps things and ideas alive, continually transplanting them into contexts that give them new life and sustain them.

More complex and more unfortunate are the inevitable refutations and denials, which followed in a steady stream. This chapter does not seek to prove that Naki was involved in the operation – the facts seem beyond question. But I attempt to trace how and when Naki's life work became so significant, and to whose benefit. Barnard's first autobiography (published in 1969) was called, fittingly, *One Life*. In the choice of title, it already seems as if Barnard was anticipating revisions and a second version. This first autobiography was co-authored by a writer called Curtis Bell Pepper, who worked and lived in Rome

('*Newsweek*'s man in Italy' from 1957 to 1969, the dust jacket informs us). That places the co-authoring of the novel in the European summer of 1968 when Barnard was being photographed with Gina Lollobrigida and Sophia Loren. The context for the writing was a stay in society homes and expensive hotels in late 1960s Milan and Rome, the cultivation of an international audience (*Newsweek* readers, perhaps) its primary desire. In the autobiography, Barnard presents the first heart transplant as a morality tale and a transformation tale – of the heart transplant, but also of himself. His barefoot beginnings in a religious and 'simple' Afrikaner home are emphasised, and early memories centre on the value of human life and the location of the soul. In the narrative of religious conversion, the reader is shown the germs of the later enlightenment, as if the life story was always already yearning towards the moment of transformative illumination that would change all. Barnard's narrative relies on a repetition of such moments of insight, inching towards the great moment of the operation. This first autobiography is shaped like a *bildungsroman*, the man at the end always prefigured in the child we see in the early pages, although there are false knowing moments that undercut this progression in the narrative arc.

The consciousness that the reader sees develop in the pages of this book is that of a provincial boy growing up to be an international celebrity. The world in which Barnard is seen to move in South Africa is an aspirational white Afrikaner one, small-minded and rather unsophisticated. There is very little reflection on the political situation in South Africa, which is taken as a natural and naturalised backdrop. Where any awareness of racial ideology enters the autobiography, it is through a perplexed and betrayed account of international media (mis)perception. The development of the man is charted in almost unreadable accounts of sexual adventures. The change one sees is from a provincial boy to someone comfortable in Euro-modernist gatherings, meeting with film stars and directors in particular. It is this access to screen and print that thrills Barnard, and he often describes his new life in terms of filmic metaphors (James Bond is a favourite twin). During the course of the autobiography, the discourse shifts from missionary's son to sexual adventurer, and this is his access to an international world. Media attention shifts from questions of *apartheid* to the many beautiful women with whom he surrounds himself, thus deflecting attention from politics.

One Life, the first draft of the life and of the heart transplant, is part of this project of placing the South African discovery on an international stage. Afrikaner, and *apartheid*, modernity of this time saw itself as a vanguard and not as something regressive. Barnard's own understanding of and approach to *apartheid* is a theme running through his work, in complex and revealing ways. In his first autobiography, he presents himself to an imagined international audience. His 'poor boy' upbringing is invoked as a way of underlining his achievements. The tone of the text is often false, when references to experience of a larger a world are included for atmosphere and effect. The uneven tone accentuates the role of the text in documenting an extraordinary life transition, but also bears traces of the repackaging and recycling of the life story, and its constant rejuvenation in new contexts.

The 'life' is skilfully constructed, and included are many lyrical passages about the worth of a life and where the real self is to be found. Thus the autobiography is best read as a quest tale, in search of the true self and its simple origins in the barefoot boy. The genres of life-writing are also brought, repeatedly, in relation to the meaning and worth of a human being. The religious discourse of his father is interwoven with medical discourses, as if building up evidence that the boy was always divinely predestined to be a medical genius. In this way the writer of the autobiography creates for the reader a context for the decisions that we see Barnard making – as if in a pre-emptive defence against the ethical objections to the heart transplant operation. Questions of wider identity and *apartheid* are part of the sections centred around family, and the most problematic and racially hostile comments are ascribed to Louwtjie, his first wife from whom he was separating as the book neared completion. The book thus also helps him chart, much in the way a relationship counsellor might, an exit strategy from his marriage.

The opening pages create for the reader a rather naïve, small-town world in which Christianity and racial divisions structure everyday life and conversations. In Part Two, we read how Barnard befriended at university an educated and worldly Harry Kahn (the first of a number of significant Jewish men in the heart transplant story, a sub-narrative often suppressed in versions of the operation that celebrate Afrikaner achievements). Descriptions of their friendship and conversations frame a burgeoning self, more politically aware and more conscious of a world beyond South Africa. Each section of the autobiography develops and complicates this meta-narrative. In Part Three, Barnard describes a moment of insight (one of many – this is a recurring trope) when he nearly administered morphine to a woman begging for euthanasia. Here again we are meant to infer that his decisions are always informed by a rigid ethical code, in an attempt to pre-empt possible criticism. Part Four concerns the dog laboratories where early research was done on animals, and it is in this section that the theme of racial identity is most fully developed. This section of *One Life* maps a number of themes that Barnard takes up in later writings, and it is in this laboratory that Hamilton Naki worked. Naki's name is not, however, mentioned in *One Life*. In later accounts, Barnard claims for Naki a centrality to his, Barnard's project – but this is not evident in the account given here.

In Part Five, Barnard and his young family's relocation to the USA brings South African politics into focus, and Barnard's then wife Louwtjie is the main vehicle through which this is done. In this version, it is Louwtjie (a nurse he met at Groote Schuur) who is unwilling to make a life in the USA because of the way South Africa is represented in the international press. Louwtjie's role in this text is to defend the Nationalist Party project, while the narrator keeps his distance from these values. She is depicted as naïve and unworldly, but through her the author is able to defend the nationalist project without himself being tainted by it. My earlier point about how a ghost-written project allows us to access a collective voice is here seen again, as Louwtjie's words run like a submerged strand through this text, expressing racist and xenophobic sentiments from which Barnard can distance himself, while still including them in the narrative.

In a particularly charged passage, Louwtjie is asked whether she is speaking Zulu (Barnard and Pepper 1969: 299) when someone overhears her speaking in Afrikaans. This misidentification of her language (and more importantly, mistaking her proudly Afrikaner identity as Zulu) becomes (in the words ascribed to Louwtjie) evidence of how South Africa is misunderstood. The way in which South Africa is misrepresented in the press is, to her, a personal affront. She returns to South Africa with the children, and on the way to fly home the family stop off in Washington. The visit to the Lincoln Memorial acts as a transit point in the narrative, making sense of the leave-taking from the USA and of the way South Africa's racial dispensation is regarded elsewhere. Unmentioned are the 1963 events at the Lincoln Memorial and Martin Luther King's impassioned and famous speech, which Barnard refers to obliquely when he writes about the 'freedom not to mix', using the Afrikaner Nationalist discourse of the time.

These references to South Africa's pariah status become more explicit in the later section of the book. On his own return to South Africa, Barnard reports conversations about the fact that the first transplant could not have been from a black person, as the international press would have accused him of experimentation (1969: 229). After the first transplant, Barnard received a phone call from 'London' and the first question – which angered him greatly – was whether the donor heart was from a black or a white person (1969: 387). Thus we see the narrative of Afrikaner modernity from the beginning at war with other readings of the heart transplant that take into consideration the different values *apartheid* assigned to bodies.

In the final pages of *One Life*, Warchansky's death poses for a moment a challenge to the narrative of scientific breakthrough and success. 'Where does Warchansky end and I begin?' (1969: 454) asks Barnard, as if it were his heart that had been transplanted into Warchansky. Barnard leaves the hospital after hearing that Warchansky has died, and his route takes him past the cemetery below Groote Schuur – now home to a number of itinerant homeless Capetonians – and he walks down a corridor between the dog laboratories and the post-mortem block. His route towards the animal laboratory is a narrative strategy to link, geographically and thematically, the post-mortem room which reminds him of the failure to keep Warchansky alive with the ongoing narrative of the necessity for experimentation. It is in the eyes of a rabbit that he finds the message he needs to end his book: 'they [the animals] wanted only to live' (1969: 464). This desire, read in the eyes of an animal, turns Warchansky's death into a narrative not of loss but of success. Through the eyes of the animals Barnard sees the continuing worth of his work. We do not read of him meeting or speaking to the caretaker; Naki and his fellow animal laboratory workers remain invisible as the surgeon communes with the rabbit.

This narrative of revival and reanimation is couched in religious terms, reminiscent of the mode of the Christian conversion narrative. These self-transformation genres rely on a narrative that draws for the reader moments of doubt and earlier, pre-conversion, moments of darkness and lack of insight. The narrative of religious conversion has the purpose of documenting and illustrating newness and the radical transformations brought by conversion; but the challenge is also to provide a link with the earlier sinful life, to show by what means the transformation took place. In this early autobiography, Barnard uses tropes of Christianity and a series of insights about the value of human life. The death of his own father, and of a brother who died young of heart disease, are the foundational experiences on which he builds himself as a medical doctor. The narrative is that of a personal and professional quest, of someone who always chooses life and tries to save it where he can.

In 1977 Barnard published the next and rather less personal instalment of his autobiography, and the function of this version was to develop a much clearer apology for Afrikaner nationalism and the *apartheid* project. Barnard was recruited as part of a sprawling propaganda machine, the details of which remain murky today (Logan's chapter 'Info' provides a useful background to Barnard's involvement), and in *Sharp Dissection* the heart transplant project is reinterpreted as part of the narrative of Afrikaner super-modernity. The cover already sets up this interpretation, showing a photograph of a kind and protective Barnard holding a small and unwell African child, whose sad eyes stare out past the viewer while his or her little hand rests on the good doctor's heart. This book revisits again the humble barefoot beginnings, as do all of Barnard's autobiographical writings. This time, however, the barefoot childhood functions as part of two linked narratives – the first is the rootedness of his family in South Africa, his own barefoot childhood connecting him back to 'the beginning of time' when the first Barnard arrived. This is a familiar narrative from white South African writing, and Afrikaner-identified writing in particular (see Coetzee 2001). The narrative of the Barnard family's 'long life' in South Africa informs the polemical tone of the book, and justifies his 'right to write about the future' of South Africa (1977: 8). Here we see the heart transplant integrated into a story about modernity and indigeneity, of Afrikaners as transplanted hearts from elsewhere who have come to revive the ailing body of Africa and of South Africa in particular.

In the by now familiar trope of the return, Barnard visits the mission church where his father used to preach to the black parishioners of the district. Barnard finds to his horror that the church has been turned into a badminton court (for the benefit only of white sports enthusiasts, although the text does not make this explicit and this is not what bothers him) (1977: 8). The modernisation project here is clearly related to the forced removal of the black community, and the relocation of their worshipping activities to an area beyond the gentrifying white community. Barnard's outrage is not directed at the disinvestment and displacement of the black community; instead, the anger is that his own 'barefoot' past has been erased: 'I wrote to the newspapers at the time, objecting strongly, and vowed not to return to Beaufort West until my father's church had been restored. It was subsequently decided by the Beaufort West Municipality that both the church and the house be restored, and this work is now in progress' (1977: 8). The moment that is commemorated is cleansed of the ugly realities of the forced removals of communities of black South Africans. Today the church houses a display dedicated to Christiaan Barnard and includes some of his many awards and the machines used for the first heart transplant. The church has been 'healed' from its unhealthy period as a badminton court, and is now healthy again – with the transplanted content that redefines its significance as linked to the story of the barefoot white boy who became the world-famous surgeon.

The second narrative inserts his own personal development from barefoot boy to world-renowned surgeon into what one might call the Afrikaner modernity narrative. Here, we see his own autobiographical *bildung* as evidence of, even exemplary of, what the 'white tribe' has brought to Africa. Barnard sees his white tribe as the defenders of values that elsewhere have been put at risk. In other words, South Africa is the operating theatre of the world, the place where civilisation and modernity are being preserved. The enemies of this civilisation are free speech, the 'liberal' media and the spectre of communism.

What the 'doctor' prescribes is a 'sharp dissection' and an intervention. Whereas it may seem as if *apartheid* is the disease, it is clear to him that it is instead the enemies of free speech and the defenders of communism who are making the patient terminally ill. He presents himself, as does the image on the cover, as someone with a concern for 'human suffering' (1977: 7). The suffering, in his analysis, is caused by the 'politics of hypocrisy' which threatens Western civilisation with extinction (1977: 14). The argument contrasts two kinds of modernity. The one kind is that exemplified by the dangerously self-destructive impulses of 'the technological age' (1977: 35) and press freedom (1977: 60), and in particular television, which trivialises everything (1977: 38–41). The twin to these forces of destruction is communism, in particular as it is interpreted through what he calls the 'viewpoint of the third world' (1977: 14, 102).

Compared to this sick modernity is the good and humane modernity of *apartheid*. South Africa's white tribe are held up as the defenders of Christian civilisation, at once the custodians and the hyper-modernisers; the way in which the heart transplant is used here is as a metaphor for a healthy heart that revitalises an ailing body. In South Africa, so this version goes, the true meanings of modernity and civilisation are preserved and humanely exercised. The controversy, he (or his ghost-writer) writes, 'is whether human life is being debased in South Africa by deliberate government policy or whether, as the Government maintains, it is pursuing a course that will ensure a better life for all' (1977: 31).

The rootedness of the white tribe returns as part of the modernisation narrative (1977: 80). The white nation, in this version, brought not only peaceful humanitarian help, but even 'peace' itself (1977: 89). South Africa (by which he means the South Africa of the white tribe) is 'the powerhouse of Africa', the very fulcrum of modernity (1977: 98–9). The modernity narrative is used to defend the right of the white tribe not only to be in South Africa, but to lead it and to determine the nature of the 'sharp dissection' needed to keep the country (and the larger continent) healthy. The rooted histories of whiteness are emphasised, as is Barnard's own life as exemplary of this rapid development, both narratives serving to defend and extend white privilege.

'I am just as much an African as Hamilton Naki' (1977: 77), Barnard writes, and here in this strangely uneven text is the beginning of what was later to become a controversial rival narrative in which Naki, a black South African, was placed at (and then removed from) the scene of the first successful human-to-human heart transplant. Naki's name and reputation are not discussed further, and he disappears until just before the first democratic elections in South Africa, when the sensational revelation was made: the person who had performed the first human-to-human heart transplant in Groote Schuur Hospital in 1967 was not – as the whole world had thought – Christiaan Barnard but in fact an as yet unknown black South African, Hamilton Naki.

In *The Second Life*, an autobiography published in 1993, a reference appears that gives an illuminating insight into the revisionary impulses behind much white life-writing of the time. This was the time of confessional white writing, such as Mark Behr's *The Smell of Apples* and Rian Malan's *My Traitor's Heart*, the scramble for salvation and revisionist white-authored autobiography across all media. Barnard's revised autobiography covers the same ground as the first, in fact provides the back story to the writing of the first. Here, though, the drama of personal revelation and enlightenment is missing. Instead, the meta-narrative running through this volume is the increasing sense of the international media as an enemy and the destroyer of his life and privacy. The treatment of sexuality and women is astonishing, and makes the volume almost unreadable. Most fascinating is the attempt to revise the material in another, new and differently political, context. When *apartheid* is mentioned, Barnard describes how he was always against it; a common enough theme in white writing from South Africa. The nature of this opposition is brought into question by the dismissive and patronising way in which he describes black South Africans. In short, the nature of his opposition to *apartheid* is most clear when he refers to being slighted by the international media and how he, as a white South African, was punished and denied the Nobel prize that was his due.

In *The Second Life* Naki is not only named but described as an excellent 'surgeon' (1993: 246). Here Naki emerges clearly, and his role is to supplement and defend Barnard's own failing reputation. For a short while, Naki was celebrated as the invisible member of Barnard's transplant team, brought now heroically to light by Barnard. Naki's role in the heart transplant team had a brief high flowering in the heady days of the early 1990s, and it was soon followed by an opportunistic (and again co-authored) novel by Barnard about 'the dog man'. Barnard's novel, *The Donor*, provides a version of Naki's life through the invented character 'Mbeki', but like that other 'dog man', *Petrus*, in J. M. Coetzee's *Disgrace*, Mbeki remains a shadowy figure. It is an extraordinarily unimaginative name; only the name Mandela could perhaps rival it for its obviousness. The character is extremely poorly drawn, but there is a clear development of the myth of the good white surgeon who saves Mbeki.

The novel is part of a discourse of reinserting Naki into history, but it is crucial to stress that Naki is in fact inserted where he never was. The novel is interesting for developing a discourse around zombies before they became fashionable in scholarship and popular culture. Heart transplants always raise the question of the relationship between the host and the donor, and one of the medical dangers concerns hostile bodies rejecting the transplanted organ. Written from a moment post 1994, Barnard again seeks to reanimate and re-enliven the meanings of his pioneering act. Here is where he begins to need Naki, to bring Naki back in order to salvage the meanings of his own past. Barnard, at this time married to a very young third wife named Karen, who typed his novel, unkindly kills off the character named Karen, and it is she who becomes the zombie waiting for a heart.

The story (pieced together from the novel and from *The Second Life*, and from the many interviews Barnard gave) captured the international imagination. Barnard's death in 2001 and Naki's in 2005 fuelled fresh rumours, and obituaries repeating the story of Naki's centrality to the operation were printed in reputable newspapers such as the London *Times* and the *New York Times*, repeating, recirculating and reviving the claim. A scholarly article appeared in the *Bulletin of the Royal College of Surgeons of England* in 2014, and in the history of the heart transplants by Donald McRae (1997) the many references are meticulously listed. The article in the *Bulletin* was illustrated with a picture of Naki as an older man, dressed in a blue surgical gown (from the reconstruction of the operation it is clear that sea-green gowns were worn; the blue colour transplants for us the photograph's context to the present).

McRae includes a stream-of-consciousness reverie from Barnard that sums up this newly edited past:

> The surgeon could not look any longer at the majesty of that Cape morning. He walked back inside and headed for his office. Barnard lay down on the brown couch and covered his eyes with an arm. His numbed reverie was broken by the appearance of Hamilton Naki, the former gardener whom he had trained to transplant dog kidneys and hearts in the Animal House. If not for the colour of his skin, Barnard knew, Naki would have been part of his surgical team eighteen days earlier. He had a touch and a gift which was the equal, if not superior, to that of most of the white surgeons who worked at Groote Schuur.

The passage continues, and the 'famous Afrikaner' is too exhausted to say the words he wishes to say ('Hello, Hami'). Instead, we hear Naki speak, murmuring that the doctor works too hard before he tiptoes out and closes the door gently (Barnard 1993: 231). The thoughts ascribed to Barnard come from the 1990s, transplanted to this moment in the 1960s. McRae did not intend this passage to be read as I do here. But what is clear from this passage is that Naki enters the room (and the narrative) to serve a particular purpose, to show Barnard's worth; and then to serve by exiting.

For a short while the gossip and myth-making seemed to honour Naki's contributions to the project. Yet soon an unpleasant and humiliating clean-up began, and a number of documents asserted that Naki could not, of course, have performed the operation: he had no training, he was a dog carer, no black people would have been allowed into the operating theatre, and so on went the list of reasons why the rumours were inaccurate. These refutations overlooked the fact that most people accepted that this was the case, knowing the limitations imposed on black South Africans. But in the rumours, Naki was celebrated not for what he *had* done but what he *might* have done given a different context. If Denise Darvall's reconstructed room could contain dresses she had neither made nor worn, why could Naki not be imagined as the world-famous surgeon he never was able to become? In the many official versions (such as a refutation in the *South African Medical Journal*), Naki's name was deleted again, leaving a near unreadable trace of his career.

Yet in the nature of rumour and gossip, these refutations again fuelled the rumours that continued to transplant Naki into the surgery team. In a 2007 documentary made by the Swiss team Werner Schweizer and Cristina Karrer, 'Hidden Heart', Naki is shown holding an imaginary heart in his hands and is heard saying 'I … I removed the heart.' The way the film is edited makes it unclear whether Naki did in fact say that he removed Darvall's heart, or whether he said that his own work was crucial in the scientific developments that made it possible, and that he was possibly holding an imaginary dog heart in his hands. In another interview, made by a US television station in 2003 when he was nearly 80 years old, Naki did state that he had been the one to lift the first transplanted heart out of the chest of Denise Darvall. It is perhaps not surprising that a man entering his ninth decade, having suffered a lifetime of small and large denigrations under *apartheid*, would eventually begin to repeat the story he had been told so often.

While Naki, as an old man, misremembered being part of the operating team, the meaning of his words is clear – his work with the dogs in the laboratory made possible the work of the transplant men. The Heart of Cape Town museum documents (without acknowledging this) the absence of black bodies during the original operations. Naki's work in the dog laboratory informed and supported the story of the glorious white tribe's hyper-modernity, and in this sense 'his' hands were in the operating room. Yet the absence of his embodied presence haunts present-day attempts to remember and celebrate the operation. The hunger for the story of Naki's presence led, to some extent even in Naki's own mind, to a false memory of black cooperation and presence at this moment of scientific breakthrough – a false memory that works in a forgiving way, covering up the dishonour of the all-white history. In order to retain the glorious modern moment, the *apartheid* past needed to be revised, and the appeal of Naki's transplanted presence was almost impossible to resist.

I end this chapter with a reflection on the museum and the invisible 'whites only' sign on the door. One approaches the hospital from the main road to find a small sign indicating the location of the museum inside the hospital complex. As one turns up the hill and towards the mountain, the road leads to the original and oldest building of Groote Schuur Hospital, built in the 1930s, where the museum is housed. As one enters the building, a reception desk much like those found in any hospital serves as a welcome desk to the museum, and here visitors can buy tickets for the tour; at the end of the tour, 'ladies' receive a plastic keyring in the shape of a heart.

I went with my mother, whose main memories of the 1970s are of a period of quick upward social mobility for her and my father, and an uncomfortable sense now of the naivety of their acceptance of the National Party's defence of increasing militarisation and a belief in the saving value of Afrikaner modernity. I had hoped she would remember what it was like to hear the news reports, on the radio at home with two small daughters, and that she would be able to evoke for me the excitement of the day. But instead of remembering the day of the transplant and its announcement, arriving at the hospital instead made her remember the many visits she had made to this same building with my gravely ill younger brother. Her arrival at the museum evoked a troubled and desperate time in her life; we entered the museum foyer without any of the intimacy I had hoped for from this mother and daughter outing. It was only later that I grasped how these separate entries into the museum were in fact very fitting, that the disturbed date stamp on the visit was at the heart of the project that is this strange and haunted museum.

On the right-hand side of the entrance a staged car crash recreated the sense that we, the visitors, had walked in at the very moment when the heart became available. The little blue car's boot was open, and a young woman was taking rolls of toilet paper and cleaning materials from it; for a moment it was not clear whether this was a re-enactment or simply an opportunistic use of the space provided by the car's boot. We were escorted into an elevator by an anachronistically flirtatious man (I later worked out that this was Don MacKenzie, a man who was never far from Barnard's side and acted as his media advisor; see Logan 2003: 173). We were left in front of the double doors that lead to the operating theatre. On walking through, we found ourselves in a room empty of any living being, with only the model of the anaesthetised waxwork dog on an operating table. While we were making sense of this strange apparition, another set of doors opened and we were invited in hushed tones to enter a film auditorium where a film had already started. It turned out we were not the only ones on the tour; a group of about 60 well-behaved Wynberg Boys' school pupils were already seated and watching an educational film. The guide asked two of them to get up and offer their seats 'for the ladies', which they uncomplainingly did.

The film was about Christiaan Barnard, but my mother and I saw only the end section, which was about Hamilton Naki, whose role had for a brief time been a source of great debate. At the end of the film, a tour guide addressed the auditorium, mainly to discount any rumours that Naki had ever assisted Barnard in his operations. Naki had never worked in Groote Schuur, she stressed, had never entered this operating theatre. What then was his role in the film, I wondered? It was, of course, an attempt to arrest once again the gossip mill. More importantly the inclusion of Naki was an attempt to revise, edit and make palatable what was to come – the all-white world we were about to enter. It is worth mentioning that by far the majority of the well-behaved school boys were not 'white'.

On completion of the film viewing, we were invited to enter, first, Christiaan Barnard's office, where he (a waxwork, fixed forever at this glorious moment) sat, presumably the day after the operation, receiving a phone call of congratulation. On the walls of the office and in the corridor were seemingly endless rows of telegrams and letters of congratulation. On the desk was a briefcase identical to the one I remember my father using in the 1960s and 70s (and which still stores the expensive mathematical drawing set that he bought at the beginning of his career but never used). Seeing the briefcase, transplanted here from my life into the museum, brought home the overlap between the lives of my parents and the ways in which my own early childhood had as its backdrop this period of incredible upward mobility for Afrikaners. The museum's retro look was disturbing also in terms of how much nostalgia there is in popular cultural forms for the 1960s, in ways that often (but not always) delete the parallel ugly archives. In her *Retro: The Culture of Revival* (2006), Elizabeth Guffey makes the useful observation that nostalgia can be a symptom of being drawn to past successes, because society's visions for the future remain unclear, a statement that might have been written about this strange museum.

Barnard's revision of his life is here given posthumous attention very much in keeping with the grammar of his own projects. The museum stages yet another transformation narrative, and these narratives concern a 'donor' whose absence is redacted to re-enliven the glorious narrative of Barnard's life, and to salvage this moment of *apartheid* modernity as a story about how the political transformation of the 1990s was in fact always part of the heart transplant project.

The transplant museum re-enacts the original heart transplant with an ambivalent and anachronistic memory of the events. The insights of scholars researching re-enactment are useful here for understanding how the museum reanimates events in ways that 'transplant' the original events into a contemporary social and political context. Robert Rosenstone's analysis of historical cinema as works of history that engage with 'the ongoing discourse surrounding its subject' (2003: 61) is useful as a methodology for interpreting the museum. Its attempt to record and stage a historical moment needs to be interpreted as part of ongoing, and competing, discourses about the meaning of the period in South African history. The meanings of Naki's present absence raise issues not unrelated to those debated just a little way further up the mountain at the main campus of the University of Cape Town, where the statue of Cecil John Rhodes was wrapped up, hoisted from its plinth by a crane and removed. That site of multidirectional memory is explored in the next chapter.

Part II

Show Them What Cleaning Is: This Time It's for Mama

5

Many accounts of the South African student movement locate the beginnings of the #RMF and the later #FMF (Rhodes Must Fall and Fees Must Fall) movements in the bucket of human excrement that Chumani Maxwele brought on to the campus of the University of Cape Town on 9 March 2015, and emptied on to the statue of Cecil John Rhodes (Booysen 2016: 3). While origin narratives can never be trusted completely (there are, for example, other versions that locate the beginnings of this wave of student activism elsewhere, that start earlier, or that relate his actions more clearly to service provision protests involving excrement), it is nevertheless a powerful story, drawing attention to questions of dirt, cleansing and the often disjointed and disorienting journeys many students have to make between home and the university campus.

In this chapter I make two linked arguments. The first is that discourses around cleaning, cleansing and dirt are suggestive as a way of understanding some of the demands of the student movement. The first part of the chapter traces the life cycles of various forms of dirt and cleansing in the debate about the nature of the university and its historic and symbolic legacies. The second part of the argument is that these dirt discourses are informed by notions of blood and belonging. In other words, I read the student movement through blood and not through shit. It is not unusual for student movements to claim allegiance to workers' movements (Ayelew n.d.; Zeilig 2007), and this was the case too in South Africa. Striking in the South African student movement of 2015 and onwards have been the utterances of identification with 'our mothers the domestic workers' (and sometimes, but less frequently, 'our fathers'). Through these statements, students were making a complaint about fees and the economic barriers faced by those from cash-poorer homes trying to enter tertiary education. This aspect of the student movement has often been interpreted through the lens of class struggle, and I return to this point below. What is striking here is the assertion of intergenerational allegiance, and the ways in which kinship and blood ties figure.

There is a conceptual gain in reading this proclaimed affiliation of blood and belonging alongside and over the dirt discourses. The journey from home to campus, then, is not only about bringing a bucket of shit from 'home' to the 'clean' campus; it is also about finding ways to link home and school, and to link home to what is read and learnt in the classroom. Bringing a bucket of waste from home is a way of stressing the necessity of bringing home (and one's kinship relations and ancestors) on to campus and into the circulatory flows of tertiary education.

The bucket of shit brought on to campus by Chumani Maxwele has had many afterlives, and Maxwele himself has often been in the news since, through his various and sometimes contentious roles in and outside the #RMF and #FMF movements. Many scholars writing about dirt in African contexts have theorised the relationship between shit and resistance, and between dirt and activism, in discussions of what Driss el Marouf has memorably called 'po(o)pular' politics (2016). Stephanie Newell's 'Politics of Dirt' project (2016, 2017, 2018) and Ken Harrow's *Trash* (2013) have developed challenging new ways of interpreting the social meanings of trash and dirt. Perhaps more than any other form of dirt, human excrement is feared as source of contamination, for obvious health reasons but also symbolically.

Chumani Maxwele's bucket was brought to campus in the same way that he would normally travel: by minibus from Khayelitsha. The bucket and its contents reference a home where there is no flush toilet, and instead a box or a bucket is used as the receptacle for the inhabitants' excrement. In an article in the *Guardian* newspaper, it was reported that Maxwele shouted 'Where are *our* heroes and ancestors?' as he 'opened the bucket and hurled its contents into Rhodes's face' (Fairbanks 2015). The title of the article – 'Why South African Students Have Turned on Their Parents' Generation' – rather contradicts this lament for absent ancestors. Reading the events as a generational conflict narrative (as others have also done), Eve Fairbanks writes:

> The story of why these generations are now at odds has deep implications for how a freed people, generation by generation, continues to relate to its history – implications that are relevant everywhere else in the world where the children of the oppressed are coming of age in what are supposed to be better circumstances.

This reading of the events, so intent on seeing disappointed 'born-frees' turn on their elders, is the *opposite* of the reading I give here. By asking 'where are our ancestors', Maxwele was not saying that our ancestors have let us down; he was making a rhetorical statement about the absence of his ancestors from campus, and about the cost of a university education, and how it requires one to enter a world cut off from the bloods of home and kinship.

The 'cost' of being at university, as everyone knows, is not only financial. Many people have analysed this, but perhaps no one as memorably as Kopano Ratele in a paragraph in which he reflects on the many reasons why African students from rural areas and townships become 'terribly confused' when they enter university:

> What confuses them? Well, we teach students to get rid of everything they have been taught about the nature of social relations, about themselves, and about other people ... What students from rural areas or townships have to learn in the very first weeks of their studies in order to stand a chance of mastering their new world is that they cannot regard their teachers as their 'fathers' or 'mothers', *'ooms'* and *'tannies'*. (Antjie et al. 2009: 59)

What Ratele is talking about here is the way social and intellectual (or disciplinary) codes rely precisely on an explicit *lack* of kinship between students and their teachers, and students and the disciplines they study. But there is a further and heightened version of this for those students who understand how these codes also reinforce a sense of exclusion (of themselves, their homes and their ancestors) from the symbols and heritage of university life. This absence of parents and kin, more than a sense of being betrayed by ancestors, is what I interpret Maxwele's lament to be. The shit he brought on to campus was, understood this way, his way of marking the long journey from home to university.

The spectacular fall of the statue of Rhodes has a large and conflicted literature and photographic archive attached to it, and has become a reference point for activists elsewhere who wish to interrogate the symbolic meanings of statues and the histories they carry. Rhodes and his friend Leander Starr Jameson, the two so-called 'benefactors' of the University of Cape Town (who 'generously donated' the land, as has often been pointed out, provoking general fury and incomprehension), are commemorated in the statue and the main hall, which used to be called Jameson Hall but is now in the process of being renamed. The histories of institutions such as the University of Cape Town and the University of the Witwatersrand show evidence of clear and direct links between higher education and colonial history. The founding of these universities coincided with the decades at the opening of the twentieth century when black South Africans were increasingly divested of (already limited) avenues to property ownership and citizens' rights. The university as an idea and as an ideal thus had its origin moment in South Africa precisely during this time of increasing racial and social inequality. To pour/hurl/deposit/smear (all of these verbs occur in the news accounts) shit on to Rhodes is to draw attention to historic dirt, in other words to *show up* the historic dirt that is already there (Rothberg 2009: 273).

Maxwele's actions can in this way be understood to mean that he felt treated 'like shit', his heroes and his ancestors absent from campus. There have been countless interpreters of these actions, and of the subsequent ways in which dirt and accusations of dirt have played out on South African campuses, and also of the ways in which these actions are linked to the continued service-provision protests. Matter out of place is how Mary Douglas defined dirt in her classic study *Purity and Danger*; to feel like dirt (to feel 'out of place') is, one could argue, expressed here by *bringing* dirt on to campus. I want to provoke, and to imagine the act of bringing a bucket of shit on to campus as a form of *cleansing*. Alongside the cleansing shit, one can also see examples of activist and performance events that attempt to cleanse campus, such as when purification and other rituals have been performed at graduation ceremonies by graduands holding burning *impepho* as they walk to the podium. At Wits University, Swankie Mafoko, Zukolwenkosi Zikalala and Matshepo Khumalo responded to the sense of the erasure of black experience in course materials by devising a performance artwork in which they were seen washing their 'colonial course packs' (Godsell et al. 2016: 110). The water in which the books had been cleaned was then used to wash their bodies and hair, a cleansing in which audience members were invited to participate. The actors had painted their bodies and faces white, and it was this 'whiteface' that was being removed to expose underneath the 'clean' black skins. The chapter 'Documenting the Revolution' in the edited collection *Fees Must Fall* (Godsell et al. 2016) gathers together anecdotes, analyses of tweets and descriptions of ephemeral events such as these performance pieces; it is an inspired contribution, and one that will become an important archival resource in future.

Writing under the pen name 'Shobane', a commentator who describes herself as '*umuntu omnyama*' (the phrase can be translated as a person who is black, although the translation cannot convey the density of meaning and the many cultural reference fields activated by the descriptor) and as 'a member of the Black Academic Caucus'. Shobane's piece, published in the *Mail & Guardian* newspaper on 8 March 2016, analyses responses to those things that were 'lost in the fire' on the night that commemorated a year's passing since the bucket arrived on campus. The fire she references was the burning of artworks from the collection of the University of Cape Town, events that were covered extensively in news media worldwide. Her opinion piece starts with a reflection on the links between art and violence:

> First, let's really think about the things that were lost in the fire. Let's think about the things that were lost through violence in the name of civilisation. In 1874, Kumasi was blown up and destroyed by the British. In 1897, Benin City and its artworks were burned down and looted under the administration of Admiral Harry Rawson. Throughout the 19th and 20th centuries, missionaries who saw African wooden sculptures as 'fetishes' systematically burned them down. There are too many examples of colonial violence – citing all of them would leave us a continent of ashes. These were of course fires that did not only decimate valuable art and architecture but lives were lost. (Shobane 2016)

Her first argument is that art and violence are often intimately linked, as Simon Gikandi in *Slavery and the Culture of Taste* has shown so strikingly in his discussion of the rise, in eighteenth- and nineteenth-century Britain, of a certain taste in clothing, furniture and art. Gikandi's argument is that this pursuit of beauty was not only made possible by the profits made from slavery and empire, but that these aesthetes were aware of and in fact responding to the horrors (burying the 'dirt') associated with their own and their peers' profits from slavery. Absent from the laments about the artworks destroyed on UCT campus, Shobane's argument goes, was any mention of the destruction of the artwork that was 'Shackville'. Shackville was a structure, but also a performative event, and has been documented in photographs by academic and activist Wandile Kasibe. It was a dwelling erected on upper campus, close to where Rhodes's statue had sat gloomily and where its now empty plinth remains. The building was made of the same found and reclaimed materials typically used to build the homes called 'shacks' in South Africa. Painted on the corrugated wall of the shack were the words 'UCT Housing Crisis'.

The shack, built in the heart of campus at the bottom of the steps that connect Jameson Hall and the empty plinth, commented on the absence of adequate student housing and symbolically placed this dwelling (which evokes other dwellings and at the same time references the symbolic and intellectual homelessness of students) at the centre. Shobane writes: 'Shackville radically and frankly re-opened the question of violence and whose lives matter. Suddenly the univer-topia divulged the dead bodies that lie at its foundations. It revealed that transformation had been like mowing the lawn with blunt-nosed scissors in order to maintain the duality that constructs value through devastation.' The shack's incongruity, like the bucket of shit, was a reminder of the ugliness that is *already* on and underlying the campus, and of the fact that the very idea of the university (or the univer-topia as Shobane calls it) is intimately linked with violence. Shobane writes of Shackville as an 'opening', as if the door and windows of the shack could give us access to another version of the university and to another future.

Shobane's piece calls for a reconstitution of Shackville, and cleverly uses the language of the need to preserve art to defend this position, talking back to the defenders of the art that had been burnt. Shackville is not only an important artwork, she writes; the 'juxtaposition [with] the ill-named Jameson Plaza and the shack where many came to gather – is really an important point of departure', and points a way forward. For Shobane, then, the arrival of Shackville on the campus created a new gathering place from which to set forth – a new origin myth to complicate the one that has Rhodes and Jameson as the moment zero of the value system of the campus.

While Virginia Woolf is an unlikely reference point for the South African student movement, the words of her treatise about the pernicious effects of an exclusive (male and of a certain class) university education have a clear echo. In *Three Guineas* Woolf describes the university of the future:

> [i]t is clear that you must build your college differently. It is young and poor; let it therefore take advantage of those qualities and be founded on poverty and youth. Obviously, then, it must be an experimental college, an adventurous college. Let it be built on lines of its own. It must be built not of carved stone and stained glass, but of some cheap, easily combustible material which does not hoard dust and perpetrate traditions. Do not have chapels. Do not have museums and libraries with chained books and first editions under glass cases. Let the pictures and the books be new and always changing. Let it be decorated afresh by each generation with their own hands cheaply … the poor college must teach only the arts that can be taught cheaply and practiced by poor people. (1986: 39–40)

The burning of artworks and books and the violence dreamt of by suffragists and twentieth-century feminists are cousins to this tradition of cleansing and new beginnings. The library that is continuously renewed is a place where knowledge is reinvigorated for each generation, repurposed from the requirements of the present.

These ways of thinking about dirt and cleanliness on campus bring into much sharper focus the statements about the links between the student movement and the workers' struggle. The relationship between students' and workers' movements elsewhere in Africa has been well documented, and remains an important way of understanding these forms of resistance. Leo Zeilig, in his *Revolt and Protest: Student Politics and Activism in Sub-Saharan Africa* (published in 2007, it does not deal with the most recent protests), offers a useful survey of student politics in sub-Saharan Africa, as well as a discussion of the historical literature. In a section called 'Class Suicide and the Intelligentsia', Zeilig writes that in the early years of the post-independence period in Africa, the geographical separation from the communities they had left often meant that students became 'alienated from the social world from which many had emerged' (2007: 32–4), seeing themselves as the vanguard of modernisation. The term 'class suicide' does not mean that students abandoned the class of their parents and communities, but instead was an activist call from Amílcar Cabral that students should perform the 'superlative act of the imagination' of consistently and consciously viewing the world from the angle of vision of the workers and peasants. Zeilig writes that the world of this early generation of post-independence African student activists 'oscillated between visions of workers and peasants and urban privilege, contradictions that help to determine the nature of their activism in the first decades of independence' (2007: 35). Vishga Satgar's chapter in *Fees Must Fall* (Satgar 2016) summarises the current debates usefully, and Bwesigye Bwa Mwesigire's research on student activism and class at Makerere and UCT will open up new ways of thinking about #RMF, as will Semeneh Ayelew Asfaw's work complicate the ways in which we understand the role of students in the Ethiopian Revolution of 1974.

At various stages of the South African student protest movement of 2015 and up to the present, cleaners and cleaning staff were invoked as allies of the students. On campuses worldwide, the alliance between workers and students is a familiar trope, and this is an aspect of these movements that has attracted much scholarly as well as media attention. The student protests included demands that the outsourcing of cleaning and maintenance staff be ended (a demand that has been partly successful). Against the background of these demands, the labour involved in keeping campus 'clean' and not letting 'standards' drop is rich with symbolic meaning. References to the invisible labour of outsourced workers provided a language through which to talk about historical dirt, and the costs of the 'clean' library and campus. What kind of reading and learning can one do in a university where all the cleaners look like (and in some cases actually *are*) one's parents and kin, while few (if any) of the professors are black? This question links the discourse of cleaning and dirt to those of academic 'standards' and the excluding traditions of the university.

Some months before Shackville, on 18 November 2015, a video appeared on the internet with a yellow banner running across the top saying 'WARNING: REPORT CONTAINS GRAPHIC CONTENT'. The news clip showed some Afri-Forum (pro-Afrikaans) aligned students cleaning a statue of J. H. Marais ('*Ons Weldoener*', which means our benefactor) on Stellenbosch campus. In the footage we see a few white women students, dressed in leggings and T-shirts, rather ineffectively washing the base of a statue which is covered in grey paint or an oily-looking liquid. As the video opens, a black woman is seen dragging away what looks like a tyre, and for a moment it seems that she is helping to clean the statue. But soon she returns, with the tyre newly soaked in paint (or dirt of some kind), which she throws like an ironic funeral wreath on to the base of the statue. In a longer video, taken later that day, the remains of the tyre are lifted over the head of the statue, chillingly evoking the 'necklacing killings' associated with South Africa. Faintly in the background one can make out laughter and jibing, and the words that can be heard are 'Girls, show them what cleaning is! They must clean!' What is invoked in this moment is the incongruity of a group of black folks watching white folks clean. And what the women are cleaning is a symbol of Afrikaner separatism and supremacy, which stands (still) in the centre of Stellenbosch campus.

The clip shows these cleaners (all white women) surrounded by a group of mostly black students, who are complimenting the cleaners on their cleaning skills. One of them is heard saying 'We must give them a name!' (https://www.enca.com/south-africa/watch-stellenbosch-university-students-face).   This comment is a reference to the distinctive naming traditions of women who clean. 'Girl' is one such a word that has been used, but there are also generic names such as 'Sophie', which artist Mary Sibande uses for her monumental 'Sophie' series in which elaborately clothed and posed casts made from her own body commemorate the women of her family who were domestic workers.

There is perhaps no more explosive figure as a rhetorical device than that of black women performing domestic labour in white homes, and in particular those who look after white children while their own children have to be left alone or cared for by other (often rural, and typically older) relatives (Cock 1980; Ally 2009). The members of the student movement were not the only ones to pick up on the significance of this figure, who stands on the threshold between spaces, skilled at reading multiple worlds and interpreting the codes through which power is structured and replicated. To clean a home is to know its secrets, and the domestic worker is a staple in literature in South Africa, as elsewhere, where economic inequality makes domestic labour readily available to some, and its provision a necessity for others. Jacklyn Cock's *Maids and Madams: A Study in the Politics of Exploitation*, published in 1980, was for long the benchmark work on domestic labour in South Africa, and its evocation of the late 1970s contains much that is still relevant today.

In a recent book-length study of domestic workers in South African writing, *Soos Familie: Stedelike Huiswerkers in Suid-Afrikaanse Tekste* (Like Family: Urban Domestic Workers in South African Texts) (2015), Ena Jansen has written a near-encyclopaedic overview of the literature on domestic workers, which includes interviews with and writings by women who have experience as domestic workers and are also creative writers. She analyses some of the novels that have become internationally famous, notably Marlene van Niekerk's *Agaat* (translated as *The Women*) and Elsa Joubert's *Poppie Nongena*. Jansen shows that ethnographic descriptions of conversations with domestic workers have long been a mainstay of Afrikaans-language non-fiction and journalism, in particular in writings by women. To claim that these accounts reveal intimacy and are a form of gratitude is a self-forgiving theme that runs through many of these texts written by white (women) employers. Jansen's dust jacket includes a self-exposing picture of the author herself with an arm around the shoulder of her own domestic 'helper', as acknowledgement of the ways in which this woman's 'help' has made possible the book we are holding. In these kitchen table ethnographies, it was historically the white 'madam' who recorded and shared the stories told to her in the ambivalent intimacy of the encounter. This 'loving' trend always risks eliding the lack of reciprocity, and significantly deletes the children not included in the ambiguous intimacy of the home. Perhaps the greatest contribution of Jansen's book is the chapter analysing representations of domestic workers by black writers, some of whom have worked as domestic workers or are the children of women who did.

Zukiswa Wanner's hilarious *Maid in SA: 30 Ways to Leave your Madam* is described on the dust jacket as a 'quirky, lighter look at one of the most important, yet most overlooked, relationships: that between a domestic worker and her madam'. Wanner gives thanks to the successful crime novelist and media personality Angela Makholwa and her 'domestic helpers and to Ange herself for employing them so that I could get material for this book' (2013: v). The humour of the project relies on the inversion of the ethnographic genres of domestic workers (she interviews 'maids' in order to gather information about 'madams'); the implied reader for this 'how-to' guide is the 'maid' who needs to navigate the tricky terrain of domestic relations. There is a further level of humour in the implication that the reader might see herself in more than one role, or have intimate knowledge of a number of the scenarios described: 'In this book you'll find the women in your life – your mothers, your sisters, your cousins, friends and yourself.'

In the discourses of the student movement, and in the artworks and literary products of black artists and writers, we see a powerfully articulated counter-archive, reading the meaning of the work of women who clean and maintain homes that are not their own from a different perspective. What we see in references to 'our mothers, the domestic workers' is a rhetorical and political gesture that draws these mothers back into their own domestic space, one that is too often unimagined in the 'big house'. It is a gesture that clarifies the activist potential of the labour that can be performed through intergenerational and multidirectional memory.

Gabeba Baderoon has called the histories of domestic labour a form of haunting, and in her article 'The Ghost in the House: Women, Race, and Domesticity in South Africa' she writes about the 'complex cultural meanings that have resulted from the central role of household labor in mediating black women's access to public space in South Africa' (2014: 175). Black women's lives as domestic workers are described in a useful phrase as 'hinge experiences', living as they do in the overlapping and contradictory spaces between the public and the private. Baderoon reads the works of artists Zanele Muholi and Mary Sibande as art that 'engages with the long, uneven context of the household and explores the notion of black women servants in white households as objects of fantasy, erasure, curiosity, anxiety, comfort, memory, origin and ambiguity' (2014: 181). She describes a telephone conversation she had with Muholi, in which the artist reported that her late mother (Bester Muholi) raised the children of her life-long employers 'at the expense of her own', and that as the child of a domestic worker Muholi felt she 'did not have a mother really' (2014: 182). For Baderoon, this absence is a form of haunting or hauntedness, and Muholi's work is interpreted as a record of the 'absence of an intimate archive of her own'. Baderoon quotes Muholi (in phrases that seem almost an illustration of Gabriele Schwab's theorisation of the somatised memory of trauma that I discussed in the Introduction): 'Look at me. Everything I do, it comes from my mum's sweat and blood. It's directly connected with my history, what I cannot forget no matter how hard I try' (2014: 185).

In her book *Democracy at Home in South Africa: Family Fictions and Transitional Culture* (2016) Kerry Bystrom analyses what she calls 'transitional artworks' produced in a time of 'transitional culture'. The term has the obvious meaning of artworks that respond to the political and social transitions in South Africa, but also the psychologised meaning of an object of comfort. Bystrom's book is attuned to, and seeks out, instances of comfort, moments of repair (2016: 57), recuperation (2016: 82) and recovery (2016: 85), and references the tending of wounds (2016: 79). While thus analysing artworks and projects in search of healing and repair, Bystrom's argument is that what is needed in scholarly and activist work is *more* attention to and greater emphasis on 'negative affect' (2016: 156). The emphasis falls, in other words, on the wound as much as on the healing of the wound. In a chapter called 'Keeping House', she discusses the works of Mary Sibande and Zanele Muholi, reading in the work of both artists 'new modes of relation to the past and its legacy of servitude' (2016: 106).

Bystrom spends some time discussing a performance (an ephemeral event given permanent form in its archiving and analysis by curator and academic Gabi Ngcobo) in which Zanele Muholi, dressed as a domestic worker, entered a conference room full of academics and started taking photographs of them. Ngcobo writes how:

> In a hall packed with feminists and woman's rights activists from all over the world [at the Association for Women's Rights in Development conference], the 'maid' rose to say something ... The 'maid' ... asked all the people present to acknowledge and thank all the domestic workers that had cleaned their toilets that morning. (Ngcobo 2010)

This invasion was meant as a performance artwork, with the conventions of that mode of surprising and unsettling. But Muholi's actions can also be interpreted as a commentary on invasion and privacy. In this provocative performance piece, Muholi brings the domestic worker-as-academic into the conference venue, destabilising the audience and inverting the conventions of academic and ethnographic engagement. In this staged performance, the academics become the observed rather than the observers, and we see perhaps what a research project could look like that sets out from the gaze of a woman who has the knowledge and analytical framework of someone who has experienced working as a domestic worker, or is the child of one.

At roughly the same time as the washing of the statues (18 February 2015), a video appeared on YouTube and was re-posted in a number of places, including the website 'Africa is a country', of a group of young black people walking around the wealthy Camps Bay area of Cape Town with a camera, in an inversion of the familiar trope of the 'township tour'. The video was posted by Sabelo Mkhabela, who may have been one of the film-makers. We see the film-makers enact, parodically, the same invasive actions as are performed by tourists on a 'township tour'. While the film-makers were not pretending to be domestic workers, their presence was interpreted by those they attempt to film as 'dirt': they are thrown out for invading the privacy of those who are enjoying their homes and the seafront restaurants. In this film, the activist project of the film-makers is to record and archive the reaction to their presence as they 'tour' someone else's 'township'. The effect of this performance is similar to Muholi's; Muholi impersonates, and dresses up as, a domestic worker and enters a space where she is unexpected and where her presence is an undesired and discomforting intrusion. The film-makers enter the 'township' with a camera to record not so much the lifestyles of those living there as their responses to the film crew's presence.

I want to return briefly to the scene of the white cleaners of the statue in honour of the benefactor in Stellenbosch. In the carnivalesque enjoyment we hear from those mock-praising the good cleaning, we see a reference to, and an upside-down re-enactment of, all the cleaning that has historically been done *for* white people in South Africa. But there is also in these actions a challenge to the institution, Stellenbosch University, to 'clean up' its act, and to clean up its attitudes to black students. Part of this cleaning up involves the acknowledgement of the 'dirt' of racial privilege that is under the clean and beautiful surface of this campus. The discourse about dirt on statues and symbols is an injunction to cleanse the institution, and is an attempt to make visible the ugliness and dirt that is not only in the past but informs and structures the beauty (one can read also the 'standards' that so many wish to defend) of the present. These events and performances are examples of what Michael Rothberg describes as staged memories, 'troubling, violent, or even terrorizing' (2009: 272). Like the artworks that reference the massacre of Algerians in Paris, these South African events can be seen as 'aggressively foregrounding the "haunting past"', yet they 'do not *produce* divisiveness but rather seek to uncover already existing, unresolved divisions' (2009: 272). This labour of uncovering (through dirtying, and making visible the historical dirt) is what constitutes the ethical dimension of the memory work done by the #Fallists.

When students used the phrase 'our mothers the domestic workers', their identification extended beyond the frequent alliance outlined in the literature on student movements in Africa. Their words also referenced the traditions of cleaning and invisible labour (the nature of domestic labour is by definition to delete traces of itself) as a way of understanding their complaints about their marginalisation and exclusion. To respond to the students' declared affiliation with the workers by making them sit a 'privilege' test, or to comment on the fact that some of the student leaders are from middle-class homes, is to wilfully ignore the nature of the 'dirt'. The language of the movement can be read through the references to dirt/cleanliness, but more importantly through a discourse of blood affiliation and the costs of the historical deletion of this affiliation. Bringing Shackville and a bucket of Khayelitsha shit to the university can be understood, in this way, as being about blood and kinship – about the need to feel and to be 'at home' at university, and to connect the worlds of home and campus, home and syllabus.

In Gabriele Schwab's *Haunting Legacies: Violent Histories and Transgenerational Trauma*, we read about the transfer of intergenerational trauma, and about a younger generation who are skilled interpreters and readers of historical harm. In the introduction I cited Schwab's comments regarding how the children of a traumatised parental generation are skilled readers of silences and memory traces on the bodies of their parents. This understanding of the second generation as skilled readers offers us an alternative to the descriptor, near universally rejected now, of South Africans born after 1994 as 'born-free'. Instead, what I suggest here is that we think of this generation as skilled readers of that which is written in the blood – of their parents' but also their own bodies.

#RMF and #FMF demonstrated this ability to read the traces and the dirty meanings of the present that they see around them. Instead of calling this form of reading the present 'rubbish', I want to call it blood-rich or even en-blooded reading. The use of blood here invokes, of course, the desire for change; but it also includes references to blood as affiliation, and to the journey between home and university. What the students wish to see, in this version, is that the values and symbols of campus are connected to, and joined up with, the homes that they come from, and that their parents and kin come from. The university needs to be not the big house in which they and their parents are tolerated merely as those who keep things clean, but a house that has the (symbolic and real) 'shack' central to the 'imagination' of what a university is and could be.

Such a way of interpreting the present requires building tunnels between classroom and home, between library and kitchen, between the ancestors and the syllabus and the course readers we prepare in the present day. Shobane's description of Shackville as a portal makes the point vividly. In the intellectual project of the student movement, and in the written and creative work produced by some of their peers (as well as some of their teachers), there is an *insistence* on looking back at, and forwards to, home, while holding on to home and kinship as forms of social consciousness. This 'home' is an ideological and activist identification of South Africa as home to all South Africans, in contrast to the 'old' South Africa where everything was 'clean' *because* it was kept this way for the purposes of the small group of people whose interests were protected and served by *apartheid*. To read the present like this, one cannot sit in the clean library; one needs instead to build the library that surges with ancestral blood, reinterpreted for a new generation.

In recent works on intimacy and home in South Africa, scholars have questioned assumptions about where 'home' ends, and who counts as 'family'. In the calls for curriculum change and the transformation of the university (discourses that were about access for both black students *and* black faculty), these questions of affiliation and 'home' have played a prominent role. I have written elsewhere about the ways in which 'standards' of academic excellence are often upheld through invisible powers, which reinforce zones of exclusion and inclusion seemingly without agency (Coetzee 2018). This too is part of the dirt that is being brought to the surface by the #Fallists' insistence on transformation. The invocation of 'our mothers, the domestic workers' underlined the lineage of the university as one associated with 'the big house', and many black students' (and lecturers') feelings of being tolerated, at best, in spaces that historically did not imagine them as full citizens, but instead as marginal to the home that is South Africa.

Many of these writings about the home and familial intimacies have not shown evidence of a retreat into the home secured against an imagined hostile other, but have instead developed the links between intimacy, home and activist scholarship. In this new thinking, we also see frequent references made to the role of the researcher, and to the ways in which she (or he) has gained access to the intimacy documented and analysed. These works are attuned to questions of privacy and access: who gets to write, who gets to see, who gets to be an expert on private and intimate matters. Gillian Godsell and Rekgotsofetse Chikane write that in 'public discussions, the Fallist movement and the academic project are often seen as incompatible' (2016: 54). Their chapter 'The Roots of the Revolution' argues (as I do here) that the two projects are necessarily and crucially linked.

In her 1982 foreword to Solomon Tshekiso Plaatje's *Native Life in South Africa*, Bessie Head wrote that '[m]ost black South Africans suffer from a very broken sense of history. *Native Life* provides an essential, missing link' (Plaatje 1982: xiii). The nature of this 'missing link' is, in the first place, that the text is a document about the impact of the passing of the Natives' Land Act of 1913, through which black South Africans were excluded from power and divested of rights. Plaatje's analysis of the private and intimate lives of the families he encountered while collecting material for his book make for the most memorable passages in *Native Life*, and provide us with a template for scholarship connecting up and reconstituting the 'missing links': histories of South Africa as 'home' to all, and histories of the black family in South Africa. Plaatje's writings stand like a version of Shackville, documenting and imagining the meanings of 'native life' and death, and providing an access point and portal through which one can enter to reconnect the broken links.

In *Native Life in South Africa* Plaatje places himself inside and alongside the fugitives and sufferers whose plight he documents. His own family at home are invoked in the conclusion to the book, and he writes of the cost to him (and to them) of having spent so much time away from home doing the research and interviews for the book, and later travelling as part of the delegation to the UK to appeal for support. One of the most evocative scenes finds Plaatje cycling through the landscape of his birth, which had ceased to be 'home' (1982: 83). This loss makes him experience an embodied fear he remembers feeling also when his own father died; this connection between family and nature (or land) recurs as a trope throughout the book. In his description of the landscape with which his relationship is being deleted before his eyes, Plaatje describes a personal fear and haunting, as if he is racing on his bicycle in front of a creature that wishes to rob him of his dignity and his inner life.

But there is another crucial strand to the way Plaatje imagines family, and that is through his call for black South Africans to be recognised as members of a greater family of human beings. This intention is motivated by a claim to being members of a family to whom obligations and affiliations have been proven. The severance of this 'missing link' to a shared humanity is part of what the text documents, and the fact that the plea to the British *failed* is now part of the way we read *Native Life*. The text is a letter sent, received and ignored. 'Shall we appeal to you in vain? I hope not!' (1982: 404) we read Plaatje saying to the British public, and *Native Life* is a testament to this dashed hope and severed connection. In this complexly coded missive (part record to provide a missing link for black South Africans, part plea for recognition of dignity) we see another way in which Plaatje's work stands as an ancestor text to many academic works in which authors document, join up, reclaim and reconstitute the missing links of black histories and futures, keeping alive what Walter Benjamin called the revolutionary spark.

A dominant reference in discussions about privacy and domesticity, wherever South African matters are discussed, has been Njabulo Ndebele's 1984 paper 'Rediscovery of the Ordinary', later taken up in the seminal collection *Rediscovery of the Ordinary: Essays on South African Literature and Culture*. This essay is often misquoted, or cited in defence of a certain retreat into private worlds at the cost of more engaged ways of being and writing. Rather than an escape into personal (that is, apolitical) domesticity and ordinariness, Ndebele's argument is instead an activist agenda for transformation and for the cultivation of self-reflective scholarship and modes of living. Perhaps Ndebele's most astute reader has been Pumla Gqola (in particular in her writings on spectacular masculinity and gendered violence, e.g. Gqola 2009, 2015, 2017), who has interpreted the comments about the ordinary and the spectacular in scorching feminist analyses that confirm Ndebele's insights as in fact a plea for *greater*, not *lesser*, forms of activism. The rediscovery of the ordinary, understood this way, is related to the responsibility to forge and connect the 'missing links' of the intimate lives of black individuals and families. The most innovative and urgent recent scholarship on and from South Africa interprets this to mean that the rediscovery of the ordinary requires tunnels to be built between activism, academia and personal choices. Ordinariness understood in this sense is an excavatory project that requires an insistent and activist engagement – not least with the ways in which knowledge is configured and disseminated, access negotiated and expert status established. In this sense, the ordinariness of Ndebele's title is to be read as an injunction to ways of thinking and writing about black histories in South Africa as 'ordinary', an approach that requires of the disciplines the questioning of historical legacies that characterise black histories and individuals as not-ordinary, not of 'here', not 'at home' in the academy. To put this differently, the future requires black presences in scholarship not as *subjects* to be discussed, but as agents who will determine and set research agendas, occupy professorial offices and head research units.

A word that has appeared with striking frequency in recent writings about South Africa is intimacy, and many of these references go back to Ndebele's call for introspection and self-reflection. In an influential piece published just two years after the democratic transition in South Africa ('A Home for Intimacy', 1996), Ndebele provides a narrative of returning to South Africa only to find his childhood home gone, the township redesigned so much as to be unrecognisable. This piece has deliberate echoes of Plaatje's narrative of the landscape that seems not to remember its son (1982: 83). Ndebele writes about how home, for black South Africans, became 'the shared experience of homelessness, the fellow-feeling of loss and the desperate need to regain something'. While celebrating a new sense of 'the whole land' as 'home', this capacious home has also, in the intervening decades, been emptied out of some things and values. The loneliness that results from decades of deliberate attempts at the destruction of the black family has led to what he calls 'the demise of intimacy in our history of sensibility'. Rediscovering the ordinary, interpreted in this way, is a commitment to personal and scholarly practices that excavate and build 'a home for intimacy'. This ordinary 'home' is therefore not a room in which doors and windows are shut and the interior space claustrophobically barred; instead, this ordinariness is a self-conscious place *from which* to view and analyse the home: its suppressed histories and the missing links that need connecting up. This is worth underlining: the family and the home need to be historicised, mapped and analysed *from* the 'home'.

In many discussions of a shared public life, Paul Gilroy's theorisation of 'conviviality' (2004) has been cited, but Ndebele is after something less optimistic and more unsettling. The qualifier 'fatal' to describe the intimacies of shared space is meant to mark and accentuate the ways in which the intimacies of the black family and the black self have been in conflict with, beleaguered by, and brought into question through other versions of the self, in particular hostile white selves. The intimacy that Ndebele theorises shows awareness of what he calls elsewhere the 'international umbrella of whiteness' that has protected whiteness (white subjectivity, white zones of intimacy, inherited white privilege) in South Africa. Instead, he argues for an approach that analyses intimacy as something potentially 'fatal'. This vision of the public sphere resists the utopian horizon so dominant in much writing about race in South Africa, and the book is presented as an invitation to readers to enter this intimately conflicted future, and to imagine conflicting regimes of looking as both ordinary and necessary.

Anne-Maria Makhulu, in her book *Making Freedom: Apartheid, Squatter Politics and the Struggle for Home*, uses the term 'intimate violence' (2015: xxi) to mark the many challenges to making home faced by the communities whose lives she describes, and with whom she talks about the meanings of home. Makhulu's book documents the efforts of black families to make homes in the squatter camps and illegal settlements around Cape Town, and the contingent forms of intimacy available to them. The argument is informed by the politics of shackdwellers' movements such as Abahlali baseMjondolo, often translated as 'the people of the shacks', though the collective term *abahlali* means, more powerfully, 'those who stay', stressing that these people are not passing through but are people who live here and are making homes. Mamphela Ramphele's evocatively named *A Bed Called Home: Life in the Migrant Labour Hostels of Cape Town* was a similar project and hugely important in laying the ground for studies of the kinds of 'homes' that *apartheid* prohibited as well as created. Makhulu's project is intent on the daily practices of making a home, caring for the self and for others (2015: 29). Her attention to the ways in which homes are decorated (2015: 162), for example, does not attempt to aestheticise, but instead to document the ordinary decency of everyday lives (and deaths). Here her work differs markedly from some other projects that aim a camera lens into shack homes to find in the ways that these have been decorated an inspirational 'shack chic' aesthetic. An extreme (but representative) example is the photo book actually called *Shack Chic*, with colourful decontextualised details that draw from the vernacular of aspirational home magazines, and do not encourage the consumers of the images to reflect on the ethics of thus displaying the private homes of marginalised families. Makhulu's focus is different, and aims instead to historicise these homes as evidence of resilience and resistance, and to present the individuals and families as not abject. For the cover of the book, an image from Zwelethu Mthethwa's photographic series *Hope Chest* was used, and the recurring image of the 'hope chest' (traditionally a container for linen and clothing prepared by women in anticipation of an imagined future and in hope of a home) is visually evocative of the work of recovering and rediscovering the broken chains of history.

Makhulu's book makes another important intervention. The visibility of books about the children of the struggle generation has created an archive of the impact on home life of political activism. Sisonke Msimang's book *Always*

Another Country: A Memoir of Exile and Home (2017) is one of the latest additions to this growing tradition in South African writing. Makhulu writes in her acknowledgements of the families of the disappeared, and of how she learnt only later in life of her own father's political work, invisible to a child's eye and – crucially – secret at the time, and so not part of the intimate family memory. The point she wishes to make with these references is that revolutionaries and activists are (and were) all members of families; and that these families needed and now need care.

To see those living in informal settlements as individuals entitled to dignity, and as humans with complex interiority, is part of a process of understanding how violence is expressed in contemporary South Africa, and what the prehistories are of the many intimate acts of violence that leave their mark on home lives. Kopano Ratele has written evocatively about the intimate sphere in a number of his essays, perhaps nowhere more affectingly than in his essay on being father to a black son who grows up speaking English (Ratele 2013). In his book *Liberating Masculinities* (2016), he includes a chapter called '*Ayashisa amateki*', in which he evokes vividly his birth home and the 'child behind the research' that he conducts. The *amateki* of the title are a fantasy pair, and in that chapter he explores the relationship he, as a small child from a cash-poor home, had to this imagined pair of All Star shoes.

Ratele's argument takes issue with many studies of, and on, 'the rising' black middle classes, arguing that scholars and activists have to try harder, to see more, to understand better, to 'listen up'. Writing about his own formation (and constant re-formation) from boy to man, he points out that his (fluid) class formation is just one dimension of the making of the man and scholar. Class identity and consumer patterns cannot be understood without the deeper and more complex understandings that his own book pushes forward. Ratele cautions against research agendas that will mean that disciplines merely replicate and exaggerate existing limiting assumptions, through thinking about young black men in predictive ways, and about class and consumerism as fixed and fixing categories (2016: 89). The book demands that researchers pay attention; but crucial here is also an understanding that some scholars will have an advantage, will have developed (and will continue to develop) the skills that will make their access to the intimacies documented not merely a peeping through windows, but conceptualised and written from inside the intimacies of the homes.

This does not necessarily lead us to a utopian horizon, but instead to an acknowledgement of the many broken links in access to knowledge, the violence inherent in the dissemination of knowledge and the fatal intimacies, both historical and current. In the years to come, new research agendas will be informed by scholarship not written in English and with bibliographies that build activist tunnels into many rooms and homes. If the metaphor of a house or home is to be used, as many of the writers and activists discussed here have done, knowledge will be produced from within the house, not by peeping through the window and stealing the intimate secrets of those inside. Shackville was, as Shobane has argued so memorably, a portal to this new university where the en-blooded library will carry traces of the homes and families from which students and their teachers come; and the knowledge will be to the benefit of those homes.

Who Can See this Bleeding? Women's Blood and Men's Blood in these #Fallist Times

6

On the opening night of the first Abantu Book Festival in the Soweto Theatre, on 8 December 2016, the poet Lebo Mashile was more exuberant than normal. Striking in her blood-red dress, she welcomed the audience, celebrating the importance of the occasion and saying: 'It has been a gap in our hearts for a long time', to murmurs of assent from the audience (http://www.abantubookfestival.co.za/). Her comments about a 'gap' referred to the absence of spaces such as Abantu where black South Africans could gather to discuss books and ideas. The nature of the 'gap' did not need to be glossed for the audience, although its significance might be missed by others less attuned to the ways in which the publishing industry and literary culture in South Africa have worked to marginalise Blackness/blackness and black reading audiences. On two historic days in early December 2016, Abantu Book Festival would be the venue for a number of discussions, roundtables and informal conversations about the nature of this 'gap'. Abantu's aim was to facilitate a space where Blackness/blackness was centred and assumed, and then from that centre to talk about pain, particularly black pain, testimony and 'our stories'. The website of Abantu says: 'This is the space we've been yearning for. Let there be healing.'

The inaugural edition of Abantu Book Festival made explicit the dynamic interconnectedness between reading and the continuous work of bringing a particular self into being. 'Abantu Book Festival: Imagining Ourselves into Existence', was the slogan of the festival. The location (Soweto), the name (*abantu*, the plural of the Nguni noun *umntu* which means a [black] person) and the emphasis on 'ourselves' are all distinguishing marks of the activist vision behind this literary festival. The photographs taken, and the videos made of the panels and gatherings, are now available online. These constitute an archive as well as a resource, creating and preserving beyond the physical gathering what Litheko Modisane in his book on cinema audiences calls 'black-centred publics' (2013). The archived videos emphasise, if the title of the festival did not already do so, the significance of Abantu in laying claim to a vibrant and *already existent* literary culture with long histories, and crucially as black and black-centred. The photographs, videos and blogs about this gathering around books allow us to insert ourselves imaginatively and affectively into this community, and to confront the ethics of attempting to do so.

As a teaching and learning resource, the value of this archive of the event is immense. In future years, it will (and should) be impossible to understand and to think about the South African literary scene without paying serious attention to this festival. The availability of the archive on the internet creates a resource and a time capsule: this is now, we are here. There is no better way of introducing a course on South African literature and culture than to screen these videos and to look at the photographic archive. And if viewing this archive makes some viewers feel excluded or disoriented, so much the better. That will be the lesson and, as I argue below, part of what needs to be understood about the intention of this festival.

The Soweto venues of the Abantu festival (Eyethu Lifestyle Centre in Mofolo and the Soweto Theatre in Jabulani) gave physical shape to the intellectual and political vision of Thando Mgqolozana. He was by this time already an internationally celebrated author, whose debut novel, *A Man Who is Not a Man*, had been critically acclaimed. Since the publication of that novel (and two subsequent ones, *Hear Me Not Alone* [2011] and *Un/Importance* [2014]) Mgqolozana had become widely read and frequently included (inside as well as outside South Africa) in courses that provide overviews of South African literary culture. This inclusion was often as an example of what are described as 'emergent' authors or 'new voices': descriptors that entrench ways of reading his work (like that of Kopano Matlwa, another author and public figure whom I discuss in this chapter) as always and timelessly 'new' and fresh. This way of reading the work of Matlwa and Mgqolozana ignores the deep literary and intellectual precursors in the work of these authors. The stress on the newness and freshness of the work deletes the contextual and historical bloodline; this contextual and historical bloodline is what Abantu makes evident.

The Abantu festival did not share the near-obsessive interest in the 'new' that so often characterises courses and reading lists on which black South African authors appear. Instead, writers and intellectuals were consciously inscribed into, and read against and alongside, existing and *long-heard* voices. The poet who was chosen to read her work at the opening event, Koleka Putuma, is indisputably young and her recently published anthology of poems 'new', but her *Collective Amnesia* indexes and references exactly the long histories worth remembering, and the urgency of the need to do so. In that sense, she is not a 'new' voice but perhaps better understood as a recent interpreter, one who keeps the spark alive and takes the long bloodline forward. Her acknowledgements to 'the womxn who raised me' ends with the words 'Thank you for helping me imagine myself' (2017: 5), sharing the language of Abantu. The collection is divided into three sections: 'Inherited Memory', 'Buried Memory' and 'Postmemory'. The poem she chose to read on the night was 'Water' (2017: 96–100), but many poems included in the collection would have been equally suitable. 'Lifeline', for example, lists the names of women who have provided a bloodline, and ends with the haunting chant: 'Black girl – Live! Live! Live!' (2017: 85).

Abantu as an idea can be traced back to many earlier literary and cultural initiatives, and the work of doing so will be valuable in itself. Such a history would best be written by an intergenerational team (ideally drawn from Putuma's 'lifeline' list) and would require experiential as well as linguistic knowledge. An important part of such a history would also be to map the connections with other literary and cultural festivals elsewhere in Africa. Bwesigye Bwa Mwesigire, the founder of the Writivism festival in Kampala (a festival that is in some ways an older sibling to Abantu), cautions in his history of Writivism precisely against notions of understanding Writivism as 'new', and maps instead the many precursors and influences on his own work (2014; 2017a: 1). This is characteristic of his generous intellectual approach, but it also makes of Writivism something more, not less, significant.

Descriptions that linger on the newness of Abantu and the newness of black South African authors' voices risk deleting and undervaluing the long histories and the bloodlines and lifelines, and the densely intertextual commentary that characterises much of the work. Grace Ahingula Musila, in a piece called 'Lot's Wife Syndrome and Double Publics in South Africa', describes how she (who grew up in Kenya and not South Africa) excitedly recommended a book to a friend. The friend, who was more attuned to South African township experiences, replied that she too admired the book but that it was full of *clichés* (2016: 1456). Musila's point, and the one I am making here too, is that a sense of 'newness' sometimes does not confirm the absence of precursors or ancestor texts, but instead merely confirms a reader's inability to imagine or provide a certain social or literary context for a work. This chapter, while fully appreciating the importance of Abantu as an original idea and as a reality, interprets Abantu as not-new. By saying that Abantu is not an 'emergent' form, I am arguing that it is an ongoing activist archive and that it supports an intellectual space for debating the very terms of literary culture and self-making through reading. When the website of Abantu said, after only one edition of the festival, that 'Abantu Book Festival has become an annual pilgrimage for black writers and readers held in SOWETO to celebrate the rich and diverse literary heritage … from the African continent', we understand that the confusion about the terminology (an event which has happened only once cannot strictly be described as an 'annual pilgrimage') is stressing something different, and is laying claim to longer histories. The 'gap' that Abantu has filled has reconfigured what went before, and has continued and intensified the work of reconnecting literary and intellectual bloodlines. What has been connected up was already there, under the skin and in the blood; it is not new, fresh blood without ancestors.

Countering the notion of an origin narrative becomes even more important when one traces where and when Mgqolozana first announced his vision. In

2015 he had been invited, as he frequently was, to take part in a panel at the Franschhoek Literary Festival. He arrived and found himself, as often before, one of the few black people at the festival and, on one of the panels in which he took part, he was invited to speak about 'finding his voice' as an author. The photographic archive of this festival (http://bookslive.co.za/blog/2015/05/18/look-at-yourselves-its-very-abnormal-thando-mgqolozana-quits-south-africas-white-literary-system/) makes explicit how the audience for the event was drawn from the mostly white literary classes of the nearby university town of Stellenbosch and the wealthy winelands around Franschhoek; the room has almost no overlap with the Abantu room in terms of its sociality and demographic. After one of the panels, Mgqolozana announced via Twitter that he would no longer take part in literary festivals such as the one held annually in Franschhoek (where Eugene de Kock was photographed on a date with his biographer just one year later). During this edition of the Franschhoek Literary Festival, Mgqolozana resigned publicly from this and from other similar white spaces.

In a form that convened a different public, he published his 21 Twitter suggestions for what he called the decolonisation of the South African literary scene (Malecowna 2015). The suggestions were written as a numbered list over the course of 13 inspired minutes on the afternoon of 19 May, and argued:

- Starting our own thing is the only way. 'Our own thing', in my opinion, is a whole new literary infrastructure.
- The existing literary structures remain colonial constructions – marginalising black people, even those who think they're IN.
- No amount of improvement of colonial constructions will ever be ideal for black people.
- So we need to undo this colonial arrangement. The RhodesMustFall young people call it DECOLONISATION.
- The decolonisation of the literary scene – and our society – will give us an opportunity to imagine ourselves afresh.
- This decolonisation will have to involve government. That's what we should have done 21 years ago. Hello, Mr President?
- RE: 'Our own thing' … No rich black person can afford to fund this decolonisation project. But they must stand up and contribute.
- 'Our own thing', the literary infrastructure I'm talking about, means libraries and bookstores in black communities.
- At the moment there are no bookstores in our communities, and the libraries that exist are fake. The literature in them is not our own.
- We need libraries with relevant literature i.e. Niq Mhlongo, Zukiswa Wanner, Kopano Matlwa, CA Davids, Lebo Mashile, Sifiso Mzobe etc.
- Bookstores – no Africana Section – with affordable books. Unfair to ask blacks

- who struggle to make ends meet to buy these expensive books.
- #RemoveTaxFromBooks.
- We need vibrant literary festivals in Umlazi, Soweto, Mdantsane, Gugulethu, Mafikeng, Lenyenye etc. Naphaya emvakwendlu ekhaya.
- Between festivals we need other forms of literary activity: poetry performances, readings, launches etc. We need writing competitions. We need literary magazines.
- Book shows on our radio and TV stations. Ekasi.
- All of this will be meaningless if not done in our mother tongues. Primarily.
- NOTE: 'Our own thing' must not be cut-and-paste from the colonial set up. An Exclusive Books kinda store will fail in Gugs.
- You cannot hope to establish a culture of reading unless this set-up exists.
- Your annual book donation initiative will have little/no impact. 'Cultivating' a culture of reading requires a functional support system.
- Malaika Wa Azania says we should model it on the drinking infrastructure that currently exists in Kasi. She's funny. She's right.
- You can troll me but it'll mean nothing to me. (http://bookslive.co.za/blog/2015/05/19/thando-mgqolozana-outlines-21-suggestions-for-the-decolonisation-of-the-south-african-literary-scene/)

The medium of Twitter tracks some of the ways in which these statements were taken up by others, and how a collective conversation took shape. As a teaching resource, the 21 tweets are extremely useful, making explicit how reading publics shape and are shaped. Reading this Twitter manifesto (and the comments that have been left as a trace during the days following its publication) draws attention to the particular locatedness of the debate, and makes the reader aware of her own relationship (or, equally importantly, the absence of such a relationship) to this community.

Mgqolozana's 21 tweets document an exit from one type of public space, refusing any longer to be part of a literary culture that regards him and his books as 'emergent' (that is, without context or history). Henceforth he would no longer agree when invited to speak on panels as someone who interpreted blackness for a white audience, who found all he had to say refreshingly 'new'. 'Look at yourselves! It is not normal!' Mgqolozana said to the audience, calling attention to the weirdly skewed make-up of the audience, but also to the assumption that such a room is 'normal' and normative, and asserting that there are other ways of reading and being.

For the first edition of Abantu Book Festival that took place in December 2016, Mgqolozana worked with a team, including the novelist and essayist Panashe Chigumadzi, who curated the programme. They selected 'Our Stories' as the theme of the festival, writing in the programme notes that 'the festival celebrates African stories through written and spoken word, visual arts, music and film. It will explore the ways in which our stories are told, and how these inform, or are informed by, our ways of being.' This understanding of the many modes and media through which stories are told expands and nuances the question of reading, and in particular what one might call located 'township' readings (the use of the term does not intend to restrict the location, but implies an affinity and an intellectual bloodline). The 'we' is glossed in, but at the same time also constituted through, Mgqolozana's Twitter feed, where the manifesto spread, was shared and retweeted.

Mgqolozana's Twitter revolution was a response to the absence of black audiences at existing literary festivals, and at the same time the repeated lamentations about the perceived decline in or, worse, *lack of* a reading culture among black South Africans (for discussions, see the many newspaper articles and other documents collected on the Abantu website). He makes a link between the colonised space of the festival and the infrastructural barriers to black readers' access to books. Abantu's impetus was to think differently about the ways in which reading shaped and in turn was shaped by everyday socialities, and in particular in black-centred contexts. A recurring theme at Abantu Book Festival was the prevalence of mental health issues, and specifically mental health issues in black spaces. The journalist and TV producer Tiisetso Tlelima reported that the festival was 'one of the few black spaces were mental illness is spoken about' (Tlelima 2016), drawing attention to the fact that the festival created ('imagined into existence') a format where these often hidden topics could be discussed. Panellists at Abantu spoke about the fact that 'black people are often expected to live perfectly coherent lives, even though their lives are multi-faceted and filled with unimaginable pain caused by about 400 years of oppression, colonialism and land dispossession'. At this historic inaugural festival of black-centred reading, the role of life-writing as a future-oriented form of self-imagining was a recurring theme, as was the role of writing and reading as forms of healing and collective identity formation. The festival's emphasis on story-telling not only referenced a readerly world beyond textual cultures and bookshops, but also made explicit the social functions of what Ato Quayson has called calibrated reading, 'that situated procedure of attempting to wrest something from the aesthetic domain for the analysis and better understanding of the social' (2003: xv).

Abantu's convening of a public, then, is precisely not a story of a new birth without histories, nor of emergence. A repeated emphasis on newness and emergence is a particularly pronounced discourse in writings about debut novels by black South African writers from the 'new' South Africa. These descriptors have proved near impossible to resist. Mgqolozana himself has often been included as one of these 'emergent' authors, as has Kopano Matlwa. The youthfulness (and beauty) of the authors (Mgqolozana was born in 1983, Matlwa in 1985) and their age when their debut novels were published (Matlwa was just 22, Mgqolozana 26) further encouraged a critical reception, in certain literary spheres, that read the novels as symptomatic of a 'new' and 'emergent' generation 'finding its voice'. These tropes of emergence have powerfully shaped the ways in which South African literature of these first decades since transition has been read trans-nationally. Compounding this readerly and critical sense of newness, both Mgqolozana's and Matlwa's debut novels were coming-of-age stories, and both have frequently (with significant exceptions) been read in ways that map precisely that which Mgqolozana's Abantu initiative seeks to challenge.

Bwesigye Bwa Mwesigire has written that when he uses the term 'emerging', he means 'those who are yet to have a book a published' (2014); in other words as soon as one publishes a novel one is no longer 'emerging'. Lynda Gichanda Spencer in her work on black women writers develops a useful definition of 'emergence', drawing for her definition on the writings of scholars such as Raymond Williams, Karin Barber and Njabulo Ndebele. Spencer describes the 'emergent writers in South Africa as young, black writers who emerge out of the apartheid regime, with distinct histories and experiences, and are interested in re-imagining black womanhood in post-repressive South Africa' (2014: 21) and writes of

> the emergent as a practice where women writers attempt to negotiate gendered and national identities when positions are no longer clear-cut, while trying to find ways of pushing forward a liberationist project both for women and within the nation-state, without being pulled back into the compromises of the roles that might be marked out for women. (2014: 18)

These mobilisations of the meanings of emergent and emergence form part of a discourse that seeks to reimagine publishing and reading landscapes, and that reconceptualises emergence as an activist practice. Spencer's use of the term is in sympathy with the projects of Writivism and of Abantu, and it is not with her transformative vision of emergence that I seek battle.

Just days before the first Abantu Book Festival took place, a novel about blood and bloodlines of many kinds was published by Kopano Matlwa, called *Period Pain*. It has since been published in an international edition with the less evocative title *Evening Primrose*. The author's South African publishers, Jacana, rebranded her previous two novels (*Coconut* and *Spilt Milk*), all three covers now showing young black women with intricate hairstyles in three-quarter view, seen from the back (Van Niekerk 2016). The absence of clearly distinguishable facial features suggests the universality of the young women (magnifying what younger readers sometimes call their 'relatability'), while also encouraging readers to interpret the novels as a set of interlinked narratives that have young female protagonists as their central concern. The covers also reference the author herself, a strikingly beautiful woman whose elaborate hairstyles are one of her trademarks. On the promotional pamphlets and marketing materials the author is shown facing us, making direct eye contact. The covers have been chosen to draw together her three novels as a set (siblings or friends), emphasising the themes running through them and encouraging us to see this new novel as a development on the previous two. Matlwa is an iconic figure, and a TEDx talk by her entitled 'What to do When a Moonshot Falls Short' is available on YouTube, along with many other interviews and material about her novels and also about her work as a medical doctor. Typically, these interviews have archived alongside them comments such as 'someone who I can aspire to be like ♥', making clear the inspirational and aspirational self-help protocols of these videos' reception. The genre of the TEDx talk simulates amazing intimacy, and a sense of familiarity and access which creates in the viewer an aspirational desire for what is promised as attainable self-improvement.

The featurelessness of the women on the covers of Matlwa's books invites any reader to see herself in these novels, the novels acting like mirrors and providing the pleasure of recognition that younger readers in particular often cite as a requirement in fiction. Many writers, speakers and critics mention having read Matlwa's novels (and *Coconut* in particular), and having seen themselves reflected there. In this sense, the marketing of the novels also confirms the sense that the novels are telling 'our stories'. The need for novels as mirrors in which 'we' can recognise ourselves reinforces in complex and contradictory ways that these are narratives of emergence. The responses of young readers of the novels who see 'their' stories in them confirm the sense that they are expressions of newness, and that Matlwa is interpreting a generation.

When Matlwa's first novel, *Coconut*, was published in 2007, it was met with immediate acclaim both nationally and internationally, and won the European Union Literary Award (now renamed the Dinaane Debut Fiction Award, a Setswana word meaning 'telling our stories together'). The novel's title references the familiar descriptor of 'coconut' for a person who is black on the outside and white inside. This language of outside/inside is suggestive also for reading the novel and understanding its reception. In a scholarly article published just two years after the novel appeared, Lynda Gichanda Spencer sketched out what remains a definitive reading of the novel, pre-empting the major trends that persist. The first sentence of Spencer's abstract to her article (entitled 'Young, Black and Female in Post-Apartheid South Africa') is arresting: 'A new kind of woman, one who occupies a distinctive subject position, is emerging in South African literature' (2009: 66). This new kind of woman (Spencer herself was, in 2009, a 'young, black and female' PhD student) is described as 'growing up between cultures, trying on different identities, and evaluating new forms of affiliation'. The language used in Spencer's argument is that of 'trying on' and 'evaluating', rather than being drawn from the more judgmental registers of coconut discourse. Her argument is concerned with 'the politics of representation', by which she means both the construction of a self and the construction of the text. Her analysis historicises Matlwa's novel, mapping the ways in which it is 'new'. But instead of seeing this newness as a moment of bursting on to an existing scene that had no parameters for reading it, her argument is invested in how the novel (and others by contemporary black woman writers) is not merely a reflection in an ethnographic mode, but rather develops a social critique, and plays an active part in the creation of new genres and forms.

Spencer's analysis shows how the 'young, black and female' authors 'are experimenting with form and trying out different genres, including popular fiction, and are using narrative as a tool with which to construct new and different ways of being female, in the process presenting alternative ways of looking at self and society' (2009: 67). Her insights remain extremely useful, not only for reading Matlwa's book but also for the ways in which this article emphasises the relationship between formal and genre innovation on the one hand, and social change on the other, as well as for its understanding of genre change and genre development in social contexts (for a recent discussion of some arguments around genre see the special issue of *The Cambridge Journal of Postcolonial Literary Inquiry* on genre, and in particular the afterword by Moradewun Adejunmobi [2017]).

This approach facilitates a reading that is flexible and dynamic, rather than seeing the newness, self-evident on the surface, as enough. Spencer's argument highlights the novel's restless form and develops a terminology that pays attention to genre innovation as in itself an activist form, and gives us a language for thinking about the mutual creation of reader and genre. The inspired comments on the 'look' of the book make clear that the white spaces between the two narratives (of two young women from different social classes) function to represent the socio-economic divisions between the two protagonists, revealing division *within* as well as *between* (Spencer 2009: 70), making clear that 'young, black and female' is a complex and dynamic descriptor.

Spencer's understanding of the language of coconuttiness is that the coconut's 'blackness is only skin deep, while the inner self is reconfigured by education, social and cultural hegemony' (2009: 68). Inside the coconut, under the thin skin, it is 'hollow in the centre', with 'no core to ground' her (2009: 74). In the subsequent scholarly literature on *Coconut*, the relationship between inside and outside dominates discussions. Tlhalo Raditlhalo, in an influential article entitled 'An Indefensible Obscenity: Fundamental Questions of Being in Kopano Matlwa's *Coconut*', reads the novel as a reflection of a South African society in which black people 'suffer from a debilitating sickness of whiteache, in which they do not wish to "pass for white" but to "be white"' (2010: 21). Aretha Phiri's and Gugu Hlongwane's articles pick up these themes, and they read the novel as both reflection and symptom of South Africa. Phiri opens her article with a useful survey of the state of whiteness studies scholarship, and argues that the novel 'lends itself to an analysis of the issues that trouble current academic and cultural attentions to whiteness', and 'expos[es] a dialectical relationship between whiteness and blackness' (2013: 163). She writes about blackness as 'porous, performative and evolving', and her argument is that by taking a 'fresh approach' to blackness, the novel yields new insights into whiteness. Her gloss of the term coconut is that it refers to 'racial duplicity' (2013: 166). Phiri quotes theorists who discuss race as performance and as practice, and that always list 'blackness and whiteness' as pairs connected as well as divided by a 'porous' skin. This understanding of the coconut is one that sees its outer skin as thin, porous and open to absorbing and filtering elements from elsewhere. The argument's dialectical understanding of blackness means that her reading of *Coconut* stresses race as a series of performances, and her argument reads the novel's innovation as indexing new instances of porous duplicity.

Gugu Hlongwane's interest, like Phiri's and Raditlhalo's, is in the 'power of whiteness', but in other ways the argument is very different. She argues that 'Matlwa's characters are not only culturally lost and painfully ashamed of their blackness, they live in a country where they are seemingly not allowed to be black' (2013: 9). Hlongwane acknowledges critical whiteness scholar Henry Giroux who has, she writes, urged 'us to move beyond the view of "whiteness" as simply a trope of domination' (2013: 9), but her argument is that whiteness is precisely that – overwhelming *and* dominant. She reads the novel as a 'timely investigation of the power of whiteness even in a black governed South Africa'. The abstract of Hlongwane's article features a curious typographical glitch. In the last sentences of the abstract, in a different typeface and font size, she grudgingly agrees with scholars who argue that whiteness and blackness are 'ideas, lived experiences, and practices in the making', quoting directly from Sarah Nuttall's formulation in her influential and award-winning book *Entanglement*. The change in typography may be incidental and unrelated to the change of tone in the abstract; what it looks like here is that an editor or peer reviewer has insisted on the inclusion of this argument, and that its late inclusion has left a trace. Hlongwane's understanding of race is more interested in untangling than in understandings of race that see identity as entangled; for her it is precisely the harmful tangle that is the cause of nervous conditions.

Hlongwane's reading singles out the 'depressed and suicidal characters' in Matlwa's novel: 'uncomfortable in their own black skins, they desire the very whiteness that is the cause of their agonizing identity complexes' (2013: 11). Her argument is insistent that there is *no* symmetry between whiteness and blackness. Her analysis spirals back to her main argument, which is that black people (and hence also Matlwa's characters) are hardly free in what is a 'supposedly free, post-apartheid country' (2013: 13), in a state that is divided rather than symmetrically entangled. Hlongwane describes Fikile and Ofilwe, the two female characters in the novel, as one another's alter egos: 'although they come from opposite sides of the economic fence, they have much in common in that they both hate themselves' (2013: 14). They are both damaged and traumatised, she argues, and this shared, mirrored trauma is due to colonialism and *apartheid* (2013: 15). Ofilwe's self-hatred is explained thus by Hlongwane: 'When she thinks critically about her so-called privileged education, she sees herself as a traitor, a sell-out, a coconut who is sleeping with the enemy' (2013: 18). These moments are, according to Hlongwane, when Ofilwe can recognise that she has not been 'true to herself' but has played the part her white friends expect her to play. Hlongwane does not make this explicit, but the comment about the true self versus the play self seems to borrow the language of performativity of race used by critical race theorists. To develop a 'healthier identity' would be not to 'play'. It is, in other words, the false 'play' identity that characterises the coconut. Hlongwane's concluding sentences make clear that her reading of the novel is one that wishes to keep race alive as a category, in schools and in scholarship: children are dying, this is not a game.

The arguments in these articles are revealing of discussions of the significance of skin, indexed here through the term coconut. In the first place skin is understood as a racial category (however race is understood in the many theoretical models invoked and cited), and the coconut's skin is brown or black, but her 'inside' has been infected or reconfigured under the membrane of the coconut shell. Hlongwane and Raditlhalo use the language of poison and forgery, Phiri uses a language that draws its terminology from porousness and seepage. What unites these scholars' insights, while they are in other ways very different, is a language of dangerous membranes that separate inside and outside. For Phiri, the inside of the coconut is restless and in motion, but also always in contact with the inside of other coconuts; for Hlongwane and Raditlhalo, the coconut's inside has been violently invaded by whiteness, the inside and outside at war with one another and the whiteness inside determining the values and holding all the power. This discourse of coconuttiness sees the coconut as an impostor, an actor 'playing' a role. Writings about coconuts often use the insidious language of inflammation and infection, or of skin that is too porous or has become diseased. The coconut's skin cannot protect the fruit from absorbing or allowing the whiteness to penetrate under the skin, seeping or filtering in.

When Panashe Chigumadzi delivered the Ruth First lecture at the University of the Witwatersrand in August 2015, she chose for the title of her talk 'Of Coconuts, Consciousness and Cecil John Rhodes: Disillusionment and Disavowals of the Rainbow Nation', drawing together the very lively debates about the statue of Rhodes (which had fallen in April of that same year) with her understanding of what a coconut is. In her lecture, she spoke about her own life (in terms that make clear she is in many ways an uncanny sister to some of the characters in Matlwa's novels):

> [I]n my final year of high school I began to actively seek out books that deal with my experiences as an African in the world. It felt as though the earth underneath my feet moved and revealed a new world. For the first time I encountered books by African authors. I furiously highlighted sentences and paragraphs, even pages, in books such as *I Write What I Like*, *Things Fall Apart*, *Coconut* and *I Know Why the Caged Bird Sings*. (Chigumadzi 2015a)

Chigumadzi explores these ideas across many genres. Her political memoir *These Bones Will Rise Again* (2018) interprets Zimbabwean history through the eyes of 'little people' like her own grandmother; she is finalising work on a collection of essays called *Beautiful Hair for a Landless People*; and her short story 'Small Deaths' (published in *Transition* magazine) picks up on themes of representation and black womanhood. The editors of *Transition* illustrated the story with a selected set of 'retro-futurist collage' artworks by Khan Nova (the artist name of Mathieu Saunier), all using the faces and bodies of black women, underlining the themes of black girl/womanhood.

The narrator of 'Small Deaths' is a film studies student, and in a section of the story we read over her shoulder part of her term paper on the ending of the 1966 film *La Noire de ...* by Ousmane Sembène. We see these lines from her assignment: 'Just before she takes her life, Diouana declares, "If I could write, I would tell them ..." I'm writing now: In Death, this Black Girl ... becomes Her Own Black Girl, Belonging to No One but Herself' (Chigumadzi 2016: 116). The story's conclusion brings the narrator back from contemplating her own 'small death', and she walks instead toward a group of Fallists, hearing in her head the repeated phrase 'Welcome Black'. To accompany an interview in the *Guardian* newspaper in 2015, Chigumadzi was photographed in a white dress, her smooth brown arms and neck stretching beyond the white fabric, as if she was a coconut that had been turned inside out or, as she terms it, a 'deconstructed', radical coconut. In her self-identification as a coconut, she redefines the term, adding the qualifier 'radical'. While the coconut's class privileges cannot be denied, Chigumadzi's redefinition of the term suggests that the coconut nevertheless has a choice. Yet the coconut discourse, even when deconstructed and radical, remains invested in its relation to whiteness. No matter how deconstructed the coconut, the trope speaks more eloquently of race than of class divisions or of imagined pan-African identities. Coconut discourse is a discourse of skin, whether skin is seen as porous or adjacent, or the layer of the body that is able to retain a 'true' self.

In the next section I want to read *Coconut* through its sister novel, *Period Pain*, from inside blood rather than the potentially contaminated coconut milk, and to explore how Abantu can shift how we read this novel. It is tempting to read the development from *Coconut* to *Period Pain* autobiographically, the author herself moving from 22-year-old medical student to doctor, healthcare activist and mother. Inspirational and self-help genres often rely on this conflation of life and text, and on the testimonial mode of writing and reading. Despite the fact that *Period Pain* was published just before Abantu Book Festival, the author was not present for the panel discussions, nor is she on any of the photographs of the historic gathering. From interviews and photographs taken around the same time, it is evident that she was heavily pregnant in late 2016, and she typically describes herself as a writer, a doctor and a mother. At the second edition of Abantu, Matlwa gave a talk called 'Medicine is my wife and writing my mistress; I love them both', and was described on the programme as 'a medical doctor and author of three novels, among other things' (Abantu Book Festival programme, 2017).

In my discussion, I shall avoid reading the novel biographically (despite the marketing campaign's invitation that we see Matlwa alongside the other young women who adorn her covers). Instead I shall read the novel against the background of Abantu and its creation of black-centred space, with Spencer's formal and genre comments in mind, and I shall relate the novel finally to a writing and reading tradition by doctors and midwives in South Africa. In these writings, we see not only the documentation of patients' lives and deaths, and notes containing their case histories, but also a discussion about what the appropriate ways are through which to make sense of such case histories. I relate this approach to genres of self-help writing, and to the making of a self through reading and writing. This discussion returns us to the concerns of this book: the ethical protocols required in order to read the bloods of the present.

In *Period Pain*, we read what is presented as a journal written by a young woman who is a medical doctor. The intimacy of the voice is familiar to readers of Matlwa's other novels, and her ability to create such intimacy is one of the reasons why younger readers in particular feel such recognition in and through reading them. The novel is marketed in South Africa as a 'youth novel', and the importance of Matlwa's novels for younger readers (in particular young black women) is enormous. The novel's form is fragmented, and many quoted texts and fragments interrupt and splice the narrative of the diary. The title references in the first place the pain associated with menstrual periods, but there are other ways of interpreting these words as describing a historical period of pain, a reference to the political and social state of South Africa that the novel diagnoses. Zanele Muholi's photographic *oeuvre* (which I discuss in the next chapter) includes an ongoing series of works entitled *Isilumo Siyaluma*, which translates in English as 'Period Pain'; Matlwa does not cite the work, and it is not clear whether her title is a reference to the art, but there are powerful resonances between these artists' projects.

Documenting menstrual cycles is a form of self-regulation used by many women, a documenting of the self in search of patterns that can explain and prepare us (that is, women of a certain age) for changes in the body. Matlwa's novel inventively logs these menstrual bloods alongside other bloods. The main character is (like Matlwa herself) a medical doctor. The diary oscillates between the private and excessive menstrual bloods of her body, which sometimes almost make her feel as if she is drowning in blood, and the public bloods of the hospital where she works. The bloods of the hospital are inside and on the bodies of sick patients, but the poorly resourced hospital itself seems to be bleeding, with blood left on the floors and walls. The narrator, allegorically named Masechaba (the Sesotho word for nation) reads the one type of blood (internal, personal) through the other (public, the blood of others), connecting them up.

Self-help texts promise to provide us with ways of reading the self, and reading in turn provides parameters for creating a self. Self-help texts have this double-sidedness: they are chosen in hope, and read for improvement or healing of some kind. Is it far-fetched to make a connection between South African readers' hunger for self-help books and the many younger South Africans one meets who report they have had a calling to become a 'traditional' healer? How I interpret these phenomena is that we are witnessing a generation taking up the responsibility for the work of diagnosing selves and others, and of logging the bloods in order to do the dangerous and multidirectional memory work that will allow the new selves to be 'imagined into being'. These are the skilled readers of the emergent present, to use Gabriele Schwab's useful insight.

The prominence of self-help genres for African readers has been noted, and a scholarly literature is beginning to respond to the ways in which these texts shape and are shaped by readers. The journalist Khanyi Ndabeni, in a newspaper article from 2015, reported that Bibles and self-help books (followed by Steve Biko's *I Write What I Like*, Nelson Mandela's life and Chinua Achebe's *Things Fall Apart*) were the most frequently shoplifted items from South African bookshops. The photograph accompanying this story showed a serious young man holding in one hand Nelson Mandela's *Long Walk to Freedom* and in the other hand a Bible, as if weighing up which one would offer him the most intellectual and spiritual sustenance. This anecdote about patterns of shoplifting emphasises a need for self-help books, a need so great that one would be willing to steal in order to improve oneself.

Stephanie Newell finds that many self-help texts show a preoccupation with the theme of marriage and the linked hope for a stable and happy home (2008: 15), and her article maps the inseparability of locally published self-help pamphlets and processes of urbanisation, in an argument that carefully weighs the meanings of modernity, misogyny and gendered urban life in Ghana. Rebecca Jones in her work on self-help genres in Nigeria argues that such texts also assert 'a metatextual claim about the power and authority of the written word, in doing so wrangling with an argument that has interested West African writers for over a century: how to justify the value of the written text' (Jones 2019). In a discussion of Lola Akande's novel *What it Takes*, I developed a different argument, linking self-help genres to the kinds of activist aims we also see in Abantu (Coetzee 2017). All of these approaches agree about the importance of self-help texts, and on the need for new scholarly approaches to them.

South African self-help texts are diverse and the capacious genre can be related to many discourses. One might, for example, think about the crowd-sourced syllabus that emerged from #RMF as a form of self-help, and the theft of *I Write What I Like* alongside the Bible is suggestive, too, of what Biko has to offer readers in terms of self-help. In my own article on Sihle Khumalo's travel writings (Coetzee 2013a), I suggested that one way of approaching Khumalo's unusual text would be to read it as a self-help manual (and like many self-help books, Khumalo's includes a description of him reading yet other self-help manuals). This self-replicating pattern of self-help genres is both its promise and its template. Elizabeth Olayiwola, writing on Mount Zion Evangelical church's attitude to the proliferation of its inspirational video films, coined the memorable phrase 'the goodness of piracy' to explain that this proliferation is part of the vision of spreading the 'good message' (2017). Self-help genres rely on this same urge to replicate and even to 'pirate' or steal a better self.

Period Pain moves between reading and documenting in this way, the reading as well as the writing providing formations of self. As we move through the novel, what we are reading is an intimate and private journal in the process of being written. Although the entries are not dated and seem to flow in one stream, we know they are written over the course of weeks and months. The journal writer is a young woman, Masechaba, who makes notes about the many other texts she reads and writes, and through which she interprets and structures her life. We see how this text incorporates instructive texts (the Bible, other spiritual and self-help books, and medical textbooks), entextualising them and continuously creating the self (of the narrator, but also of the reader). This form of reading (in search of a self, but also in search of the most appropriate ways of 'reading' the self) shape this novel, and make it an ideal text for young readers and particularly suited to the classroom. But this way of reading the novel exists alongside the less 'emergent' reading that links up the bloods of the novel with the bloods of Abantu. Abantu can be understood as bringing to the surface the need for conversations about care, care of the body and care of the self. This community of care extends beyond that which often sees self-help texts as shallow or trivial; what I am arguing is that Abantu and self-help genres can be read as forms that achieve and shape care, while *at the same time* reflecting on and debating the very terms of the care. The reader of such texts (and perhaps this same reader also attends Abantu) is encouraged to reflect on the ways of making, as well as the terms for understanding, a 'better' self. Thus reading becomes a regime of care that creates and sustains the making of self. These ethical protocols of reading complicate a narrative of emergence, emphasising instead the deeply contextualised and contextualising work reading performs for the self and the community – in particular in 'periods of pain'.

Period Pain opens with a quotation from the US theologian and spiritual writer Frederick Buechner: 'The only books worth reading are books written in blood' (Matlwa 2016: 7). The spiritual orientation is reinforced by the opening words about a woman who touched the garment of Jesus and was healed from a malady of bleeding from which she had suffered for twelve years (Mark 5:25–34). These two quotations are included here as the reader begins to orient herself, but we are not certain whether they come from the author (Kopano Matlwa) or are part of the notebook we are reading, written in the first person by the narrator. The opening section has us read (over the shoulder of the diarist, so to speak, as if we are reading over the shoulder of the young woman we see on the cover) about the onset of her first menstrual period. The bleeding, she remembers knowing 'immediately', was a 'punishment from God'. Reading further, we see that it is more complicated, that it is in fact her Ma's judgement and punishment she fears. When her mother notices the spots on her tights, it was as if 'a flood gate opened within me, and the blood poured out between my thighs, down my legs and onto my Jelly Baby shoes, and continued to do so for weeks, easing up for a few days at a time, only to gush out again with even more intensity, charging past the clots in its way' (2016: 12).

Night after night, the narrator goes home and tells her Ma about 'the many horrific things our people overcome daily that go undocumented. I tell her that somebody must list them, all the bad things that are happening to them, to me, to us. Somebody needs to write them down' (2016: 29). Ma, listening at the end of her own demanding day, is the recipient of this documenting – and we alongside her, as we read. The story-telling at the end of the day is also a document of the ways in which training as a doctor (reading medical textbooks) does not prepare one for the realities of working in a poorly resourced state hospital. The learning and reading needed to become a doctor, we realise, is no guarantee that the healing aim of the work will be achieved. 'Patients die all the time. Nobody expects you to save them all the time. We do what we can' (2016: 27).

The first few pages provide us with an origin narrative for why the writer of the notebook decides to become a doctor: she wants to make a friend in the medical profession who will perform for her the hysterectomy that other doctors have been unwilling to perform, which will stop the excessive periods from which she suffers. She registers for a degree at 'Seriti University' (a Setswana word that means 'dignity', alerting us to the themes of the novel). Father Joshua at her church asks the newly qualified doctor to speak to the youth at church about careers, one of the many instances of teaching and learning in the novel. These inspirational speeches are clearly related to self-help genres, the speaker's own success and achievements acting as an encouragement to the listeners. And so begins another set of writings, her emails to the account of her deceased brother, Tshiamo. These email messages include practice versions of the short speeches she prepares for Father Joshua's youth meetings, but also smiley face emoticons and photographs (which we never see – the emails to Tshiamo remain private, as letters sent to the dead tend to be). These letters (visible briefly in the 'Sent' folder of her phone, detected and then deleted before others, including us, can read them) are replaced by 'this stupid journal that is read by no one but God' – and of course, us. The notebook entries are interrupted by quotations from the Bible, creating a sense of daily readings that accompany life events and through which the journal writer tries to 'read' her life's meanings. The reader of the novel, like the reader of the Bible, is encouraged to find the parallels – to read *Period Pain* for instruction and improvement.

With good intentions, the diarist ends her day by planning the next day:

> Tomorrow I'm going to wake up early and get to hospital on time. I'm going to be in the lab first thing in the morning and make sure I have all the patients' results before the ward round. I'm going to check their temperatures myself if the nursing sisters haven't done them yet. I'm going to stop others discharging them before they're well enough to go home. I'm going to ask them how they feel, instead of making it up. (2016: 45)

This ethical protocol requires of her that she reads (her notes, relevant scientific journals) and writes (making a list of 'all the things I need to do for the day'), reinforcing the idea of reading and writing as modes of imagining a better self into being, as well as protocols for better forms of care (2016: 45).

The novel is explicit in its use of the metaphor of blood and menstrual periods, and the author perhaps was sensitive to the fact that the novel would probably be read by younger readers. So in response to a nurse's racism against her Zimbabwean friend Nyasha, we read a conversation between Masechaba and Nyasha: '"It's just a period South Africa's in," [Nyasha] said matter-of-factly. "Growing pains." // "Like period pain," I said, trying to make a joke' (2016: 65). The racism against non South Africans, and the indignities suffered in a poorly resourced state hospital, are logged as versions of 'period pain', alongside the literal period pain from which Masechaba suffers. Nyasha's name links her to another text about female self-making, the narrator in the influential 1988 novel *Nervous Conditions* by the Zimbabwean author and film-maker Tsitsi Dangarembga. The format of *Period Pain* is, in the mode of self-help genres, in search of the most suitable text or quotation through which to 'read' the present.

The narrative of the logging of various forms of pain is interrupted by an event which is at first unclear to the reader. Part 3 of the novel starts with a series of sharp and sorrowful, unanswered notes to God. The spiritual texts though which to 'read' the life seem to have been rendered meaningless by the strength of the sorrow she feels, and by her lack of comprehension. 'There is no vocabulary for the pain', the journal entry reads (2016: 109). Gradually the reader pieces together that the narrator has been raped. We read a gruelling account of the attack, and the description lingers on the neck of the victim, uncomfortably echoing the image on the cover of the South African Jacana edition – as if we are seeing her neck as the rapists did, but perhaps also echoing my interpretation above that we are observing her life (reading it even) over her shoulder.

Ma, whose opinions are a constant reference field (her knowledge and world view, too, constitute one of the resource texts through and against which the journal writer guides her life) has a simple explanation: she thinks these things happened because of a lack of connectedness to 'the ancestors'. This cryptic response seems at first to be unfeeling, but if we accept Ma's analysis as referencing the long history of suffering carried in the blood, she guides the reader in a different direction. The journal entries return to this topic:

> how viscous our blood must be. It carries so much in it. Stories swirling round and round our veins, up into our hearts at least a zillion times a day. Stories of men going into cities, men in men, men in women, women in men, sharing intimacies, sharing pain, sharing anger, sharing hatred, sharing resentment, sharing loss. (2016: 118)

The blood becomes a library and an archive of circulating experience, transmitted generationally. The rape results in a pregnancy, and the journal writer becomes – not by choice – one in the line of ancestors handing on these stories in the blood. The swirling stories of her life have already been documented in the journal we read, but now are also handed on to her unborn child through the placental and umbilical transmission of blood. When the baby (a girl child) is born, we read she 'looked like nothing, like a blank page. Like a fresh start' (2016: 149). She looks like a blank page, but we know that underneath the page of skin, history-rich blood courses. In turn, this baby will become a 'skilled reader' of her own as well as her ancestors' lives and stories.

The novel ends with some journal entries on the baby girl's early days – some initial paragraphs written about and on to the unmarked page of her life, in the tradition of new parents documenting (as form of self-surveillance, but also in celebration) the little achievements and milestones of the child's development. In the final entry we read how her mother (the journal writer) takes her to the clinic to have an inoculation shot. The needle that will pierce her unmarked skin, which is like a blank page, brings prophylactic care, and those administering the syringe's contents into her bloodstream wish to protect her body against future harm and disease. In this projection of future care there is not a deletion of the histories already in the blood, since those meanings are already written under the skin. But the care of the next generation, Matlwa's novel shows, is a source book and self-help guide to reading our times. That, we realise, is the care that is needed: imagining the next generation into being, and transmitting this care up and down the bloodlines..

The trope of the coconut relies on a tension between inside and outside: the brown skin outside and the white liquid inside. The inside of the coconut is judged as a contamination or an impostor – something that has somehow managed to get under the skin. The thinking about identity and the notion of the coconut is a discourse not about entanglement or contact, but about its opposites: conflict and division. In Matlwa's novel the inside is understood differently, and in a rather literal way: it is the baby growing inside Masechaba. As the baby was conceived during a rape, there are obvious reasons for regarding it as a form of contamination; yet in the final pages of the novel we see Masechaba give birth to a baby she claims and loves as her own. The ways in which this image of the inside becoming manifest on the outside differ from the coconut discourse are worth spelling out. The baby's presence inside Masechaba is at first like a contamination, and the rape has left her traumatised and alienated. The final pages, with the loving descriptions of the small girl's birth and early developmental stages, offer an optimistic alternative. The protagonist whose diary we have been reading has, through the text, developed a consciousness that hosts new modes of shaping the reader, as her body hosts the growing baby.

While Matlwa was writing this novel, she was completing a doctoral dissertation on public health policy (2018) and also conducting research for a project on maternal scanning in the Democratic Republic of the Congo (DRC), with her colleague, friend and fellow medic Chrystelle Opope Oyaka Wedi. The project's name ('Ona mtoto wako') means, translated from Kiswahili, 'see your baby'. On the website, Matlwa (or Matlwa Mabaso, the name under which her medical work is done) and Wedi's professional and activist projects are outlined on a page headed (in the welcoming and intimate language of such information pages) 'Who we are' (http://www.onamtotowako.com/who-we-are). The project addresses the fact that

> 800 women die every day due to complications in pregnancy and childbirth and 99% of these deaths occur in developing countries. What is most tragic about these deaths is that they occur from preventable and treatable conditions, conditions for which we have existing and effective solutions. When a mother dies during childbirth, her infant's odds of making it to their second birthday are grim, and her existing children face a life of considerable vulnerability. (http://onamtotowako.com/why-we-do-it)

The emphasis is on preventing maternal mortality, making visible the plight of the many women who die every day because of the absence of medical care for easily treatable pregnancy-related conditions.

The project is called see your baby, but the technological imaging that allows women to 'see' their babies functions also as a way of convening publics – bringing women into circles of care and information. Wedi and Matlwa's idea was to take a mobile scanning unit to rural areas as a way of bringing life-saving antenatal healthcare to women living in remote or rural areas of the DRC. When pregnant women came to the mobile clinic to see their babies on the scan, they would become aware of other forms of care available to them. Through the imaging technology, women were able to 'see' their babies inside; but the visit to the mobile clinic also had other benefits for how the women would imagine and see their pregnancy and their future. The website for the project makes evident these discourses of futurity and self-care.

Matlwa is one of a long tradition of South African women writers who are also medical practitioners and healthcare activists. When she was a medical student, she co-founded WREMS (Waiting Room Education by Medical Students), a health promotion organisation which used a similar approach to provide health education to families who were in the waiting rooms of mobile clinics. A recent trend in South Africa has seen memoirs by medical practitioners, such as Maria Phalime who wrote *Postmortem: The Doctor Who Walked Away* (2014), and autobiographies by those living with cancer and HIV, for example Lauren Segal's *Cancer: A Love Story* (2018). Medical humanities constitutes a growing area of scholarship in South Africa, and the research group housed at WiSER (http://wiser.wits.ac.za/medical-humanities) hosts discussions and research projects on a number of themes including medical memoirs. Shula Marks's 1994 study *Divided Sisterhood: Race, Class and Gender in the South African Nursing Profession* is an impressively comprehensive history of the nursing profession in South Africa. These projects and texts can be brought into productive relationship with self-help genres, which are often ignored as being superficial or as promoting neoliberal agendas.

A particularly interesting set of South African texts are those written by scholars and creative writers who are also midwives. Midwives as characters in novels are intermediaries between worlds and discourses, and approaches to childbirth index all sorts of historical and social concerns. Mamphela Ramphele, healthcare professional and medical doctor, writes in her autobiography about her own mother's experience of giving birth that

> the midwife who attended to her at my birth was, according to my mother, most unhelpful. She disparaged any request from my mother for help during labour as the cry of a spoilt schoolteacher seeking special attention. As a result my mother delivered me without any assistance from the midwife. She only came in later to cut

the umbilical cord, heaping more scorn as she tidied up. I was to bleed heavily from the improperly tied stump of cord that night and, according to my mother, nearly died over the next few days from a combination of neo-natal jaundice and the after-effects of blood loss. (1995: 2)

Makhosazana Xaba, a prominent gender activist and creative writer who has published scholarly as well as policy documents about birth control, has written an extraordinary autobiographical piece about giving birth and about being born. Her story 'Midwives, Mothers, Memories' appeared in a collection called *Just Keep Breathing* (edited by Sandra Dodson and Rosamund Haden and published in 2008). Xaba's narrative opens with the striking words: 'In my early twenties, I delivered hundreds of babies. Naturally, my interest in my own birth and that of my daughter tends towards the technical' (2008: 1). Xaba's writing style is often surprising, and frequently intertextual; for example, her short story 'The Suit Continued: The Other Side' responds to the misogyny in Can Themba's 'The Suit' and rewrites it in another register.

In the short story on midwives, mothers and memories, Xaba writes how she wishes that she knew the length of her mother's labour, what her own position as foetus was as she was being born, and what her Apgar score was. She would like, she writes, 'to see the record of all this'. Xaba turns this narrative of a bloodline of women, a narrative that brings together her own and her daughter's births, into a richly historicising description of the conditions of pregnancy and birth-care. Her mother was fortunate to be cared for by a trained midwife, her aunt Mrs Sanah Mamashela, called 'Staff':

Getting hold of those records of my birth would be a treat. I am curious about the kind of records Sanah would have kept in the fifties. How did she monitor labour? What charts did she use? The mere thought of looking at the papers – yellowing, time-crumpled – excites me. Most of all, I wish to see Staff's signature attesting to her professional presence at my arrival. (2008: 1)

The story thus brings together two bloodlines: that of the mother, daughter and granddaughter, and also that of the midwives and nurses, and the knowledge passed on through their lore. These different ways of knowing the body, and more importantly the different modes of charting and monitoring the welfare of the body, are presented as a bloodline (broken, in need of re-membering) of women's forms of care for one another. The medical knowledge held by midwives, across generations, is a version of the protocols of ethical care, through writing and reading practices that can preserve and enable life.

The blood of childbirth is often associated with newness and emergence. Here we see midwives and medical practitioners record and document the birth, and inscribe the births into longer histories, not only of genealogical bloodlines but also of scholarly and knowledge bloodlines. The discussion up to now has privileged women's bloods: the blood of pregnancy, menstruation and childbirth. I want to go back now to another kind of blood, the manly blood associated with rituals of *ulwaluko* and certain traditions of becoming a man through cutting the skin of the penis.

I return to the man who created Abantu, and to Abantu as a space of imagining a certain self into being, and explore how this visionary project relates to Mgqolozana's other work, which has been in medical and care registers. Mgqolozana's name appears in 2008 and 2009 (when he must have been finalising the novel *A Man Who is Not a Man*) in bibliographies of academic and policy research on 'Nursing in a new era' and 'Public nursing in neglect', literature reviews and research notes published by the South African Human Sciences Research Council (Breier et al. 2008; 2009) where he worked as a researcher. Mgqolozana's academic research focused on the ethics and practice of medical care, and the reports made suggestions for how to address structural challenges to nursing during a time when it was hoped that inequalities in access to health provision for black South Africans would come to an end. These research reports share many of the concerns of *Period Pain*, and suggest productive ways for reading *A Man Who is Not a Man* through blood and through Abantu.

In a review cited on the home page of the publishers of Mgqolozana's novel, we read the words of a reviewer describing how the novel 'exposes the unpalatable face of Xhosa circumcision' (review by Diane Awerbuck). The reviewer also argues that '[t]he incompatibility of custom with modern norms is at the heart of the book', using the language of dehistoricising judgement that is a frequent strand in writings about circumcision and initiation practices. In a review by Gail Smith, the author (Mgqolozana) is described as '[s]carily eloquent and intense considering his age – 26 – the young author embodies a new South African masculinity grappling with the wisdom of customs and culture as they pertain to manhood'. Here too, we read about the author that his 'new' identity puts him in conflict with 'customs and culture', implying that a necessary break with the past is how we are to read the novel. Smith describes the heated discussions at Mgqolozana's book launch at Xarra in Johannesburg, quoting the writer:

> I'm starved for engagement. I don't know if I can write well or not. People just want to talk about the political issues. I want to know if my book is a good contribution to literature, if it works as a novel, as a work of art. I want to know about my writing. Of course I'm interested in the subject matter, but I'm yet to get a critical review that engages with the text, rather than the subject matter. (http://www.ukznpress.co.za/?class=bb_ukzn_reviews&method=view_reviews&global[fields][_id]=104)

The tropes that recur in the discussions are those of the author's evident youth and the newness of his 'voice'. There is often an urge to read the novel autobiographically (as some have done; see, for example, Hinz and Hangula 2009: 268). The fact that the text is a debut novel brings another set of metaphors into play, about coming of age. Such responses conflate the publication of the novel with an authorial coming of age, emphasising the author's own emergence into 'manhood'. A similar comment was made by the art historian Sue Williamson about a series of artworks by Thembinkosi Goniwe (then in his twenties) that engaged with representations of *ulwaluko*: 'Goniwe has undergone his artistic *ulwaluko*. So far, so good. It will be interesting to see how he develops' (Williamson 2002). The language describes his early artworks as works of transition, and the artworks as new and as a break with history. But the language of initiation limits what we are able to see.

In the interview with Smith, Mgqolozana is quoted as saying: 'I'd like to find out if there is an irrefutable correlation between an accepted definition of manhood and traditional male circumcision compared to being circumcised surgically or not circumcised at all. I'd like to find out if, and how, traditional male circumcision defines manhood today.' This comment can be interpreted in many ways, but I wish to read it through an unusually illuminating discussion of the novel by Nonhlanhla Dlamini (based on a chapter from her recently completed PhD) that was published in *Postamble*, a trans-disciplinary postgraduate journal housed at the University of the Witwatersrand (Dlamini 2014). Dlamini's is the only discussion that places the hospital scenes as central to reading the novel. She argues that the hospital is positioned 'at the centre of its hero's recovery', and that Mgqolozana portrays the hospital as 'a place of restoration and rescue'. Dlamini relates the novel to genres of trauma narration, and concludes that 'Mgqolozana's is an activist novel that stages a political intervention and holds out the possibility of empowered healing'. This emphasis on healing rather than damage brings a crucial reorientation to how one reads the novel.

The subject of *ulwaluko* (a complex cluster of rituals that includes circumcision as one component) is fiercely debated in South Africa. The feature film *Inxeba* (The Wound) was chosen to represent South Africa at the 90th Academy Awards in the category of Best Foreign Language Film, and it was also chosen as the inaugural film for the Film Africa festival in London in September 2017. Thando Mgqolozana is credited as a co-writer, alongside John Trengove (who also directed) and Malusi Bengu. The film is not directly based on Mgqolozana's novel, but his academic expertise about the medical dangers faced by young men in some of the initiation schools makes him an expert on the topic. The film's reception in South Africa has been controversial, with responses typically concentrating either on the queer love story or on the invasion of the privacy of the schools. Representations of *ulwaluko* in the media have received a great deal of attention, and *Inxeba*'s makers and writers have had to engage with this in interviews and in the many social media comments about the film.

Ulwaluko rituals mark an entrance into manhood, and historically women and children were prohibited from observing men during their period of seclusion, as well as other aspects of the *ulwaluko* school. Through the representation of the rituals in the work of many photographers, film-makers and artists, the tropes of *ulwaluko* have become part of a shared visual archive (for an insightful discussion of the debates, see Goniwe and Gqola 2005). Discussions about the appropriation of the rituals by some photographers and artists have added important themes to the discussions around representation, knowledge and power. There is another aspect that has come to dominate scholarship, and that is analyses of the problematic media representations of *ulwaluko* schools, in particular those in the Eastern Cape region of South Africa.

Pumla Gqola and Lilian N. Ndangam have both analysed the ways in which *ulwaluko* has been portrayed across various South African media. Ndangam's concern is with the 'mediated gaze on the black African male body' (2008: 210). Her interesting study contextualises this media gaze within discussions of female genital mutilation (FGM), Foucauldian understandings of the gaze and notions of secrecy and privacy. She provides an overview of how initiation is represented in African literary texts, and weighs up the many arguments about the 'modalities of secrecy' around these practices (2008: 221). In her concluding paragraphs she makes a suggestive observation about how all these many media texts are themselves a kind of school, where 'the uninitiated come to learn about this rite of passage' (2008: 224). This 'school' (the media archive), she shows, is a site where the very terms through which to understand socio-political transformation are debated through attention to black male bodies. The blood of the ritual of manhood, in this interpretation, becomes a vast and contested circuit, with conflicting and contradictory discourses 'schooling' us in the complex and conflicted ways in which we can read the present.

In Gqola's chapter, part of an edited collection containing challenging pieces on manhood, she analyses the ways in which media representations of *ulwaluko* have 'developed an idiom in their coverage of what has come to be known as "botched circumcisions", a set phraseology that relies on heavily medical language to frame and comment on a masculine crisis of identity' (2007: 143). Gqola points out how the 'shamed body on display' is often also interviewed, filmed or photographed in a hospital or medical setting. News reporters foreground discourses of health (often expressed in terms that borrow from saviour discourses). Gqola asks: 'But who may come to the aid of these bodies? Who are the appropriate doctors and through what kinds of medicine and terms can they intervene?' (2007: 148).

The narrative of emergence (being a new voice, finding a voice, coming out) and its conflation with damaged masculinity is part of what Gqola analyses in her brilliant argument. One of her concerns is the nature of the gaze, and for whose benefit the damage is being catalogued. If we place this novel adjacent to Mgqolozana's research into the quality and availability of nursing, and his investigations of the types of care available to initiates, the novel's focus shifts from the spectacular fascination with 'botched circumcision' (whole archives of images exist on the internet to catalogue scarred penises, disturbing not only for what they catalogue but for the registers of disembodied spectacle they invoke and echo) to forms of care. This is the issue engaged by the writers whose work I have discussed in this chapter: to debate and negotiate the kinds of knowledge and the kinds of care that are required. Countering a narrative of emergence and newness, this chapter has argued that *Coconut*, *Period Pain* and *A Man Who is Not a Man* are not reflections of emergent new identities. Instead these works must be read as part of a well-developed intellectual tradition. They are not instances of new blood appearing on the surface, but instead constitute activist attempts to connect the intergenerational bloods.

I read Mgqolozana's novel as part of the labour of formulating caring protocols (of writing and of reading) and as a text attuned to the various ways in which the self can be catalogued, recorded and understood. In this reading the hospital is not the coldly clinical place that has to mend the broken 'boy', but becomes instead the centre from which the novel defines a vision of change – both genre innovation and social activism. Such a reading places the hospital nurse not as an outsider to the *ulwaluko* school, but as an insider in a range of forms of care that seek to connect and interpret, rather than obliterate, other forms of schooling. The title of Gugu Hlongwane and Khondlo Mtshali's 'Mentoring, Masculinity and Reparation in Mgqolozana's *A Man Who is Not a Man*' promises to contribute to such a project, but the authors rely on a psychological model developed by Donald Winnicott and Melanie Klein, and their article thus works in the opposite way to the deep contextualisation for which I am arguing.

In this final section I have argued how *A Man Who is Not a Man* could be read from the space of Abantu, through Gqola's insights, and alongside Mgqolozana's academic research on nursing and care protocols. When Mgqolozana announced his departure from a certain literary culture, he used the language of the gaze, demanding that his surprised hosts and audience examine themselves and look at themselves. It was a call for a recalibration, and an injunction to reassess the terms through which we regulate and understand encounters, and how we define that which is described as new and emergent. This raises challenging questions for how South African literature is to be read, in South African classrooms and kitchens and in a wider world. The bloodlines logged in Koleka Putuma's poem 'Lifeline' (2017: 85) find a close sister in the list of names of women and girls to whom Kopano Matlwa dedicates *Period Pain*. These communities of mutual care list the names of women: friends, mothers, midwives, sisters, daughters. Anyone can read the books, but when the reader closes her copy of *Period Pain*, she would do well to think about her relationship to the woman on the cover, over whose shoulder we seem to be looking into the book.

The Bloody Fingerprint: 7
We Must Document

The South African visual artist Zanele Muholi mobilises the complex meanings of a bloody fingerprint in her series of artworks called *Isilumo Siyaluma* (period pain, or the pains associated with periods), the prototype of which provides the cover for this book. Muholi's menstrual artworks are made with a particular kind of blood, blood that in some languages is named differently so as to distinguish it from other bloods. Menstrual blood is differently valued symbolically, and its relation to the skin or surface of the body is distinct. The bleeding of menstruation is the result of the body naturally shedding the thickened (invisible and internal) womb lining, which replenishes itself after being shed, then grows and is shed again cyclically (periodically, as the name indicates). Menstrual blood is the body's mode of self-regulation, but it also structures and punctuates time. It is different from the other bloods that flow in a closed circulatory system through our bodies and which are brought to the surface in a blood test.

The menstrual cycle has an invisible phase (unremarkable, and unremarked upon), followed by the hyper-visible phase when bleeding occurs. This bleeding has, at various times and in various contexts, required menstruating women to be separated or to bring ourselves and our blood into invisibility. A vast scholarly and activist literature has reflected on and analysed these prohibitions, and the shame and embarrassment associated with visible menstrual blood. When menstrual blood rises to the surface (on clothing or on furniture) it has extraordinary power to unsettle and cause discomfort. It is these meanings of blood that are brought to the surface of the canvas in Muholi's work.

To make the *Isilumo Siyaluma* series, Muholi collected her own menstrual blood, pressed her finger into the fluid and then made prints, using her finger dipped in the blood as paint. The viscosity of menstrual blood makes it different from other human bloods as a painterly medium, and most women are used to touching this blood (at least from our own bodies). There is a well-documented tradition of menstrual art by women artists, and Muholi's work is informed by this tradition but with activist agendas shaped and inflected by her own location. In discussions by Pumla Dineo Gqola (2006) and Nomusa Makhubu (2012) these situated agendas are shown to be central to Muholi's activist project. Gqola's argument makes evident the arresting link between menstruation and women's lives as lesbians on which Muholi's work relies.

The flow of menstrual blood, Gqola writes, marks a woman as 'useless', since 'under patriarchy she has failed to marshal her body parts to act in accordance with the rules that govern how such a society replicates' (2006: 85). Menstrual blood *on display* thus becomes an activist form of documenting women's lives, but also a provocation to patriarchy. Makhubu writes that Muholi's use of menstrual blood to make art functions 'to question hetero-patriarchy' (2012: 518).

In an earlier series of works with the names *Period I*, *Period II* and so on, Muholi had photographed blood-stained sanitary pads and tampons, and one image shows a heavy trail of menstrual blood running towards the plug-hole of an otherwise empty bath tub. These are images familiar to women of menstruating age, but the display of these moments of private bleeding has a power very different from mere archives of the everyday. Makhubu's analysis of Muholi's menstrual artworks transgresses the normally well-behaved language of academic scholarship when she writes:

> Blood is indexical of a wound as well as menstruation. The sanitary pad in Muholi's work seems to take on the same semiotic function as that of a plaster and a bandage: it functions as an aid. It holds back, restricts, hides. It is uncomfortably corrective. It protects others from the uncontainable self. The vagina in Muholi's artwork appears as this kind of intimidation where the viewer is confronted with blood that flows uncontrollably in an uncompromisingly realistic, aesthetically repulsive and unapologetic manner. (2012: 517–18)

Makhubu's analysis and her choice of language themselves function as a 'kind of intimidation', provoking and prodding the reader.

Muholi has described the menstrual project as a form of testimony, as she also characterises her other artistic work in which she creates photographic portraits of black LGBTI subjects. Her series of *Faces and Phases* portraits, she has said often, is an ongoing document of the pain of black lesbian lives in South Africa. In presentations and lectures, Muholi always carefully individualises and names the people in her photographs, gives information about the context of the photographic session and testifies about the subjects' lives and in some cases deaths. She typically also includes the dates on which these women were raped, or when they died as a result of violence. The effect is striking, and transgressive of the discourses that photographic artists normally use to discuss and comment on their work. Talking about her art is a central part of Muholi's practice as activist, and her statements about this series are characterised by a heightened self-referentiality, the framing lectures repeating and reinforcing the themes of testimony and documentation.

The *Isilumo Siyaluma* works are non-representational and have been described as kaleidoscopic (Salley 2012) or as flowers (Selvick 2015), both of these images emphasising the disjunction between the deceptive beauty of the repetition and patterning of the works and the suffering (period pains and the violence done to women's bodies) that Muholi always mentions. The artworks in the series are described as memorials: 'each patterned piece in this series represents a "curative rape" survivor or a victim of hate crime, the physical and spiritual blood that is shed from our bodies' (Muholi 2011). The repetition of the small menstrual blood markings in each artwork, digitally manipulated to form the patterns, reinforces the sense of the multiplicity of attacks on black lesbian women, and the fragmentation of self that results from such violence, while also invoking the repetition of the harm caused. Since the blood is menstrual, a temporal (and even cyclical) repetition is part of the meaning of the work.

The template for these composite artworks is the bloody fingerprint, indexing not forensic criminal evidence but instead claiming a defiant and transgressive identity. Muholi's fingerprint is an authenticating mark left to show she was there, she witnessed these things, and she will bring them to the surface (here literally on to the surface of her artworks) to be seen. The blood on the fingerprint is a disturbing and confusing image, showing that which should be *inside* the body (namely the blood) now *on the surface* of the body (on the whorls and ridges of the skin of the finger which are used for biometric data gathering as well as forensic science). In South Africa as elsewhere, pressing an inked finger on to a piece of paper, or holding a hand over the screen of a biometric fingerprint scanner, are frequently used methods of verifying one's identity. In this case, the fingerprint is not an identifying ink imprint or an optical scan, but a print pressed on to the skin/surface of the canvas and made using the artist's own blood. The encrypted meanings in blood thus are brought to the surface (of the body, but also the page) in a tautological identification mark. Keith Breckenridge in his book *Biometric State: The Global Politics of Identification and Surveillance in South Africa, 1850 to the Present* provides a history of the development, over the last 150 years, of biometric identification systems largely based on fingerprint registries (and the cover of his book blends a fragmented world map with fingerprints created using tiny binary code symbols). Breckenridge's argument is that while biometric registration systems claim to be able to identify individuals for life, these identification systems in fact reject any knowledge about individuals beyond the physical body.

The use of menstrual blood to document evokes Sara Ahmed's memorable description of emotions as 'sticky' and 'leaky' in her writings about the embodiedness of intimacy. She writes:

> Emotions tell us a lot about time; emotions are the very 'flesh' of time. They show us the time it takes to move, or to move on, is a time that exceeds the time of individual life. Through emotions, the past persists on the surface of bodies. Emotions show us how histories stay alive, even when they are not consciously remembered; how histories of colonialism, slavery, and violence shape lives and worlds in the present.

> The time of emotion is not always about the past, and how it sticks. Emotions also open up futures, in the ways they involve different orientations to others. (2004: 202)

My own argument develops a theory of embodied remembering, but through and in blood rather than on the skin's surface. Ahmed's argument here is interested in 'skin' as that which is shaped by contact with others, but for reasons I explained in the introduction, my approach wants to pierce the skin to access what is underneath, namely the history-rich blood. The sticky and leaky emotions of Ahmed's metaphor bring the bloods above the skin; for skin to be slippery and leaky, there has to have been a tear or rupture. Or, in this case, a menstrual period.

The authors of *The Curse*, in their chapter 'Absent Literature: The Menarche' (Delaney et al. 1988: 171), write that documenting menstrual blood is a tradition found more often in diaries than in literature. This means that blood logs are typically part of a private archiving of the self, and are not meant to be brought to the surface and into public gaze. Logging the cycle of blood has long been a way for women to predict their bodies' behaviour, whether to prevent (or enable) pregnancy, or simply to regulate and calibrate ordinary life. In South African writing by women, there are many references to menstrual blood, and logging these bloods will in itself be a valuable academic exercise. In Winnie Madikizela-Mandela's harrowing account of her excessive menstrual bleeding in incarceration (2013), the bleeding is logged as an accusation against her torturers, but also as a way of asserting personhood and dignity in the face of tormentors who wish to use the menstrual blood to further humiliate her.

In Mamphela Ramphele's account of her first period, she writes of her shock at finding blood on her clothes and of running to church to ask God to make the blood go back where it came from. Her mother's reluctance to discuss this topic with her meant that it never occurred to her to tell her mother she was menstruating. Instead, a young woman living with the family becomes her confidante and caring educator (1995: 33–4). More recently Redi Tlhabi published an autobiographical account of her complex friendship with Mabegzo, a man she knew to be a rapist and killer, but who tenderly cared for her and even bought her sanitary pads when she had her first menstrual flow. The book returns to blood of all kinds, and the opening pages describe Mabegzo's dead and bloodied body (2012: 1). Tlhabi's account of her friendship with Mabegzo is an autobiographical account of the care shown to her by someone who was also responsible for deeds of extreme violence to others:

> I cannot remember a time when I was not thinking about Mabegzo, the subject of my book. Long after he had died, I wondered if his life could have been any different had he been brought up differently. With every news item about a young man who

raped, murdered or robbed someone, I have found myself asking, is this another Mabegzo? (2012: vii)

Tlhabi's title, *Endings and Beginnings: A Story of Healing*, seems to promise one of the Rainbow Nation stories through which South Africa has often been understood. 'Writing about Mabegzo has been a gift to me. A gift of healing and maturity' (2012: viii), her preface reads. Yet the 'healing' discourse is more complex than a story of forgiveness or restorative truth-telling. In an opening that is striking in its echoes, Pumla Dineo Gqola begins her book *Rape: A South African Nightmare* with an anecdote of a half-remembered television programme: 'Many years ago, I watched a television programme where a journalist and cameraperson sat around and talked to a group of young men who had readily admitted on camera to having raped. It was a strange and unsettling encounter. It was also illuminating' (2015: 1–2). Gqola's reflections on the meaning of her project are not in the register of the 'gift', yet there are similarities in these projects that allow us to gloss Tlhabi's 'gift' in a different way.

Gqola writes of the cost, to her and those around her, of writing this book on rape. This may sound like the often-read expressions of appreciation for the support of friends and family while someone (the acknowledging author) completed a manuscript. These comments have a different valence, however. In her conclusion Gqola summarises the impetus for writing the book, and comments on how the work for the *Rape* book supports and is supported by the many feminist individuals and groups with whom she works and lives. She thought it would be an 'easy' book to write:

> Yet, many times I have told everybody in my life how I do not want to write it. I wish that I did not have to think about rape, that it was not so close to home, that I did not have to think about the many times I have felt the difficult combination of rage and tenderness as I sat across from someone as they talked about how someone had raped them. (2015: 168)

In the preface that she wrote for Eusebius McKaiser's *Run Racist Run: Journeys into the Heart of Racism* (2015), which was published around the same time as *Rape*, Gqola links her book to his, as intellectual siblings, and connects them both to Njabulo Ndebele's often misunderstood essay 'Rediscovery of the Ordinary' (McKaiser 2015: vii). Gqola references Ndebele here as part of a reflection on the role of public intellectuals such as herself and McKaiser, and their books (on racism and rape): 'In an ideal world, [these topics] would be out of our systems and we would now have the freedom to write creatively about more mundane human stuff' (2015: vii–viii), and would be 'free of the burden' of writing about race and rape. Here we see a more emphatic expression of the cost of writing the book, which (like Tlhabi's) engages with the ongoing legacies of the South African past. Tlhabi's account of her relationship with a man she knows to be a rapist and murderer, but who was a caring friend to her, is an introspective reading (under the skin) of how we are to understand a man like Mabegzo and hence ourselves. Gqola's book maps the ways in which rape and race have been mutually constitutive, and that it is the enduring legacy of the past that has created the 'South African nightmare' that her book documents and analyses.

Rape, her argument goes, is not incidental to South African lives, but is a central discourse in how we think about the relationship between knowledge and care. Gqola's book is an analysis of rape, but it is also a reflection on the ethics of scholarship and knowledge. Who is to document, who should see suffering, who must be believed, and why do we write; these are questions germane to her project. In chapter 5, I wrote about scholarship that excavates tunnels between home and university, connecting the bloods. Gqola's activist project and Muholi's artworks bring into view that which is often not spoken of. They do so through placing at the centre of our knowledge and experience the 'tunnel' or passage through which women's menstrual blood flows. In a document written for an exhibition of *Isilumo Siyaluma* at Blank Gallery in Cape Town, Muholi wrote: 'The passage in which we bleed // The passage where we are/were born // The passage through which we become (wo)men? // The erotic passage meant to be aroused, is raped // The passage we love is hated and called names // The sacred passage is ever persecuted' (Muholi 2011). Muholi's poetic text draws together the painfully layered meanings of the word 'passage', a corridor or tunnel that connects each one of us to the mother whose body hosted us during pregnancy.

A curious feature of the many scholarly and activist responses to Muholi's menstrual work is the fact that it typically elides the references to mothers ('The passage where we are/were born') in favour of the activist LGBTI+ agenda. Gabeba Baderoon (2014) provides an insightful analysis of how mothers figure in the work of Muholi and Mary Sibande, but her article does not include a discussion of the bloods artworks. In chapter 6 I cited Muholi saying to Baderoon that all her work is about her mother. How do we interpret this absent presence, and how can it generate new insights for the project of reading the bloods? The outflow of menstrual blood is normally a marker of an absence of pregnancy, and many women have waited anxiously for the 'blood test' that is the onset of a menstrual period – either wishing for it to come as a sign of lack of pregnancy, or in hope of its absence. Menstrual blood is a blood of reproduction (of itself, as it is cyclically renewed, but also because menstruation marks the body's potential to host life) and also a marker of time. It is the blood that transmits that which is carried on, and in which the lost mother whom Muholi writes about can be recuperated symbolically. When Koleka Putuma thanks the 'womxn' who made her, she is thinking back through this bloodline, documenting and acknowledging the flows of love and care.

In Makhosazana Xaba's moving wish to have been present at her own birth, we see another version of this care. Xaba imagines having been there to be the midwife accompanying her mother while she gave birth. The midwife would be able to document, through caring protocols, the mother's labour and so, backwards through the bloods, to extend care to her. Xaba imagines the different forms of knowledge (knowledge as care) that she would have brought to that scene. Here is a way of countering the tropes of newness and 'birth' of a new nation, through the retrospective care, up and down the bloodlines, of the 'womxn' who cared for us. This retrospective care is what Muholi's testimony, and her injunction that 'we must document', replicates and advocates.

'Pain', writes Pumla Gqola, 'is a valid form of knowledge, whether it be the pain of firsthand experience or empathetic pain' (2015: 169). In the activist forms of art and scholarship analysed in my concluding chapter, there is a commitment to documenting forms of knowledge that are the result of pain. Part of this activist project of knowledge production includes attention to the moment when the pain is logged and documented. The personal cost of this kind of scholarship is high, and the process fraught with dangers. When the phrase 'telling our stories' is used, it is often understood as positive, or at least neutral – a mirror held up in which 'we' see our faces. Through the self-reflective words of Gqola and Muholi we are urged not only to witness that about which they tell us, but also to consider the costs of the way knowledge is produced and circulated.

I return here to the comments on self-help genres, and to self-help as a model for activist and regenerative scholarship. The needle that pierces the skin so that the blood sample can be taken, in this version of scholarship, returns the knowledge to the body from which the bloods came. Reading the bloods, listening to (and believing) the stories, creating ethical protocols for knowledge production and dissemination: this is scholarship as ongoing form of care. In this book I have referred to the many writers and intellectuals whose work does precisely this, to chronicle as a way of extending care. Reading the bloods with these protocols of care means to read the blood not as 'emergent' or as 'new' and 'free', but instead as part of the project of keeping alive what Walter Benjamin describes as the revolutionary spark of the past.

This book has argued that blood, rather than the skin that has been a dominant category through which to understand South Africa, provides us with a way of reading the unfolding and surging present. Blood is hidden and invisible, but always richly encrypted with meanings. To document and to log the bloods is part of convening communities of care. I have shown that in the work of many writers and thinkers the urge to archive and to log is accompanied by fierce debates not only about *what* should be remembered, but what the very terms are of documenting and reading these events. An important consideration in these debates is for whose benefit the bloods are collected and read. A blood test gives us this language through which to talk about reading (reading the social, reading texts) as test event. In blood testing, there is often a lag between what is occurring in the body and what can be read in the blood; the date stamp on the blood is as important as the careful logging of the moment of testing. In the 1990s it seemed that memory and commemorative projects were the key to making the future. In the thinking and writings of a younger generation, it has become evident that the making of the future is stickier and bloodier, the terms of its making an ongoing form of warfare. The chapters in this book have shown that the multidirectional and intergenerational meanings of the past in the present sometimes surge and flow in reinvigorating currents. At other times they are arrested or blocked; but they always leave a mark.

Bibliography

Abantu Book Festival programme (2017), http://www.abantubookfestival.co.za/images/Abantu%20PDF.pdf (accessed 5 September 2018).

Adejunmobi, Moradewun (2017), 'Afterword: Genre Queries, African Studies', *The Cambridge Journal of Postcolonial Literary Inquiry* 4(2): 258–64.

Agnew, Vanessa (2007), 'History's Affective Turn: Historical Reenactment and its Work in the Present', *Rethinking History: The Journal of Theory and Practice* 11(3): 299–312.

Ahmed, Sara (2004), *The Cultural Politics of Emotion*, Edinburgh: Edinburgh University Press.

Ahmed, Sara (2010), *The Promise of Happiness*, Durham, NC: Duke University Press.

Ahmed, Sara (2015), 'Selfcare as Warfare', post on *Feministkilljoys*, https://feministkilljoys.com/2014/08/25/selfcare-as-warfare/ (accessed 5 September 2018).

Alexander, Neville (1994), *Robben Island Dossier, 1964–1974*, Cape Town: UCT Press.

Alexander, Peter, Thapelo Lekgowa, Botsang Mmope, Luke Sinwell and Bongani Xeswi (2012), *Marikana – A View from the Mountain and a Case to Answer*, Auckland Park: Jacana.

Ally, Shireen (2009), *From Servants to Workers: South African Domestic Workers and the Democratic State*, Ithaca, NY: Cornell University Press.

Altman, Lawrence K, (2001), 'Christiaan Barnard, 78, Surgeon for First Heart Transplant, Dies', *The New York Times*, 3 September.

Ancer, Jonathan (2017), *Spy: Uncovering Craig Williamson*, Auckland Park: Jacana.

Anderson, Benedict (1983), *Imagined Communities: Reflections on the Origin and Spread of Nationalism*, London: Verso.

Anonymous (2016), 'Eugene de Kock Asked to Leave *Sunday Times* Literary Awards Shortlist Event', https://www.businesslive.co.za/bd/national/2016-05-16-apartheid-assassin-de-kock-asked-to-leave-award-shortlist-announcement/ (accessed 19 September 2018).

Anouilh, Jean (2008), *Antigone*, Paris: La Table Ronde.

Apel, Dora (2014), 'Torture Culture: Lynching Photographs and the Images of Abu Ghraib', *Art Journal* 64(2): 88–100.

Arendt, Hannah (2006 [1963]), *Eichmann in Jerusalem: A Report on the Banality of Evil*, New York: Penguin.

Ayelew Asfah, Semeneh (n.d.), 'The Young and the Urban in Addis Ababa: Towards a Popular History of Revolution in Ethiopia, c. 1950–1974', incomplete and interrupted PhD project, MISR Makerere University.

Baderoon, Gabeba (2014), 'The Ghost in the House: Women, Race, and Domesticity in South Africa', *The Cambridge Journal of Postcolonial Literary Inquiry* 1(2): 173–88.

Baderoon, Gabeba (2017), 'Animal Likenesses: Dogs and the Boundary of the Human in South Africa', *Journal of African Cultural Studies* 29(3): 345–61, http://www.tandfonline.com/doi/abs/10.1080/13696815.2016.1255599 (accessed 5 September 2018).

Barber, Karin (2007), *The Anthropology of Texts, Persons and Publics: Oral and Written Culture in Africa and Beyond*, Cambridge: Cambridge University Press.

Barnard, Christiaan (1977), *South Africa: Sharp Dissection*, Cape Town: Tafelberg.

Barnard, Christiaan (1993), *The Second Life: Memoirs*, ed. Chris Brewer, Cape Town: Vlaeberg.

Barnard, Christiaan (1996), *The Donor*, London: Penguin.

Barnard, Christiaan, and Curtis Bell Pepper (1969), *One Life*, Toronto: Macmillan.

Barnard, Christiaan, and Siegfried Stander (1975), *The Unwanted*, London: Arrow.

Barnard, Rita (ed.) (2014), *The Cambridge Companion to Nelson Mandela*, Cambridge: Cambridge University Press.

Bell, Terry (2003), *Unfinished Business: South Africa, Apartheid and Truth*, New York: Verso.

Benjamin, Walter (1973), *Illuminations*, London: Fontana.

Benthien, Claudia (2002), *Skin: On the Cultural Border Between Self and the World*, New York: Columbia University Press.

Best, Stephen, and Sharon Marcus (2009), 'Surface Reading: An Introduction', *Representations* 108(1): 1–21.

Blignaut, Charl (2016), 'Black to the Future: Why You Should go to the Abantu Book Festival', *City Press*, 27 November, http://www.w24.co.za/Entertainment/Books/black-to-the-future-why-you-should-go-to-the-abantu-book-festival-20161127-2 (accessed 5 September 2018).

'Blood as Archive of Dignity and Intimacy' (2017), workshop held at Princeton Institute for International and Regional Studies, http://piirs.princeton.edu/event/blood-archive-dignity-and-intimacy (accessed 5 September 2018).

Booysen, Susan (ed.) (2016), *Fees Must Fall: Student Revolt, Decolonisation and Governance in South Africa*, Johannesburg: Wits University Press.

Branch, Adam, and Zachariah Mampilly (2015), *Africa Uprising: Popular Protest and Political Change*, London: Zed Books.

Breckenridge, Keith (2014), *Biometric State: The Global Politics of Identification and Surveillance in South Africa, 1850 to the Present*, Cambridge: Cambridge University Press.

Breier, Mignonne, Angelique Wildschut and Thando Mgqolozana (2008), *Nursing in a New Era*, HSRC Research Brief, no. 1, http://repository.hsrc.ac.za/handle/20.500.11910/6610 (accessed 5 September 2018).

Breier, Mignonne, Angelique Wildschut and Thando Mgqolozana (2009), *Public Nursing Training in Neglect*, http://repository.hsrc.ac.za/handle/20.500.11910/4793?show=full (accessed 5 September 2018).

Buxbaum, Lara (2017), 'Risking Intimacy in Contemporary South African Fiction', *Textual Practice* 31(3): 523–36, http://www.tandfonline.com/doi/full/10.1080/0950236X.2017.1295613 (accessed 5 September 2018).

Bwa Mwesigire, Bwesigye (2014), 'On Writivism: Promoting Literature by Africans to Africans on the Continent', *Sunday Times* BooksLive, 13 June, http://tiahbeautement.bookslive.co.za/blog/2014/06/13/ssda-guest-post-by-bwesigye-bwa-mwesigire-on-writivism/ (accessed 5 September 2018).

Bwa Mwesigire, Bwesigye (2017a), 'A Brief History of African Literary Festivals', unpublished paper prepared for Africa Writes Festival, London, July 2017.

Bwa Mwesigire, Bwesigye (2017b), unpublished manuscript on #RMF.

Bystrom, Kerry (2016), *Democracy at Home in South Africa: Family Fictions and Transitional Culture*, New York: Palgrave Macmillan.

Bystrom, Kerry, and Sarah Nuttall (2013), 'Introduction: Private Lives and Public Cultures in South Africa', *Cultural Studies* 27(3): 307–42.

Carsten, Janet (2013), 'Introduction: Blood Will Out', *Journal of the Royal Anthropological Institute*, Special Issue, S1-S23.

Chauke, Clinton (2018), *Born in Chains: The Diary of an Angry 'Born Free'*, Johannesburg: Jonathan Ball.

Cheng, Anne Anlin (2009), 'Skins, Tattoos, and Susceptibility', *Representations* 108(1): 98–119.

Chicago, Judy (1996), *Beyond the Flower: The Autobiography of a Feminist Artist*, New York: Penguin.

Chigumadzi, Panashe (2013), 'A New Self-identity for Africans', TEDx talk delivered in Johannesburg, https://www.youtube.com/watch?v=hemD116ipcg (accessed 5 September 2018).

Chigumadzi, Panashe (2015a), 'Of Coconuts, Consciousness and Cecil John Rhodes: Disillusionment and Disavowals of the Rainbow Nation', Ruth First Memorial Lecture, 18 August, http://vanguardmagazine.co.za/of-coconuts-consciousness-and-cecil-john-rhodes/ (accessed 19 September 2018)

Chigumadzi, Panashe (2015b), 'Why I Call Myself a "Coconut" to Claim my Place in Post-apartheid South Africa', *The Guardian*, 24 August, https://www.theguardian.com/world/2015/aug/24/south-africa-race-panashe-chigumadzi-ruth-first-lecture (accessed 5 September 2018).

Chigumadzi, Panashe (2016), 'Small Deaths', *Transition* 121: 148–63.

Chigumadzi, Panashe (2018), *These Bones Will Rise Again*, London: Indigo Press.

Clifford, James (1988), *The Predicament of Culture: Twentieth-Century Ethnography, Literature, and Art*, Cambridge, MA: Harvard University Press.

Cock, Jacklyn (1980), *Maids and Madams: A Study in the Politics of Exploitation*, Johannesburg: Ravan.

Coetzee, Carli (2001), '"They Never Wept, the Men of my Race": Antjie Krog's *Country of my Skull* and the White South African Signature', *Journal of Southern African Studies* 27(4): 685–96.

Coetzee, Carli (2013a), 'Sihle Khumalo, *Cape to Cairo*, and Questions of Intertextuality: How to Write about Africa, How to Read about Africa', *Research in African Literatures* 44(2): 62–75.

Coetzee, Carli (2013b), *Accented Futures: Language Activism and the Ending of Apartheid*, Johannesburg: Wits University Press.

Coetzee, Carli (2016), 'Academic Freedom in Contexts', *Arts and Humanities in Higher Education* 15(2): 200–8.
Coetzee, Carli (2017), 'Self-help as Warfare: Lola Akande's Campus Novel and What it Takes to be a Woman who Succeeds on a University Campus', *Africa in Words*, 11 September, https://africainwords.com/2017/09/11/self-help-as-warfare-lola-akandes-campus-novel-and-what-it-takes-to-be-a-woman-who-succeeds-on-a-university-campus/ (accessed 5 September 2018).
Coetzee, Carli (2018), 'Unsettling the Air-Conditioned Room: Journal Work as Ethical Labour', *JALA*. DOI: 10.1080/21674736.208.1501979.
Coetzee, J. M. (1999), *Disgrace*, London: Vintage.
Collis-Buthelezi, Victoria J. (2017), 'The Case for Black Studies in South Africa', *The Black Scholar: Journal of Black Studies and Research* 47(2): 7–21.
Comaroff, Jean, and John Comaroff (2002), 'Alien-Nation: Zombies, Immigrants, and Millennial Capitalism', *South Atlantic Quarterly* 101(4): 779–805.
Connor, Steven (2004), *The Book of Skin*, London: Reaktion.
Cooper, David K. (2001), 'Christiaan Barnard: Flamboyant Surgeon Famed for First Heart Transplant Operation', *The Guardian*, 3 September, https://www.theguardian.com/news/2001/sep/03/guardianobituaries.medicalscience (accessed 5 September 2018).
Cotton, Michael, Rosemary Hickman and Anwar Suleman Mall (2014), 'Hamilton Naki, his Life and his Role in the First Heart Transplant', *Royal College of Surgeons of England Bulletin* 96: 224–7.
Dahlqvist, Anna (2018), *It's Only Blood: Shattering the Taboo of Menstruation*, London: Zed Books.
Dangarembga, Tsitsi (1988), *Nervous Conditions*, London: The Women's Press.
De Kock, Eugene, and Jeremy Gordin (1998), *A Long Night's Damage: Working for the Apartheid State*, Johannesburg: Contra Press.
Delaney, Janice, Mary Jane Lupton and Emily Toth (1988), *The Curse: A Cultural History of Menstruation*, Urbana, IL: University of Illinois Press.
Digby, Anne, and Howard Phillips, with Harriet Deacon and Kirsten Thomson (2008), *At the Heart of Healing: Groote Schuur Hospital*, Auckland Park: Jacana.
Dlamini, Jacob (2009), *Native Nostalgia*, Auckland Park: Jacana.
Dlamini, Jacob (2014), *Askari: A Story of Collaboration and Betrayal in the Anti-Apartheid Struggle*, Auckland Park: Jacana.
Dlamini, Nonhlanhla (2014), 'Ironies and Contradictions in Neo-traditional Xhosa Masculinity: Silence and Shame', http://postamble.org/portfolio/neo-traditional-xhosa-masculinity/
Dlamini, Nonhlanhla (2015), 'The Transformation of Masculinity in Contemporary Black South African Novels', PhD thesis, University of the Witwatersrand.
Dodson, Sandra, and Rosamund Haden (eds) (2008), *Just Keep Breathing: South African Birth Stories*, Auckland Park: Jacana.
Douglas, Mary (1966), *Purity and Danger: An Analysis of the Concepts of Pollution and Taboo*, London: Routledge and Kegan Paul.
Dovey, Lindiwe (2009), *African Film and Literature: Adapting Violence to the Screen*, New York: Columbia University Press.

Driver, Dorothy (2005), 'Truth, Reconciliation, Gender: The South African Truth and Reconciliation Commission and Black Women's Intellectual History', *Australian Feminist Studies* 20(47): 219–29.
Dubow, Jessica, and Ruth Rosengarten (2004), 'History as the Main Complaint: William Kentridge and the Making of Post-Apartheid South Africa', *Art History* 27(4): 671–90.
Dubow, Saul (2006), *A Commonwealth of Knowledge: Science, Sensibility and White South Africa, 1820–2000*, Oxford: Oxford University Press.
Dubow, Saul (2014), *Apartheid: 1948–1994*, Oxford: Oxford University Press.
Ebewo, Patrick J. (2015), 'Mandela's Funeral as Community Performance', *Pula: Botswana Journal of African Studies* 29(2), http://journals.ub.bw/index.php/pula/article/view/747 (accessed 19 September 2018).
Ehrenreich, Barbara, and Arlie Russell Hochschild (eds) (2003), *Global Woman: Nannies, Maids and Sex Workers in the New Economy*, London: Granta.
Elkins, Caroline (2005), *Imperial Reckoning: The Untold Story of Britain's Gulag in Kenya*, New York: Henry Holt.
Erasmus, Zimitri (2017), *Race Otherwise: Forging a New Humanism for South Africa*, Johannesburg: Wits University Press.
Fairbanks, Eve (2015), 'Why South African Students Have Turned on Their Parents' Generation', *The Guardian*, 18 November, https://www.theguardian.com/news/2015/nov/18/why-south-african-students-have-turned-on-their-parents-generation (accessed 5 September 2018).
Falola, Toyin (2017), 'In Memoriam: Barbara Harlow, 1948–2017', https://groups.google.com/forum/#!topic/usaafricadialogue/_1GtirdJNJ8 (accessed 5 September 2018).
Farber, Leora (2015), 'Archival Addresses: Photographs, Practices, Positionalities', *Critical Arts* 29(1): 1–12.
First, Ruth (2010 [1965]), *117 Days: An Account of Confinement and Interrogation under the South African 90-Day Detention Law*, London: Virago.
Fonn, Sharon, and Makhosazana Xaba (2001), 'Health Workers for Change: Developing the Initiative', *Health Policy and Planning* 16(1): 13–18.
Fontein, Joost, and John Harries (2013), 'Editorial: The Vitality and Efficacy of Human Substances', *Critical African Studies* 5(3): 115–26.
Frank, Anne (2007), *The Diary of a Young Girl*, London: Puffin.
Frankel, Glenn (1999), *Rivonia's Children: Three Families and the Price of Freedom in South Africa*, London: Weidenfeld and Nicolson.
Fugard, Athol (1993), *Township Plays*, Oxford: Oxford University Press.
Gallop, Jane (1988), *Thinking Through the Body*, New York: Columbia University Press.
Gamedze, T., and A. Gamedze (2015), 'Salon for What', *Johannesburg Workshop in Theory and Criticism* 9, https://jwtc.org.za/the_salon/volume_9/thuli_gamedze.htm (accessed 19 September 2018).
Gikandi, Simon (2011), *Slavery and the Culture of Taste*, Princeton, NJ: Princeton University Press.

Giliomee, Hermann (2003), *The Afrikaners: Biography of a People*, Cape Town: Tafelberg.
Gilroy, Paul (2004), *After Empire: Melancholia or Convivial Culture? Multiculture or Postcolonial Melancholia*, London: Routledge.
Glaser, Linda B. (2016), '"Skin" Was Theme of Society for the Humanities Event', *Cornell Chronicle*, 23 January.
Gobodo-Madikizela, Pumla (2003), *A Human Being Died that Night: Forgiving Apartheid's Chief Killer*, London: Portobello Books.
Godsell, Gillian, and Rekgotofetse Chikane (2016), 'The Roots of the Revolution', in Susan Booysen (ed.), *Fees Must Fall: Student Revolt, Decolonisation and Governance in South Africa*, Johannesburg: Wits University Press, 54–73.
Godsell, Gillian, Refiloe Lepere, Swankie Mafoko and Ayabonga Nase (2016), 'Documenting the Revolution', in Susan Booysen (ed.), *Fees Must Fall: Student Revolt, Decolonisation and Governance in South Africa*, Johannesburg: Wits University Press, 101–24.
Goldblatt, Beth, and Sheila Meintjes (1997), 'Dealing with the Aftermath: Sexual Violence and the Truth and Reconciliation Commission', *Agenda: Empowering Women for Gender Equity* 36: 7–18.
Goniwe, Thembinkosi, and Pumla Dineo Gqola (2005), 'A Neglected Heritage: The Aesthetics of Complex Black Masculinities', *Agenda* 19(63): 80–94.
Gqirina, Thulani (2016), 'Eugene de Kock Spotted in Franschhoek', http://www.news24.com/SouthAfrica/News/eugene-de-kock-spotted-in-franschoek-20160514 (accessed 5 September 2018).
Gqola, Pumla Dineo (2006), 'Through Zanele Muholi's Eyes: Re/Imagining Ways of Seeing Black Lesbians', in Sophie Perryer (ed.), *Zanele Muholi: Only Half the Picture*, Cape Town: Michael Stevenson, 82–9.
Gqola, Pumla Dineo (2007), '"A Woman Cannot Marry a Boy": Rescue, Spectacle and Transitional Xhosa Masculinities', in Tamara Shefer, Kopano Ratele, Anna Strebel, Nokuthla Shabalala and Rosemarie Buikema (eds), *From Boys to Men*, Cape Town: UCT Press, 145–59.
Gqola, Pumla Dineo (2009), '"The Difficult Task of Normalizing Freedom": Spectacular Masculinities, Ndebele's Literary/Cultural Commentary and Post-apartheid Life', *English in Africa* 36(1): 61–76.
Gqola, Pumla Dineo (2010), *What is Slavery to Me? Postcolonial/Slave Memory in Post-Apartheid South Africa*, Johannesburg: Wits University Press.
Gqola, Pumla Dineo (2015), *Rape: A South African Nightmare*, Johannesburg: MF Books.
Gqola, Pumla Dineo (2017), *Reflecting Rogue – Inside the Mind of a Feminist*, Johannesburg: MF Books.
Graybill, Lynn (2001), 'The Contribution of the Truth and Reconciliation Commission toward the Promotion of Women's Rights in South Africa', *Women's Studies International Forum* 24(1): 1–10.
Gready, M., B. Klugman, M. Xaba, E. Boikanyo and H. Rees (1997), 'South African Women's Experiences of Contraception and Contraceptive Services', https://www.popline.org/node/274318 (accessed 5 September 2018).

Gready, Paul (2007), 'Autobiography and the "Power of Writing": Political Prison Writing in the Apartheid Era', *Journal of Southern African Studies* 19(3): 489–523.
Green, Louise (2016), 'Apartheid's Wolves: Political Animals and Animal Politics', *Critical African Studies* 8(2): 146–60.
Green, Louise, and Noëleen Murray (2009), 'Notes for a Guide to the Ossuary', *African Studies* 68(3): 370–86.
Guffey, Elizabeth (2006), *Retro: The Culture of Revival*, London: Reaktion.
Harlow, Barbara (1992), *Barred: Women, Writing and Political Detention*, Hanover, NH: Wesleyan University Press.
Harlow, Barbara (1996), *After Lives: Legacies of Revolutionary Writing*, London: Verso.
Harlow, Barbara (2009), 'Tortured Thoughts: From Marshall Square to Guantánamo Bay', *Biography* 32(1): 26–42.
Harraway, Donna (2003), *The Companion Species Manifesto: Dogs, People, and Significant Otherness*, Chicago: Prickly Paradigm Press, http://xenopraxis.net/readings/haraway_companion.pdf (accessed 5 September 2018).
Harraway, Donna (2006), 'Entangling Dogs, Baboons, Philosophers, and Biologists', *Configurations* 14(1, 2): 97–114.
Harraway, Donna (2016), *Staying with the Trouble: Making Kin in the Chthulucene*, Durham, NC: Duke University Press.
Harrow, Kenneth W. (2013), *Trash: African Cinema from Below*, Bloomington, IN: Indiana University Press.
Hassim, Shireen (2014), 'A Life of Refusal: Winnie Madikizela-Mandela and Violence in South Africa', *Storia delle Donne* 10: 55–77.
Hergé (2012 [1949]), *Tintin: Prisoners of the Sun*, Copenhagen: Egmont.
Hill Collins, Patricia, and Sirma Bilge (2016), *Intersectionality*, Cambridge: Polity.
Hinz, Manfred, and Moudi Hangula (2009), '"A Man is not a Man Unless …": Male Circumcision – A Legal Problem?', in Oliver C. Ruppel (ed.), *Children's Rights in Namibia*, Windhoek: Konrad Adenauer Stiftung, 267–82.
Hirsch, Marianne (1997), *Family Frames*, Cambridge, MA: Harvard University Press.
Hlongwane, Gugu (2013), '"In Every Classroom Children Are Dying": Race, Power and Nervous Conditions in Kopano Matlwa's *Coconut*', *Alternation* 20(1): 9–25, http://alternation.ukzn.ac.za/Files/docs/20.1/Alternation%2020.1%20(2013).pdf#page=14 (accessed 5 September 2018).
Hlongwane, Gugu, and Khondo Mtshali (2016), 'Mentoring, Masculinity and Reparation in Mgqolozana's *A Man Who is Not a Man*', *African Identities* 15(1): 100–11, http://www.tandfonline.com/doi/abs/10.1080/14725843.2016.1175922 (accessed 5 September 2018).
Hodes, Rebecca (2017), 'Briefing: Questioning "Fees Must Fall"', *African Affairs* 116(462): 140–50.
Houppert, Karen (1999), *The Curse: Confronting the Last Unmentionable Taboo: Menstruation*, New York: Farrar, Straus and Giroux.
Iqani, Mehita (2015), 'The Consummate Material Girl? The Contested Consumption of Winnie Madikizela-Mandela in Early Post-Apartheid Media Representations', *Feminist Media Studies* 15(5): 779–93.

Jablonski, Nina G. (2006), *Skin: A Natural History*, Berkeley, CA: University of California Press.
Jansen, Anemari (2015), *Eugene de Kock: Sluipmoordenaar van die Staat*, Cape Town: Tafelberg.
Jansen, Ena (2015), *Soos Familie: Stedelike Huiswerkers in Suid-Afrikaanse Tekste*, Pretoria: Pretoria Boekhuis.
Johnson, Christopher H., Bernhard Jussen, David Warren Sabean and Simon Teuscher (eds) (2013), *Blood and Kinship: Matter for Metaphor from Ancient Rome to the Present*, Oxford: Berghahn Books.
Jones, Megan, and Jacob Dlamini (eds) (2013), *Categories of Persons: Rethinking Ourselves and Others*, Johannesburg: Picador Africa.
Jones, Rebecca (2019), 'How to be a Writer in Your 30s in Lagos: Self-help Literature and the Creation of Authority in Africa', in Moradewun Adejunmobi and Carli Coetzee (eds), *The Routledge Handbook of African Literature*, London: Routledge.
Joubert, Elsa (1980), *The Long Journey of Poppie Nongena*, Johannesburg: Jonathan Ball.
Judt, Tony (2010), *The Memory Chalet*, London: William Heinemann.
Kasibe, Wandile, and Thuli Gamedze (2015), 'Rhodes Must Fall Photo Essay', *Johannesburg Workshop in Theory and Criticism* 9, https://jwtc.org.za/the_salon/volume_9/kasibe_gamedze.htm (accessed 19 September 2018).
Kathrada, Ahmed (2004), *Memoirs*, Cape Town: Zebra Press.
Kathrada, Ahmed (2008), *A Simple Freedom: The Strong Mind of Robben Island Prisoner, No. 468/64*, Highlands North: Wild Dog Press.
Kinney, Alison (2016), *Hood*, London: Bloomsbury.
Knight, Chris (1991), *Blood Relations: Menstruation and the Origins of Culture*, New Haven, CT: Yale University Press,
Krog, Antjie (1989), *Lady Anne*, Cape Town: Taurus.
Krog, Antjie (1998), *Country of my Skull*, Johannesburg, Random House.
Krog, Antjie (2003), *A Change of Tongue*, Johannesburg, Random House.
Krog, Antjie (2013), 'Shards, Memory and the Mileage of Myth', in Megan Jones and Jacob Dlamini (eds), *Categories of Persons: Rethinking Ourselves and Others*, Johannesburg: Picador Africa, 66–88.
Krog, Antjie (2015), 'Can an Evil Man Change? The Repentance of Eugene de Kock', *The New York Times Sunday Review*, 13 March, https://www.nytimes.com/2015/03/14/opinion/sunday/the-repentance-of-eugene-de-kock-apartheid-assassin.html?_r=0 (accessed 5 September 2018).
Krog, Antjie, Nosisi Mpolweni and Kopano Ratele (2009), *There was this Goat: Investigating the Truth Commission Testimony of Notrose Nobomvu Konile*, Scottsville: University of KwaZulu-Natal Press.
Lee, Rebekah (2013a), 'Mandela: In South Africa, Death and Politics are Bedfellows', http://theconversation.com/mandela-in-south-africa-death-and-politics-are-bedfellows-21301 (accessed 5 September 2018).
Lee, Rebekah (2013b), 'Funeral Frenzy: Mourners, Entrepreneurs and the Price of Death in Africa', http://www.huffingtonpost.co.uk/dr-rebekah-lee/africa-funerals-death-_b_3344902.html (accessed 5 September 2018).

Lindner, Christoph, and Miriam Meissner (eds) (2016), *Global Garbage: Urban Imaginaries of Waste, Excess, and Abandonment*, London: Routledge.
Lodge, Tom (2006), *Mandela: A Critical Life*, Oxford: Oxford University Press.
Logan, Chris (2003), *Celebrity Surgeon: Christiaan Barnard – A Life*, Johannesburg and Cape Town: Jonathan Ball.
Madikizela-Mandela, Winnie (2013), *491 Days: Prisoner Number 1323/69*, Athens, OH: Ohio University Press.
Makhubu, Nomusa M. (2012), 'Violence and the Cultural Logics of Pain: Representations of Sexuality in the Work of Nicholas Hlobo and Zanele Muholi', *Critical Arts* 26(4): 504–24.
Makhulu, Anne-Maria (2015), *Making Freedom: Apartheid, Squatter Politics, and the Struggle for Home*, Durham, NC: Duke University Press.
Makwabe, Buyekezwa (2013), 'We Stole Chris Barnard's Boots', *Sunday Times*, 20 October, https://www.pressreader.com/south-africa/sunday-times/20131020/281685432579794 (accessed 5 September 2018).
Malan, Rian (1990), *My Traitor's Heart, Blood and Bad Dreams: A South African Explores the Madness in his Country, his Tribe and Himself*, London: Vintage.
Malcolm, Janet (1997), *The Journalist and the Murderer*, London: Granta.
Malecowna, Jennifer (2015), '"Look at Yourselves – It's Very Abnormal": Thando Mgqolozana Quits South Africa's "White Literary System"', http://bookslive.co.za/blog/2015/05/18/look-at-yourselves-its-very-abnormal-thando-mgqolozana-quits-south-africas-white-literary-system/ (accessed 5 September 2018).
Malecowna, Jennifer (2016), 'Not Welcome: Thabiso Mahlape and Lauren Beukes on Eugene de Kock's Presence at the Sunday Times Literary Awards Shortlist Event', http://bookslive.co.za/blog/2016/05/15/not-welcome-thabiso-mahlape-and-lauren-beukes-on-eugene-de-kocks-presence-at-the-sunday-times-literary-awards-shortlist-event/ (accessed 5 September 2018).
Mall, Anwar Suleman (2007), 'Hamilton Naki – a Surgical Sherpa', *South African Medical Journal* 97(2): 95–6.
Mallinson, Theresa (2015), 'Thando Mgqolozana: "The Audience does not Treat Me as a Literary Talent, but as an Anthropological Subject"', *Daily Vox*, 15 May, https://www.thedailyvox.co.za/thando-mgqolozana-the-audience-does-not-treat-me-as-a-literary-talent-but-as-an-anthropological-subject/ (accessed 5 September 2018).
Mandela, Nelson (1994), *Long Walk to Freedom: The Autobiography of Nelson Mandela*, London: Little, Brown.
Mandela, Nelson (2010), *Nelson Mandela: Conversations with Myself*, London: Macmillan.
Mangcu, Xolela (2016), '"Mandela does not Represent Entire Liberation Struggle", Says Oppenheimer Award Winner', *UCT News*, https://www.news.uct.ac.za/article/-2016-06-09-mandela-does-not-represent-entire-liberation-struggle-saysnbspoppenheimernbspawardnbspwinner (accessed 19 September 2018).
Marks, Shula (1983), 'Ruth First: A Tribute', *Journal of Southern African Studies* 10(1): 123–8.

Marks, Shula (1994), *Divided Sisterhood: Race, Class and Gender in the South African Nursing Profession*, New York: Palgrave Macmillan.
Maroga, Kopano (2017), 'The Poetics of Remembrance as Resistance: The Work of Sethembile Msezane', *ArthThrob*, 27 February, https://artthrob.co.za/2017/02/27/the-poetics-of-remembrance-as-resistance-the-work-of-sethembile-msezane/ (accessed 5 September 2018).
Marouf, Moulay Driss el (2014), 'The Aesthetic and Practical Fields of Excrementality of L'boulevard festival', *Social Dynamics* 40(3): 575–88.
Marouf, Moulay Driss el (2016), 'Po(o)pular Culture: Measuring the "Shit" in Moroccan Music Festivals', *Journal of African Cultural Studies* 28(3): 327–42.
Martin, Emily (1987), *The Woman in the Body: A Cultural Analysis of Reproduction*, Milton Keynes: Open University Press.
Masango Chéry, Tshepo (2017), 'Beyond the Elder Statesman: Reflections on Teaching about Mandela and South Africa in Neo-Liberal Times', *The Black Scholar: Journal of Black Studies and Research* 47(2): 54–69.
Matandela, Mbali (2015), 'Stagnant Debates, Stagnant Minds', *Johannesburg Workshop in Theory and Criticism* 9, https://jwtc.org.za/the_salon/volume_9/mbali_matandela.htm (accessed 19 September 2018).
Matlwa, Kopano (2007), *Coconut*, Auckland Park: Jacana.
Matlwa, Kopano (2010), *Spilt Milk*, Auckland Park: Jacana.
Matlwa, Kopano (2016), *Period Pain*, Auckland Park: Jacana.
Matlwa Mabaso, Kopano (2016), 'What to do When a Moonshot Falls Short', TEDx talk, https://www.youtube.com/watch?v=rACJHUid7Lk (accessed 5 September 2018).
Matlwa, Kopano (2017), *Evening Primrose*, London: Hodder and Stoughton.
Matlwa Mabaso, Kopano (2018), 'External Quality Assessment of Health Facilities in South Africa: Strengths Appraised and Gaps Identified', PhD thesis, Oxford University.
Mazrui, Ali (1968), 'The Poetics of a Transplanted Heart', *Transition* 35: 50–9.
McDonald, Marianne (2006), 'The Return of Myth: Athol Fugard and the Classics', *Arion: A Journal of Humanities and the Classics*, 3rd series, 14(2): 21–48.
McKaiser, Eusebius (2015), *Run, Racist, Run: Journeys into the Heart of Racism*, Johannesburg: Bookstorm.
McRae, Donald (1997), *Every Second Counts: The Extraordinary Race to Transplant the First Human Heart*, London: Simon and Schuster.
Meyer, Melissa L. (2005), *Thicker than Water: The Origins of Blood as Symbol and Ritual*, London: Routledge.
Mgqolozana, Thando (2009), *A Man Who is Not a Man*, Auckland Park: Jacana.
Mgqolozana, Thando (2011), *Hear Me Not Alone*, Auckland Park: Jacana.
Mgqolozana, Thando (2014), *Un-Importance: A Novel*, Auckland Park: Jacana.
Mgqolozana, Thando (2015), '21 Suggestions for the Decolonisation of the South African Literary Scene', http://bookslive.co.za/blog/2015/05/19/thando-mgqolozana-outlines-21-suggestions-for-the-decolonisation-of-the-south-african-literary-scene/ (accessed 5 September 2018).

Mhlongo, Niq (2018), 'The Biography of a Generation – Niq Mhlongo Reviews Clinton Chauke's *Born in Chains: The Diary of an Angry 'Born Free'*', *Johannesburg Review of Books*, 6 June, https://johannesburgreviewofbooks.com/2018/06/04/city-editor-the-biography-of-a-generation-niq-mhlongo-reviews-clinton-chaukes-born-in-chains-the-diary-of-an-angry-born-free/ (accessed 5 September 2018).

Mkhabelo, Sabelo (2015), 'Camps Bay Reverse Township Tour', http://livemag.co.za/featured/watch-viral-video-camps-bay-suburb-reverse-township-tour/ (accessed 5 September 2018).

Modisane, Litheko (2013), *South Africa's Renegade Reels: The Making and Public Lives of Black-Centered Films*, New York: Palgrave Macmillan.

Modisane, Litheko (2014), 'Mandela in Film and Television', in Rita Barnard (ed.), *The Cambridge Companion to Nelson Mandela*, Cambridge, Cambridge University Press, 224–43.

Modisane, Litheko, Victoria J. Collis-Buthelezi and Christopher Ouma (2017), 'Introduction: Black Studies, South Africa, and the Mythology of Mandela', *The Black Scholar: Journal of Black Studies and Research* 47(2): 1–6.

Morante, Elsa (2001 [1974]), *History: A Novel*, trans. William Weaver, London: Penguin.

Mpofu, Shepherd (2017), 'Disruption as a Communicative Strategy: The Case of #FeesMustFall and #RhodesMustFall Students' Protests in South Africa', *Journal of African Media Studies* 9(2): 351–73.

Msimang, Sisonke (2014), 'Should we be Mad at Mandela?', *Daily Maverick*, 26 November, https://www.dailymaverick.co.za/opinionista/2014-11-26-should-we-be-mad-at-mandela/#.WfxEfFuoNow (accessed 5 September 2018).

Msimang, Sisonke (2017), *Always Another Country*, Cape Town: Jonathan Ball.

Muholi, Zanele (2011), *Isilumo Siyaluma*, http://www.blankprojects.com/exhibition-press/isilumo-siyaluma/ (accessed 5 September 2018).

Murphy, Philip (2015), 'Jack Gold's Early Film *Ninety Days* Deserves to be Remembered', *The Guardian*, 12 August, https://www.theguardian.com/tv-and-radio/2015/aug/12/letter-jack-gold-obituary (accessed 5 September 2018).

Murray, Jessica (2012), '"Pain is Beauty": The Politics of Appearance in Kopano Matlwa's *Coconut*', *English in Africa* 39(1): 91–107.

Musila, Grace Ahingula (2015), *A Death Retold in Truth and Rumour: Kenya, Britain and the Julie Ward Murder*, Woodbridge: Boydell and Brewer/James Currey.

Musila, Grace Ahingula (2016), 'Lot's Wife Syndrome and Double Publics in South Africa', *PMLA* 131(5): 1452–61.

Musila, Grace Ahingula (2018), 'MaKhumalo's Spaza Shop || Lena Moi's Dance', keynote speech delivered to the ASAUK2018 conference, September, Birmingham University UK.

Nathoo, Ayesha (2009), *Hearts Exposed: Transplants and the Media in 1960s Britain*, London: Palgrave Macmillan.

Ndangam, Lilian N. (2008), '"Lifting the Cloak on Manhood": Coverage of Xhosa Male Circumcision in the South African Press', in Egodi Uchendu (ed.), *Masculinities in Contemporary Africa*, Dakar: CODESRIA, 209–28.

Ndebele, Njabulo S. (1991), *Rediscovery of the Ordinary: Essays on South African Literature and Culture*, Johannesburg: COSAW.
Ndebele, Njabulo S. (1996), 'A Home for Intimacy', *Mail & Guardian*, 26 April, https://mg.co.za/article/1996-04-26-a-home-for-intimacy (accessed 5 September 2018).
Ndebele, Njabulo S. (2003), *The Cry of Winnie Mandela: A Novel*, Banbury: Ayebia Clarke Publishing.
Ndlovu, Isaac (2012), 'Prison and Solitary Confinement: Conditions and Limits of the Autobiographical Self', *English Studies in Africa* 55(1): 16–34.
Ndlovu, Musawenkosi (2017), *#FeesMustFall and Youth Mobilisation in South Africa: Reform or Revolution?*, New York: Routledge.
Ndlovu-Gatsheni, Sabelo J. (2016), *The Decolonial Mandela: Peace, Justice and the Politics of Life*, Oxford: Berghahn Books.
Newell, Stephanie (2008), 'Corresponding with the City: Self-Help Literature in Urban West Africa', *Journal of Postcolonial Writing* 44(1): 15–27.
Newell, Stephanie (2016a), 'Dirty Familiars: Colonial Encounters in African Cities', in Christoph Lindner and Miriam Meissner (eds), *Global Garbage: Urban Imaginaries of Waste, Excess, and Abandonment*, London: Routledge, 35–51.
Newell, Stephanie (2016b), 'Researching the Cultural Politics of Dirt in Urban Africa', in Shalini Puri and Debra A. Castillo (eds), *Theorizing Fieldwork in the Humanities*, New York: Palgrave Macmillan, 193–212.
Newell, Stephanie (2017), 'The Last Laugh: African Audience Responses to Colonial Health Propaganda Films', *Cambridge Journal of Postcolonial Literary Inquiry* 4(3): 347–61.
Newell, Stephanie (2018), 'Screening Dirt: Public Health Movies in Colonial Nigeria and Rural African Spectatorship in the 1930s and 1940s', *Social Dynamics* 44(1): 6–20.
Newell, Stephanie, and Louise Green (2018), 'Putting Dirt in its Place: The Cultural Politics of Dirt in Africa', *Social Dynamics* 44(1): 1–5
Ngcobo, Gabi (2010), 'It's Work as Usual: Framing Race, Class and Gender through a South African Lens', *AfricAvenir*, http://www.africavenir.org/publications/e-dossiers/revisions/gabi-ngcobo.html (accessed 5 September 2018).
Nuttall, Sarah (2006), 'A Politics of the Emergent: Cultural Studies in South Africa', *Theory, Culture & Society* 23(7–8): 263–78, http://journals.sagepub.com/doi/pdf/10.1177/0263276406073229 (accessed 5 September 2018).
Nuttall, Sarah (2009), *Entanglement: Literary and Cultural Reflections on Post-Apartheid*, Johannesburg: Wits University Press.
Nuttall, Sarah (2013), 'Wound, Surface, Skin', *Cultural Studies* 27(3): 418–37.
Nuttall, Sarah (2014), 'Surface, Depth and the Autobiographical Act: Texts and Images', *Life Writing* 11(2): 161–75.
Nuttall, Sarah, and Achille Mbembe (2014), 'Mandela's Mortality', in Rita Barnard (ed.), *The Cambridge Companion to Nelson Mandela*, Cambridge: Cambridge University Press, 267–90.
Nuttall, Sarah, and Achille Mbembe (2015), 'Secrecy's Softwares', *Current Anthropology* 56 (supplement 12), December, S317-S324.

Nuttall, Sarah, and Cheryl-Anne Michael (eds) (2000), *Senses of Culture: South African Cultural Studies*, Cape Town: Oxford University Press.
Nzerue, Chike M. (2006), 'Hamilton Naki, Transplant Surgeon', *Journal of the National Medical Association* 98(3): 448–9.
Olayiwola, Elizabeth (2017), 'We are God's Alternative: The Making of Mount Zion Evangelical Video Films in Nigeria and Beyond', unpublished paper presented at ASA of Africa Conference, University of Ghana, September.
Pauw, Jacques (1992), *In the Heart of the Whore: Apartheid's Death Squads*, Cape Town: Southern Book Publishers.
Pauw, Jacques (2011), *Dances with Devils: A Journalist's Search for the Truth*, Cape Town: Zebra Press.
Pauw, Jacques (2013a), *Into the Heart of Darkness – Confessions of Apartheid's Assassins*, Cape Town: Jonathan Ball.
Pauw, Jacques (2013b), 'Jacques Pauw on Vlakplaas' Apartheid Assassin, Dirk Coetzee', *Daily Maverick*, 8 March, https://www.dailymaverick.co.za/article/2013-03-08-jacques-pauw-on-vlakplaas-apartheid-assassin-dirk-coetzee/#.WRV6Cvnytow (accessed 5 September 2018).
Perryer, Sophie (ed.) (2006), *Zanele Muholi: Only Half the Picture*, Cape Town: Michael Stevenson Gallery.
Phalime, Maria (2014), *Postmortem: The Doctor Who Walked Away*, Cape Town: Tafelberg.
Phiri, Aretha (2013), 'Kopano Matlwa's *Coconut* and the Dialectics of Race in South Africa: Interrogating Images of Whiteness and Blackness in Black Literature and Culture', *Safundi* 14(2): 161–74.
Pinnock, Don (ed.) (2012), *Ruth First: Voices of Liberation*, Johannesburg: HSRC Press.
Plaatje, Solomon Tshekiso (1982 [1916]), *Native Life in South Africa*, Randburg: Ravan Writers Series.
Posel, Deborah, and Pamila Gupta (2009), 'The Life of the Corpse: Framing Reflections and Questions', *African Studies* 68(3): 299–309.
Putuma, Koleka (2017), *Collective Amnesia*, Cape Town: uHlanga Press.
Quayson, Ato (2003), *Calibrations: Reading for the Social*, Minneapolis, MN: University of Minnesota Press.
Raditlhalo, Tlhalo (2010), 'An Indefensible Obscenity: Fundamental Questions of Being in Kopano Matlwa's *Coconut*', *Imbizo* 1: 19–38.
Raji, Wumi (2005), 'Africanizing Antigone: Postcolonial Discourse and Strategies of Indigenizing a Western Classic', *Research in African Literatures* 36(4): 135–54.
Ramaphosa, Cyril (2015), 'Speaking Notes for Deputy President Cyril Ramaphosa at Youth Engagement at Harare Library, Khayelitsha', http://bookslive.co.za/blog/2015/02/12/cyril-ramaphosa-meets-with-lauren-beukes-and-thando-mgqolozana-to-discuss-sas-reading-culture/ (accessed 5 September 2018).
Ramphele, Mamphela (1995), *A Life*, Cape Town and Johannesburg: David Philip.
Ramphele, Mamphela (1996), 'Political Widowhood in South Africa: The Embodiment of Ambiguity', *Daedalus* 125(1): 99–117.

Rappert, Brian, and Chandré Gould (2017), *Dis-Eases of Secrecy: Tracing History, Memory & Justice*, Auckland Park: Jacana,
Ratele, Kopano (2013), 'Does He Speak Xhosa?', in Megan Jones and Jacob Dlamini (eds), *Categories of Persons: Rethinking Ourselves and Others*, Johannesburg: Picador Africa, 119–34.
Ratele, Kopano (2016), *Liberating Masculinities*, Cape Town: HSRC Press.
Rich, Adrienne (1986), *Of Woman Born: Motherhood as Experience and Institution*, New York: Norton.
Rogosin, Lionel (2004), *Come Back, Africa*, Parktown: STE Publishers.
Rosenstone, Robert A. (2003), 'The Reel Joan of Arc: Reflections on the Theory and Practice of the Historical Film', *The Public Historian* 25(3): 61–77.
Ross, Fiona C. (2003), *Bearing Witness: Women and the Truth and Reconciliation Commission in South Africa*, London: Pluto Press.
Rothberg, Michael (2009), *Multidirectional Memory: Remembering the Holocaust in the Age of Decolonization*, Stanford, CA: Stanford University Press,
Rothberg, Michael (2012), 'Progress, Progression, Procession: William Kentridge and the Narratology of Transitional Justice', *Narrative* 20(1): 1–24.
Roux, Daniel (2005), 'Aphanasis of/as the Subject: From Christopher Marlowe to Ruth First', *Shakespeare in Southern Africa* 17: 27–33.
Roux, Daniel (2006), '"I Speak To You and I Listen to the Voice Coming Back": Recording Solitary Confinement in the Apartheid Prison', *English Academy Review* 22(1): 22–31.
Roux, Daniel (2009), 'Jonny Steinberg's *The Number* and Prison Life Writing in Post-Apartheid South Africa', *Social Dynamics* 35(2): 231–43.
Roux, Daniel (2014a), 'Inside/Outside: Representing Prison Lives after Apartheid', *Life Writing* 11(2): 247–59.
Roux, Daniel (2014b), 'Mandela Writing/Writing Mandela', in Rita Barnard (ed.), *The Cambridge Companion to Nelson Mandela*, Cambridge: Cambridge University Press, 205–23.
Salley, Raél Jero (2012), 'Zanele Muholi's Elements of Survival', *African Arts* 45(4): 58–69.
Sampson, Anthony (2011), *Mandela: The Authorised Biography*, London: Harper Collins.
Satgar, Vishwas (2016), 'Bringing the Class Back In: Against Outsourcing during #FeesMustFall at Wits', in Susan Booysen (ed.), *Fees Must Fall: Student Revolt, Decolonisation and Governance in South Africa*, Johannesburg: Wits University Press, 214–34.
Schalkwyk, David (2001), 'Chronotopes of the Self in the Writings of Women Political Prisoners in South Africa', in Nahem Yousaf (ed.), *Apartheid Narratives*, Amsterdam and New York: Rodopi, 1–36.
Schalkwyk, David (2012), *Hamlet's Dreams: The Robben Island Shakespeare*, London: Bloomsbury.
Schalkwyk, David (2014), 'Mandela, the Emotions, and the Lessons of Prison', in Rita Barnard (ed.), *The Cambridge Companion to Nelson Mandela*, Cambridge: Cambridge University Press, 50–69.

Schwab, Gabriele (2010), *Haunting Legacies: Violent Histories and Transgenerational Trauma*, New York: Columbia University Press.
Segal, Lauren (2018), *Cancer: A Love Story*, Auckland Park: Jacana.
Seltzer, Mark (1997), 'Wound Culture: Trauma in the Pathological Public Sphere', *October* 80: 3–26.
Selvick, Stephanie (2015), 'Positive Bleeding: Violence and Desire in Works by Mlu Zondi, Zanele Muholi, and Makhosazana Xaba', *Safundi* 16(4): 443–65.
Shefer, Tamara, Kopano Ratele, Anna Strebel, Nokuthla Shabalala and Rosemarie Buikema (eds) (2007), *From Boys to Men*, Cape Town: UCT Press.
Shetterly, Margot Lee (2016), *Hidden Figures: The Story of the African-American Women Who Helped Win the Space Race*, New York: William Morrow/HarperCollins.
Shipley, Jesse (2015), 'Selfie Love: Public Lives in an Era of Celebrity Pleasure, Violence, and Social Media', *American Anthropologist* 117(2): 403–13.
Shobane (2016), 'The Art of Hypocrisy: Appeal to Reconstitute Shackville', *Mail & Guardian*, 8 March, http://thoughtleader.co.za/blackacademiccaucus/2016/03/08/the-art-of-hypocrisy-appeal-to-re-constitute-shackville/ (accessed 5 September 2018).
Slovo, Gillian (1997), *Every Secret Thing: My Family, My Country*, London: Little, Brown.
Slovo, Gillian (2010), 'Introduction', in Ruth First, *117 Days: An Account of Confinement and Interrogation under the South African 90-Day Detention Law*, London: Virago.
Slovo, Shawn (1988), *A World Apart*, London: Faber and Faber.
Smith, Margaret (1964), 'Ruth Slovo and her Children Quit S. Africa for Good', *Sunday Times*, 15 March, p. 5.
Sosibo, Kwanele (2016), 'Thando Mgqolozana on How Can We Decolonise SA Literature', *Mail & Guardian*, 14 March, https://mg.co.za/article/2016-03-14-author-mgqolozana-how-can-we-decolonise-sa-literature (accessed 5 September 2018).
Soyinka, Wole (1975), 'Neo-Tarzanism: The Poetics of Pseudo-Tradition', *Transition* 48: 38–44.
Spencer, Lynda Gichanda (2009), 'Young, Black and Female in Post-Apartheid South Africa: Identity Politics in Kopano Matlwa's *Coconut*', *Scrutiny2* 14(1): 66–78.
Spencer, Lynda Gichanda (2014), 'Writing Women in Uganda and South Africa: Emerging Writers from Post-repressive Regimes', PhD thesis, Stellenbosch University,
Starr, Douglas (1999), *Blood: An Epic History of Medicine and Commerce*, London: Little, Brown.
Steiner, George (1984), *Antigones*, Oxford: Clarendon Press.
Stone, Amanda (2014), 'Negotiating Feminine Absence: Menstruation and Visual Culture', MA thesis, Savannah College of Art and Design, http://ecollections.scad.edu/iii/cpro/DigitalItemViewPage.external;jsessionid=79B5F3A0AF813DB308 A9EBCE7D486873?lang=eng&sp=1002674&sp=T&sp=1&suite=de (accessed 19 September 2018).

Tattersall, Robert (2009), *Diabetes: The Biography*, Oxford: Oxford University Press.

Tlelima, Tiisetso (2016), 'Mental Illness in the Spotlight at the Abantu Book Festival', *This is Africa*, 14 December, https://thisisafrica.me/mental-illness-spotlight-abantu-book-festival/ (accessed 5 September 2018).

Tlhabi, Redi (2012), *Endings and Beginnings: A Story of Healing*, Auckland Park: Jacana.

Tucker, Bruce, and Sia Triantafyllos (2008), 'Lynndie England, Abu Ghraib, and the New Imperialism', *Canadian Review of American Studies* 38(1): 83–100.

Van der Leun, Justine (2015), 'The Odd Couple: Why an Apartheid Activist Joined Forces with a Murderer', *The Guardian*, 6 June, https://www.theguardian.com/global/2015/jun/06/odd-couple-apartheid-activist-madeleine-fullard-convicted-policeman-eugene-de-kock (accessed 5 September 2018).

Van Niekerk, Garreth (2016), 'Book, Art, Alchemy', *City Press*, 9 July, https://citypress.news24.com/Trending/book-art-alchemy-20160630 (accessed 5 September 2018).

Vokes, Richard, and Katrien Pype (2018), 'Chronotopes of Media in Sub-Saharan Africa', *Ethnos* 83(2): 207–17.

Wa Azania, Malaika (2014), *Memoirs of a Born-Free: Reflections on the New South Africa by a Member of the Post-Apartheid Generation*, Auckland Park: Jacana.

Waldby, Catherine, and Robert Mitchell (2006), *Tissue Economies: Blood, Organs and Cell Lines in Late Capitalism*, Durham, NC: Duke University Press.

Wanner, Zukiswa (2013), *Maid in SA: 30 Ways to Leave your Madam*, Auckland Park: Jacana.

White, Luise (2000), *Speaking with Vampires: Rumor and History in Colonial Africa*, Berkeley, CA: University of California Press.

White, Luise, and Miles Larmer (2014), 'Mobile Soldiers and the Un-National Liberation of South Africa', *Journal of Southern African Studies* 40(6): 1271–4.

Wieder, Alan (2013), *Ruth First and Joe Slovo in the War against Apartheid*, New York: Monthly Review Press.

Wildschut, Angelique, and Thando Mqolozana (2008), *Shortage of Nurses in South Africa: Relative or Absolute?*, Case Study Report HSRC, http://www.labour.gov.za/DOL/downloads/documents/research-documents/nursesshortage.pdf (accessed 5 September 2018).

Williamson, Sue (2002), 'Artbio: Thembinkosi Goniwe', *Artthrob* 62, https://artthrob.co.za/02oct/artbio.html (accessed 19 September 2018).

Wolpe, Annmarie (1994), *The Long Way Home*, London: Virago.

Woodward, Wendy (2008), *The Animal Gaze: Animal Subjectivities in Southern African Narratives*, Johannesburg: Wits University Press.

Woolf, Virginia (1986 [1938]), *Three Guineas*, London: The Hogarth Press.

Xaba, Makhosazana (2008), 'Midwives, Mothers, Memories', in Sandra Dodson and Rosamund Haden (eds), *Just Keep Breathing: South African Birth Stories*, Auckland Park: Jacana, 1–10.

Xaba, Makhosazana, and Laetitia Rispel (2013), 'Ensuring Women's Right to Choose: Exploring Nurses' Role in the Choice on Termination of Pregnancy Act', *Agenda* 27(4): 69–78.

Yousaf, Nahem (ed.) (2001), *Apartheid Narratives*, Amsterdam and New York: Rodopi.
Zeilig, Leo (2007), *Revolt and Protest: Student Politics and Activism in Sub-Saharan Africa*, London: Tauris Academic Studies.
Zweig, Stefan (2006), *Chess: A Novel*, London: Penguin.

Filmography

90 Days, documentary film, B&W, directed by Jack Gold, written by Ruth First, BBC, 1965.
A World Apart, directed by Chris Menges, written by Shawn Slovo, 1988.
Catch a Fire, directed by Philip Noyce, written by Shawn Slovo, Universal Pictures, 2006.
Come Back Africa, directed by Lionel Rogosin, screenplay by Lionel Rogosin, William Modisane and Lewis Nkosi, 1960.
Drum, directed by Zola Maseko, 2004.
Hidden Heart (http://lichtblick-film.com/dokumentarfilme/film.asp?id=15), a film by Werner Schweizer and Cristina Karrer, 2007.
Invictus, directed by Clint Eastwood, 2009.
Inxeba (The Wound), directed by John Trengove, written by John Trengove, Malusi Bengu and Thando Mgqolozana, 2017.
Mandela's Gun, directed by John Irvin, 2016.

Index

117 Days 61–79
90 Days 63, 68, 71, 75–78
491 Days 20, 69 (see Winnie Madikizela-Mandela)
A Man Who is Not a Man 122–146 (see Thando Mgqolozana)
Abantu Book Festival 121–127, 132–135, 142, 145
Adejunmobi, Moradewun 129
Afrikaner modernity narrative 13, 85–100
Agnew, Vanessa 24
Ahmed, Sara 55, 149–150
Akande, Lola 135
Alexander, Neville 33
amnesia and Rainbowism 12, and #Fallists 35
Antigone 32–33, 35
apartheid encrypted effects on bodies 4
archive overlooked or forgotten 6, contested 6, compromised 7, blood as 4, skin as 11, of kinship and belonging 12, usable activist archive 13, remixed 24, of resistant prison writing tradition 42, oppositional 44, family photograph albums 57, described as a strongroom 62, Abantu web site as activist archive 121
Arendt, Hannah 48
askaris 7–8, 39, 47
Ayelew, Semeneh Asfaw 108

Baderoon, Gabeba 82, 111, 152
Barber, Karin 127
Barnard, Christiaan 13, 81–100
Behr, Mark 95
Benjamin, Walter 20–22, 24, 27, 37, 116, 153

Berman, Myrtle 77
Black studies as project 36
Black reading audiences 121–127
blood testing ethical protocols ix, to whose benefit ix, as time sensitive ix, and extractive biomedical practices ix, as trope for ethical scholarship 16
blood and intergenerational memory ix, women's embodied experiences of blood 1, as archive 4, of intergenerational care 15
born-free limitations of term ix, 5, 14–15, 35, 37, 104, 114
Bystrom, Kerry 112

Chigumadzi, Panashe 125, 131–132
Chikane, Rekgotsofetse 115
Cock, Jacklyn 110
Coconut 127–146 (see Kopano Matlwa)
Coetzee, Carli 48, 58, 93, 115, 135
Coetzee, Dirk 40–41
Coetzee, J.M. 96
Collective Amnesia 122 (see Koleka Putuma)
Collis-Buthelezi, Victoria J. 36
Comaroff, Jean and John 86
communities of care 15
Connor, Steven 10–11

Dangarembga, Tsitsi 137
Darvall, Denise 81–82, 97–98
De Kock, Eugene 7, 12, 39–60, 124
decolonisation of the university curriculum 35, of the South African literary scene 124–125
Dlamini, Jacob 6–9, 39, 42, 45, 47, 53, 55, 59
Dlamini, Nonhlanhla 143

Doherty, Christo 57–58
Douglas, Mary 106
Dovey, Lindiwe 26, 31
Drum 30–31
Dubow, Jessica 24

Ebewo, Patrick 34
Eduardo Mondlane University, Maputo 61
Endings and Beginnings A Story of Healing 151 (see Redi Tlhabi)
epigenome correlation with social and economic levels of privilege 4
Erasmus, Zimitri 11, 55
ethics of scholarship 15–16, 115–117, 153–154
Evans, Martha 26
Evening Primrose 127 (see Kopano Matlwa)

Falkoff, Nicky 57
Fallists redefining literary and cultural studies ix, debating terms of knowledge production ix, costly labour performed by 6, as skilled readers of their own bodies and those of their ancestors 6, coded through blood not shit 14, as cleansing project 14, 19, and Mandela 35–37, and discourses about ancestors 113–115, and Abantu Book Festival
fingerprint mark of identity 15, as forensic evidence 15; bloody 147, Zanele Muholi's art 149–150, made with menstrual blood 147–154
First, Ruth 12–13, 61–79, 131
Franschhoek Literary Festival 39, 124
Fullard, Madeleine 40

Gikandi, Simon 106–107
Gilroy, Paul conviviality 117
Gobodo-Madikizela, Pumla 13, 40, 42, 48–60
Godsell, Gillian 115
Gold, Jack 75
Gould, Chandré 7, 39

Gqola, Pumla Dineo 15, 25, 82, 116, 144–146, 147–154
Green, Louise 40

Harlow, Barbara 44, 61–62, 66–67, 71, 75, 79
Harrow, Kenneth 104
Hear Me Not Alone 122 (see Thando Mgqolozana)
Heart of Cape Town Museum 81, 98–100
heart transplant 13, 81–100
Hirsch, Marianne 57–58
Hlongwane, Gugu 129–131, 145

intergenerational ix, 6, 11, 15, 103, 111, 114, 123, 145
Invictus 26–31
Inxeba 143
Isilumo Siyaluma 133 (see Zanele Muholi), 147–154

Jansen, Anemari 39, 41–43, 45–60
Jansen, Ena 110
Jobson, Marjorie 42
Jones, Megan 9
Jones, Rebecca 134
Judt, Tony 64

Kani, John 32–3
Kasibe, Wandile 107
Krog, Antjie 40, 47–8, 58

Lee, Rebekah 34
libraries and activist scholarship 13, Ruth First as librarian 66–67, and decolonisation 108–109, activist intellectual tunnels between home and library 120, and Abantu 124
Long Walk to Freedom 33–4, 134 (see Nelson Mandela)

Madikizela-Mandela, Winnie 20–21, 34, 69, 150
Makhubu, Nomusa 147–148
Makhulu, Anne-Maria 118–119

Malan, Rian 83, 95
Malcom, Janet 46, 49, 50, 54
Mama, Candice 46, 59
Mandela, Nelson 12, 19–37, 44, 49
Mandela meanings of his life for #Fallist generation 20, 35–37,
Mangcu, Xolela 35
Marikana 19
Maroga, Kopano 35
Marouf, Driss el 104
Masango Chéry, Tshepo 36
Maseko, Zola 30–31
Mashile, Lebo 121
Matlwa, Kopano Mabaso 122, 127–136
Maxwele, Chumani 103–105
Mazrui, Ali 13, 85–86
menstrual blood 1, 13, 15, 68–69, 133–146, 147–154
Mgqolozana, Thando 122–146
Mhlangu, Solomon Kalushi 2
Missing Persons Task Force 39–42
Mkhabela, Sabelo 112
Mlangeni, Bheki 52
Modisane, Litheko 22, 24, 26, 30, 36, 121
Mpolweni, Nosisi 48
Msezane, Sethembile 35
Msimang, Sisonke 21, 31, 118
Mthethwa, Zwelethu 118
Mtshali, Khondlo 145
Muholi, Zanele 15, 111–113, 133, 147–154
multidirectional memory 5, ethical dimensions of 6, as activist labour 14
Murray, Noëleen 40
Musila, Grace Ahingula 8–9, 123
Mwesigire, Bwesigye Bwa 108, 123, 127

Naki, Hamilton 14, 81–100
Nathoo, Ayesha 84–85
Natives' Land Act 36, 115–116
Ndangam, Lilian N. 144
Ndebele, Njabulo 31, 47, 116–117, 127, 151
Ndlovu-Gatsheni, Sabelo J. 36
Nervous Conditions 137 (see Tsitsi Dangarembga)
Newell, Stephanie 104, 134
Ngcobo, Gabi 112

Ntshona, Winston 32–33
Nuttall, Sarah 5, 9, 11, 20, 130

Olayiwola, Elizabeth 135
Ona mtoto wako 139
Ouma, Christopher 36

Pauw, Jacques 40
Period Pain 127–146, see Kopano Matlwa
Phiri, Aretha 129–131
photographs of Eugene de Kock 13, photograph albums and kinship 13, of Nelson Mandela 22–23, 25, of the *Drum* era 30–32, of Eugene de Kock's life outside prison 39, photographs in biography of Eugene de Kock 53–54, photographs of Vlakplaas 57–60
Plaatje, Solomon Tshekiso 36, 115–117
pregnancy 1, 138–146
Prime Evil 41
prison cell 12–13, 20–23, 29, 32–3, 39–60, 61–79
prison visitors 12, 42, 46–7, 50, 71
prisoner 1323/69 See Winnie Madikizela Mandela
prisoner 46664 see Nelson Mandela
protocols of care 3, debating terms of 4
Putuma, Koleka 122, 145, 152
Pype, Katrien 21

Qunu 32

Raditlhalo, Tlhalo 129–131
Ramphele, Mamphela 118, 140, 150
Rape A South African Nightmare 151 (see Pumla Dineo Gqola)
Rappert, Brian 7, 39
Ratele, Kopano 7, 104–105, 119
reading as ethical practice ix, 121–145
reading as activist way of bringing a self into being 121
reading blood x, 1, 3
Rediscovery of the Ordinary 116–117 (see Njabulo Ndebele)
Rhodes, Cecil John and bucket of shit 14, and Mandela's death 19, and

Chapungu 35, and #RMF 100–107, and decolonisation 131
Rhodes Must Fall ix, 6, 14, 19, 35–37, 103–120, 121–132
Rogosin, Lionel 77
Rosengarten, Ruth 24
Rosenstone, Robert A 25, 100
Rothberg, Michael 5, 6, 12, 25, 29, 105, 113
Roux, Daniel 42–45, 61–62

Satgar, Vishga 108
scabs 10
Schalkwyk, David 21, 68–69
Schwab, Gabriele 4–5, 45, 58, 111, 114, 134
Segal, Ronald 64
self-help and self-care genres 15, 43, 134–146
Shackville 107, 109, 114
Sharpe, Christina 36
Shipley, Jesse Weaver 23
"Shobane" 106–108, 114
Sibande, Mary 109, 111–112, 152
skin unbroken layer holding blood inside body 1, opening the skin to read the blood 3, limitations as intellectual framework 9, as master signifier 9, as historical burden 9, as body's script 10, as screen 10–11, and constant regeneration 11, as archive 11, as lie 11, soft pale skin of Eugene de Kock 49, and coconut 129–132, as blank page 138
Slovo, Gillian 65, 67, 71–72, 78–79
Slovo, Joe 64, 78
Slovo, Shawn 71, 76
Slovo, Robyn 71
"Small Deaths" 132 (see Panashe Chigumadzi)

Soyinka, Wole 85
Spencer, Lynda Gichanda 127, 129–130
spectacular masculinity 3, 116
Spilt Milk 127 (see Kopano Matlwa)

tattoos 10–11, 56
The Black Scholar 36
The Island 32
These Bones Must Rise 132 (see Panashe Chigumadzi)
Tlhabi, Redi 150–151
transgenerational haunting 4–6, 61, 111–116
transmission of knowledge as collaboration ix, as intellectual bloodline ix
Truth and Reconciliation Commission 8, 25, 39–40–41, 47–8, 55, 61–62, 64, 69, 71

ulwaluko 142–146
Un/Importance 122 (see Thando Mgqolozana)

Vlakplaas 12, 40, 57–58
Vokes, Richard 21

Wanner, Zukiswa 110
Wedi, Chrystelle Opope Oyaka 139
White, Luise 2, 10, 47, 59, 83
Williams, Raymond 127
Williamson, Craig 61–62, 64
Wolpe, Anne Marie 68
Writivism 123, 127

Xaba, Makhosazana 141–146, 153

Zeilig, Leo 108

AFRICAN ARTICULATIONS

ISSN 2054–5673

Previously Published

Achebe and Friends at Umuahia: The Making of a Literary Elite　Terri Ochiagha, 2015. Winner of the ASAUK Fage & Oliver Prize 2016

A Death Retold in Truth and Rumour: Kenya, Britain and the Julie Ward Murder　Grace A. Musila, 2015

Scoring Race: Jazz, Fiction, and Francophone Africa　Pim Higginson, 2017

Writing Spatiality in West Africa: Colonial Legacies in the Anglophone/Francophone Novel　Madhu Krishnan, 2018

Written under the Skin: Blood and Intergenerational Memory in South Africa　Carli Coetzee, 2019

Experiments with Truth: Narrative Non-fiction and the Coming of Democracy in South Africa　Hedley Twidle, 2019

At the Crossroads: Nigerian Travel Writing and Literary Culture in Yoruba and English　Rebecca Jones, 2019

Cinemas of the Mozambican Revolution: Anti-Colonialism, Independence and Internationalism in Filmmaking, 1968–1991　Ros Gray, 2020

African Literature in the Digital Age: Class and Sexual Politics in New Writing from Nigeria and Kenya　Shola Adenekan, 2021

www.ingramcontent.com/pod-product-compliance
Lightning Source LLC
Chambersburg PA
CBHW070807230426
43665CB00017B/2514